UPSETTING THE APPLE CART

THE COLUMBIA HISTORY OF URBAN LIFE

KENNETH T. JACKSON, GENERAL EDITOR

Deborah Dash Moore, *At Home in America: Second Generation New York Jews* 1981

Edward K. Spann, *The New Metropolis: New York City, 1840–1857* 1981

Matthew Edel, Elliott D. Sclar, and Daniel Luria, *Shaky Palaces: Homeownership and Social Mobility in Boston's Suburbanization* 1984

Steven J. Ross, *Workers on the Edge: Work, Leisure, and Politics in Industrializing Cincinnati, 1788–1890* 1985

Andrew Lees, *Cities Perceived: Urban Society in European and American Thought, 1820–1940* 1985

R. J. R. Kirkby, *Urbanization in China: Town and Country in a Developing Economy, 1949–2000 A.D.* 1985

Judith Ann Trolander, *Professionalism and Social Change: From the Settlement House Movement to Neighborhood Centers, 1886 to the Present* 1987

Marc A. Weiss, *The Rise of the Community Builders: The American Real Estate Industry and Urban Land Planning* 1987

Jacqueline Leavitt and Susan Saegert, *From Abandonment to Hope: Community-Households in Harlem* 1990

Richard Plunz, *A History of Housing in New York City: Dwelling Type and Social Change in the American Metropolis* 1990

David Hamer, *New Towns in the New World: Images and Perceptions of the Nineteenth-Century Urban Frontier* 1990

Andrew Heinze, *Adapting to Abundance: Jewish Immigrants, Mass Consumption, and the Search for American Identity* 1990

Chris McNickle, *To Be Mayor of New York: Ethnic Politics in the City* 1993

Clay McShane, *Down the Asphalt Path: The Automobile and the American City* 1994

Clarence Taylor, *The Black Churches of Brooklyn* 1994

Frederick Binder and David Reimers, *"All the Nations Under Heaven": A Racial and Ethnic History of New York City* 1995

Clarence Taylor, *Knocking at Our Own Door: Milton A. Galamison and the Struggle to Integrate New York City Schools* 1997

Andrew S. Dolkart, *Morningside Heights: A History of Its Architecture and Development* 1998

Jared N. Day, *Urban Castles: Tenement Housing and Landlord Activism in New York City, 1890–1943* 1999

Craig Steven Wilder, *A Covenant with Color: Race and Social Power in Brooklyn* 2000

A Scott Henderson, *Housing and the Democratic Ideal* 2000

Howard B. Rock and Deborah Dash Moore, *Cityscapes: A History of New York in Images* 2001

Jameson W. Doig, *Empire on the Hudson: Entrepreneurial Vision and Political Power at the Port of New York Authority* 2001

Lawrence Kaplan and Carol P. Kaplan, *Between Ocean and City: The Transformation of Rockaway, New York* 2003

François Weil, *A History of New York* 2004

Evelyn Gonzalez, *The Bronx* 2004

Jon C. Teaford, *The Metropolitan Revolution: The Rise of Post-Urban America* 2006

Lisa Keller, *Triumph of Order: Democracy and Public Space in New York and London* 2008

Jonathan Soffer, *Ed Koch and the Rebuilding of New York City* 2010

UPSETTING THE APPLE CART

BLACK-LATINO COALITIONS IN NEW YORK CITY FROM PROTEST TO PUBLIC OFFICE

FREDERICK DOUGLASS OPIE

COLUMBIA UNIVERSITY PRESS   NEW YORK

Columbia University Press
Publishers Since 1893
New York   Chichester, West Sussex
cup.columbia.edu
Copyright © 2015 Columbia University Press
All rights reserved

Library of Congress Cataloging-in-Publication Data

Opie, Frederick Douglass.
Upsetting the apple cart : Black-Latino coalitions in New York City from protest
to public office / Frederick Douglass Opie.
pages cm. — (The Columbia history of urban life)
Includes bibliographical references and index.
ISBN 978-0-231-14940-2 (cloth : alk. paper)
ISBN 978-0-231-52035-5 (e-book)
1. African Americans—New York (State)—New York—Politics and
government—20th century. 2. Hispanic Americans—New York (State)—
New York—Politics and government—20th century. 3. African Americans—
New York (State)—New York—Relations with Hispanic Americans.
4. New York (N.Y.)—Politics and government—20th century.
5. New York (N.Y.)—Race relations. I. Title.
F128.9.N4O65 2014
305.8009747'1—dc23
2014012943

COVER IMAGE: Picket line at Lenox Hill Hospital, 1959.
(Courtesy of Kheel Center for Labor-Management Documentation
and Archives, Cornell University, Ithaca, N.Y.)
COVER DESIGN: James Perales
BOOK DESIGN: Lisa Hamm

References to websites (URLs) were accurate at the time of writing.
Neither the author nor Columbia University Press is responsible for URLs that
may have expired or changed since the manuscript was prepared.

In memory of my mother, Margaret Opie (1935–2014). She was an organizer supreme who used her singing voice and food to feed the Progressive movements she supported. Fried chicken, which she called the "gospel bird," served as her go-to dish.

CONTENTS

ACKNOWLEDGMENTS

S PECIAL THANKS TO the intellectual communities at Marist College, Babson College, and Harvard University for their support. A similar thanks to those who allowed me to interview them and/or suggested others to interview. Without their support, this book would not have been possible.

A NOTE ON SOURCES

I N RESEARCHING THIS BOOK, I used interviews, secondary works, published papers, and archival collections of newspapers, photos, and oral histories. I retrieved materials from the Kheel Center at Cornell University, Tamiment Library & Robert F. Wagner Labor Archives at New York University, the Archives of the Puerto Rican Diaspora at Hunter College, the archives of Lehman College and City College of New York (CCNY), and the New York City Municipal Archives. Oral histories from people involved in the events, movements, organizations, and institutions discussed are absolutely essential to the book's analysis and credibility. The book also includes oral histories of and about activists and their supporters dating back to the mid-1950s, including those of Morris "Moe" Foner and Bayard Rustin, and about A. Philip Randolph, Malcolm X, Percy Sutton, and Joseph Monserrat. I use the oral histories of students and teachers who participated in the student movement of the late 1960s and activists from political organizations, including the Young Lords (YLO); El Comité Movimiento de Izquierda Nacional Puertorriqueño (MINP); the Dominican Parade Committee in Washington Heights; the Hispanic youth organization, ASPIRA; the Hostos Community College campus takeover; and the Puerto Rican Socialist Party (PSP). The book includes interviews with members of the New York Committee in Support of Vieques (NYCSV), the National Congress for Puerto Rican Rights (NCPRR), Latinos for Jackson, and Latinos for Dinkins. I was also able to interview Mayor David Dinkins and a number of his close friends and political allies, including Basil Paterson and Denny Farrell. I spoke with key labor leaders, including the former president of District

Council 37 Stanley Hill and the former president of Local 1199 Dennis Rivera. Rivera and the political strategist Bill Lynch ran Jesse Jackson's campaign for president in 1988 and David Dinkins's campaign for mayor in 1989.

The oral histories not only add a profound richness to these stories but also provide a vital check on the accuracy of widely accepted secondary accounts. Journalists and writers from even the most prestigious institutions seem to have relied on assumptions rather than research when reporting on contentious events and alliances between blacks and Latinos in New York. Many times I found that I was the first to have asked even the most basic questions to these primary sources or to have attempted to interview people directly involved in major organizations and campaigns.

My fluency in Spanish was an asset in tackling this subject matter and conducting oral histories with native Spanish speakers. Finally, having grown up watching my mom's ardent political activity, including serving as an NAACP membership recruiter and community center director in Ossining, New York; a Westchester County delegate to the 1976 Democratic national convention; and a member of the Friends of Africa, a New York–based organization, which participated in the anti-apartheid movement, I came to this project with a visceral understanding of Progressive grass roots organizing and protest.

ABBREVIATIONS

AATA	African American Teachers Association
AAUPA	Asian American Union for Political Action
AFL	American Federation of Labor
AFSCME	American Federation of State, County, and Municipal Employees
AMCBW	Amalgamated Meat Cutters and Butcher Workmen of North America
BES	Black Economic Survival
BLAPP	Black-Latino Alliance for Progressive Politics
BPRSC	Black and Puerto Rican Student Community
BSA	Black Student Association
CASA	Center for Autonomous Action
CCNY	City College of New York
CJHW	Committee for Justice to Hospital Workers
COINTELPRO	Counter Intelligence Program (FBI)
CORE	Congress of Racial Equality
CPS	Chicago Public Schools
CUNY	City University of New York
DC 37	District Council 37
EOP	Educational Opportunity Program
FALN	Fuerzas Armadas de Liberación Nacional
FBCA	Fulton Street, Bedford-Stuyvesant Vanguard Civic Association
FCWPA	"Feeding the City Project Collection" (WPA NYC Unit)

FHS	Federation of Hispanic Societies Incorporated
GNYHA	Greater New York Hospital Association
HEOP	Higher Education Opportunity Program
HUD	Department of Housing and Urban Development
IBEW	International Brotherhood of Electrical Workers
ILGWU	International Ladies' Garment Workers Union
IPO	independent political organization
LARES	Latin American Recruitment and Educational Services Program
LULAC	League of United Latin American Citizens
LUPA	Latinos United for Political Action
MALDEF	Mexican American Legal Defense and Education Fund
MAPA	Mexican American Political Association
MINP	El Comité Movimiento de Izquierda Nacional Puertorriqueño
MPI	Movimiento Pro Independencia
NAACP	National Association for the Advancement of Colored People
NCPRR	National Congress for Puerto Rican Rights
NFA	National Farmworkers Association (renamed United Farm Workers Union)
NTA	Negro Teachers Association
NYCSV	New York Committee in Support of Vieques
NYPD	New York Police Department
OPBE	Ocean Hill People's Board of Education
PIP	Pro Independence Party
POWER	People Organized for Welfare and Employment Rights
PRISA	Puerto Rican Student Activities
PRSM	Puerto Rican Students' Movement
PRSU	Puerto Rican Student Union
PSP	Puerto Rican Socialist Party
PUSH	People United to Save Humanity
ROTC	Reserve Officers' Training Corps
SAC	Sociedad de Albizu Campos
SAS	Student Afro-American Society
SDS	Students for a Democratic Society

SEEK	Search for Education, Elevation, and Knowledge
SEIU	Service Employees International Union, Local 1199
SGA	Student Government Association
SNCC	Student Nonviolent Coordinating Committee
SSPC	Southside Political Action Committee
SUNY	State University of New York
TWU	Transport Workers Union
UAAA	United African American Association
UFT	United Federation of Teachers
UFW	United Farm Workers Union
UIC	University of Illinois at Chicago
UMAS	United Mexican American Students
UPR	University of Puerto Rico
UTT	United Tremont Trade
YLO	Young Lords Organization

UPSETTING THE APPLE CART

INTRODUCTION

ONE OF THE most headline-grabbing pronouncements from the 2000 U.S. Census Bureau was that Latinos had surpassed African Americans to become the nation's largest minority group, totaling 41,300,000 compared with 38 million. With each ethnic group making up close to 13 percent of the U.S. population, this meant that more than 25 percent of the country's residents was either African American or Latino. In several major cities in the country, this combination already comprises the majority population. With projections of continued Latino population growth, most demographers predict that this combination will rise to more than one-third of the U.S. population by the middle of the twenty-first century. The national immigration-related demographic shift has inspired a number of books on Latin American immigration to the United States and the Latino experience in the United States.[1]

This slow but steady increase in the number of blacks and Latinos in the United States has already shaped the political history of most of America's major cities. I chronicle how these minority groups pooled their power to upend politics-as-usual in New York City, thus changing the face of local politics and challenging the political status quo in the postwar era. The importance of coalitions to political success is proven by their power to raise such politicians as David Dinkins to office. Nonetheless, the fragility of these coalitions was reflected in the rivalries that sometimes ensued as well as their inability to reelect Dinkins.

This book focuses on shared grassroots movements among black and Latino workers, students, tenants, trade unionists, and political operatives in

New York City over a critical thirty-year period. It looks at black and Latino workers within New York City's labor movement, and the struggle of black and brown labor coalitions against racism in the construction trades.[2] The book calls for scholars to move beyond treating left-of-center Latino Progressives in the same way that Ralph Ellison's *Invisible Man* was treated—which is to say, as "invisible activists."[3] Finally, it focuses on times in which African Americans and Latinos came together and the lessons learned from the electoral coalition of the mid- to late-1980s.[4] By focusing on a history that resonates with the most recent New York City mayoral election of Bill de Blasio, this book is certainly not defined by that history but stands as one of the first works to explore it.

*　*　*

While in the graduate program at Syracuse University, I studied both U.S. and Latin American history and undertook intensive Spanish-language training. I first traveled to Guadalajara, Mexico, in 1992 to live with a host family and study Spanish. In 1996 and 1997, I lived in Guatemala City, Guatemala, for six months doing dissertation fieldwork and conducting archival research at the Archivo General de Centro América there. My book *Black Labor Migration in Caribbean Guatemala, 1882–1923* (2009) came out of that research. It is a study of transnational labor radicalism among railroad and banana workers at the turn of the twentieth century in the frontier towns of Caribbean Guatemala. National, ethnic, and racial identities all informed the character and strength of the coalitions among working-class black immigrants and Latin Americans living in the Caribbean borderlands of Guatemala, Honduras, Belize, and El Salvador. I also wrote *Hog and Hominy: Soul Food from Africa to America* (2008), a study of the global origins of soul food, the forces that have shaped its development, and the distinctive cultural collaborations that occurred among Africans, Asians, Europeans, and Americans (particularly the maize culture from the Maya of Central America) to create this distinctive cuisine. It draws on a wide range of sources from oral histories to traditional archival materials to examine the ways that food has been an indicator of social position, a source of community cohesion and cultural identity, and a vehicle for change and cross-cultural collaboration. Because I believe that food is a critical lens through which to view cross-cultural relationships and coalition building, I've included related recipes in this book as a way of highlighting the role of food in social movements. Napoleon once said that "an army marches on its stomach," and this is certainly true for the army of volunteers in the movements covered in this book.

During the summer of 2005, I came across a set of Works Progress Administration (WPA) records in the New York City Municipal Archives, which described blacks and Latinos in Harlem in the 1930s eating in the same restaurants, frequenting the same nightclubs and theaters, and intermarrying. I was struck by these descriptions given the degree of separation I observed between contemporary blacks and Latinos (Ecuadorians, Dominicans, some Puerto Ricans, and Cubans) in Westchester County, just north of New York City. The contrast inspired me to explore the dynamics of African American–Latino coalitions at different times and places.

* * *

In this book, I describe the dynamics among African Americans and Hispanic immigrants from the Caribbean in New York City between 1959 and 1989. While the data is site-specific, my findings suggest a tentative framework for answering the broader questions that drive this study: What forces have shaped African American and Latino coalitions at various points in history? Where and why did collaborations and political alliances emerge—or fail to emerge—between blacks and Latinos in twentieth-century America?

I found evidence dating back to 1959 that broad cross-sections of black and Latino communities did form successful coalitions to advance what Martin Luther King Jr. called "the struggle [of unorganized black and brown workers] for justice, freedom, and dignity in New York City."[5] Indeed, I found that blacks and Latinos repeatedly formed strong coalitions around struggles for justice, freedom, and dignity during the thirty years examined in this study. Blacks and Latinos developed the strongest coalitions when they shared a language, a political goal, an employer, or class status as well as when they operated within the same spaces, such as in housing projects, work places, union halls, school campuses, or public streets. Black and Latino coalitions in New York City grew around campaigns for worker rights, equality in schools, and democracy in South Africa and

Central America and led to greater participation and representation of blacks and Latinos in New York's Democratic Party.

The focus on relations between black and Latino activists fills a gap in the historiography of the civil rights movement, the labor movement, and electoral politics in post-1970s New York City and Chicago. The detailed portraits of Latino Progressives working in coalition with African American activists and elected officials serve to balance the neglect historians outside the field of Latino studies have given to Latino Progressives in organized labor, the Left, and electoral politics in New York City between 1959 and 1989. The electoral coalitions covered in the second half of the book (1970s and 1980s) did not come about easily. The left-of-center groups, unions, and civil rights groups and their leaders who formed coalitions had been the target of state repression including COINTELPRO, the FBI's counterintelligence program whose mission was to disrupt actions of the radical leftist organizations and groups such as the Black Panthers.

An important part of this story takes place not in New York City but in Chicago, which elected its first black mayor in 1983, six years before New York City elected David Dinkins. In many ways, the seeds for Mayor Dinkins's election and Jesse Jackson's presidential run were sown in Chicago where lessons learned in coalition politics were put to use in New York City.

The final three chapters in the book focus on Progressive Latino activism in the 1970s through to the election of Dinkins as mayor of New York City in 1989. These chapters provide new perspectives on electoral politics and coalitions in the 1970s and 1980s. What exists on the topics has been written through a liberal and Progressive white and black paradigm with only an occasional mention of Latino agency and involvement. This book, then, is an attempt to end the division that now exists among those writing about blacks, Latinos, and electoral politics in post-1970s New York.

* * *

Chapter 1 looks at the two waves of black and Latino migration to New York that occurred between 1930 and 1949 and from 1950 to 1970 and the subsequent patterns of resettlement. I explore how different backgrounds and reasons for emigrating shaped their relationships and participation in social, vocational, and political activities in twentieth-century New York.

Chapter 2 examines a series of strikes by low-income hospital workers in New York City between 1959 and 1962. The strikes fostered a political alliance among white labor leaders, Latino activists, black civil rights leaders, and the black nationalist Malcolm X before he left the Nation of Islam.

Chapter 3 analyzes the student movements in the 1960s and early 1970s at Lehman College, CCNY, and Columbia University, as well as events occurring at the same time in East Harlem around issues of community control. I discuss how Latino involvement in the student movement made the limitations of Black Power ideology all the more apparent.

Chapter 4 shows how political clubs and organizations trained black and Latino Progressive activists to participate in electoral politics in the 1970s and 1980s and look at the response by black and Latino members of District Council 37 (DC 37), a New York City public-employees' union, to the election of President Ronald Reagan and U.S. foreign policy in South Africa and Central America in the early 1980s. The chapter delves into the movement to stop U.S. bombing on the island of Vieques in Puerto Rico and the formation of the National Congress for Puerto Rican Rights.

The final three chapters address electoral politics from the late 1970s to the late 1980s and are based on interviews with elected officials, campaign managers, labor leaders, and activists. The book ends with a chapter on the election of David Dinkins in 1989. Until the election of Bill de Blasio in 2013, Dinkins had been the last Democrat elected mayor of in a city where registered Democrats outnumbered GOP members almost 4 to 1. Today the ratio is 6 to 1.

Chapter 5 examines the political campaigns of New York City politicians José Rivera and Major Owens in 1982, Chicago mayor Harold Washington in 1983, and Jesse Jackson in 1984, and the importance of black and Latino coalitions to their campaigns. The chapter specifically discusses the importance of unions in Democratic politics as demonstrated by the Democratic primaries for governor of New York in 1982. I also review the early contributions of Chicago-based Black Panther Fred Hampton to the notion of a black and Latino Rainbow Coalition.

Chapter 6 looks at the impact of the 1984 Jackson campaign on black and Latino Progressives in New York City. Voter registration and fund-raising drives begun during the Jackson campaign continued after 1984 in order to leverage the political power of black and Latino voters and thereby help unseat Mayor Ed Koch in 1989. I set aside the myths surrounding the Coalition for a Just New York's search for a candidate to defeat Koch in 1985 as well the group's efforts to take over the borough presidents' offices in Brooklyn, Manhattan, and the Bronx.

Chapter 7 delves into the planning and organizing that led to the election of David Dinkins as New York City's first African American mayor and the role that organized labor and Latino activists played in that effort. It also discusses Dinkins's failed reelection campaign in 1993.

The conclusion provides an overview of the post-Dinkins black–Latino coalition, a general assessment of what happened, and how this period either diverged from or continued trends from the previous decades not only in the labor movement but also in political representations for black and Latino communities.

1

JOURNEYS

BLACK AND LATINO RELATIONS, 1930–1970

THE DESIRE FOR a better life with more opportunities brought Latinos from Cuba and Puerto Rico to the United States in droves in the early part of the twentieth century, just as generations of immigrants had done before and after them.

For these immigrants, home was a place riddled with problems brought by long histories of colonialism, racism, and classism. This migration began as early as the 1860s, when political persecution, poverty, and lack of opportunity under Spanish colonialism drove Cubans to the United States. The trend continued following Cuba's independence from Spain in 1898, when Cuban oligarchs and foreign investors continued their stranglehold on the best land, jobs, and opportunities, thus prompting Cubans to head to the United States in a slow but steady stream.

MIGRATION'S FIRST WAVE, 1930S AND 1940S

Until the 1930s, Tampa was the center of the Cuban American expatriate community and home to a thriving cigar industry. After 1930, new Afro-Cuban arrivals, more diverse in their occupations than the first wave, many of them musicians, baseball players, and cigar makers, headed to New York City. Due to racist housing practices, the majority of black immigrants from the Caribbean (Puerto Rican, Cuban, and Panamanian) moved into established African American neighborhoods. Most of New York's early Afro-Cuban immigrants settled in Harlem. White Cubans tended to settle in small groups in areas of Brooklyn, Queens, the Bronx, and Staten Island. The number of Cuban immigrants in New York City is unknown, but it was only a fraction of the 18,000 Cubans in the United States in 1940, most of whom were still settling in Florida.[1]

Puerto Rican immigration to New York was similarly fueled by poverty and unemployment but Puerto Rican immigrants, in contrast to Cubans, did form tight-knit, distinctive communities upon their arrival. The first influx of Puerto Ricans to New York City occurred in 1910. Three hundred individuals settled on the Lower West Side of Manhattan along Eighth Avenue between Fourteenth and Thirtieth Streets. Shortly thereafter, one member of this Lower West Side community relocated to East Harlem to open a barbershop, thus initiating an influx of Puerto Ricans to the neighborhood.[2]

Puerto Ricans started to arrive in large numbers during World War I. Wartime restrictions on European migration caused labor shortages in the United States, so employers in the manufacturing and service industries recruited Puerto Ricans to meet their labor demands.[3] Harlem's Puerto Rican population swelled after 1917 when the U.S. Congress passed a bill granting citizenship to all native-born Puerto Ricans.

The Puerto Rican population in the United States swelled from 1,513 in 1910 to almost 53,000 in 1930. As the number of Puerto Ricans in East Harlem increased, the area became known as "Spanish Harlem" and "El Barrio" and by 1935, the Puerto Rican diaspora in New York had grown to approximately 75,000 people in three communities throughout the city. Thirty-five thousand lived in Spanish Harlem, 30,000 lived in South Brooklyn, and 10,000 lived on the West Side between Broadway and Amsterdam Avenue near Columbia University.[4] It is unknown what percentage of these Puerto Ricans immigrants were of African descent, but the historian Winston James writes that "black and brown Puerto Ricans were a significant and conspicuous presence" in Harlem in the 1920s and 1930s.[5]

Many of the same factors that drew Cubans and Puerto Ricans to the United States also attracted African Americans from the rural South to the urban North. During the first Great Migration between 1910 and 1930, more than 1.5 million African Americans fled persistent food shortages, low wages, and underemployment in the South where those economic forces and mistreatment pushed African American wageworkers, sharecroppers, and tenant farmers out of the South. Glowing reports of job opportunities and a better life pulled them to the North.[6] By 1917, almost 500,000 of these black southerners had migrated to the North and Midwest to work in fast-growing industries such as meat packing, steel, and automobiles. They created new lives for themselves in major urban areas such as New York City, Kansas City, Chicago, Philadelphia, and St. Louis.[7] The majority of the southern-born migrants to Harlem came from Virginia although many came from North Carolina, South Carolina, Florida, Georgia, and Maryland.[8] African American migrants tended to settle in clusters in urban communities, largely because white landlords would not rent to blacks and Latinos outside certain areas.[9]

During the 1930s, the majority of New York's African American and Latin American residents lived a precarious existence. The Great Depression devastated the nation's economic system, reinforcing a "protect one's own" mentality among white business owners and employers. Whites who owned profitable businesses refused to give their better jobs to African Americans or Latinos. Institutionalized racism stymied the development of businesses and housing to serve the region's nonwhite residents.[10] Ghetto landlords charged high rents for living quarters that were vastly inferior to those available to white residents in other parts of the city. These were hard times under the best of circumstances, but even more so for new immigrants and migrants trying to make a living in a racially fragmented city.[11]

MIGRATION'S SECOND WAVE, 1950S AND 1960S

In the 1950s and 1960s, a second wave of African Americans and Hispanics arrived in New York. Five million African Americans fled the Deep South and moved to a wide variety of destinations across the country. In New York City, the overwhelming majority of new arrivals were from Puerto Rico due, in part, to San Juan's status as the "international training ground" for the U.S. government's Point Four Program in the 1950s. Point Four was an explicitly anti-Communist program couched as an early technical assistance program intended to show developing countries that American capitalism was superior to Communism.[12] As part of the deal to provide assistance in Puerto Rico, the Truman administration negotiated with the Puerto Rican colonial government to empty the island's poorest sectors and encourage the inhabitants, "many of them mulattos," to migrate to urban centers in the United States, including New York, Chicago, and Philadelphia. Participants received reduced airfare between the island and the mainland, and these 600,000 "mostly rural unskilled" Puerto Ricans helped fill the demand for cheap labor in the U.S. manufacturing sector. The hope was that exporting the poor would boost mobility among those Puerto Ricans who remained, burnishing capitalism's image in the Third World, but it did not work.[13]

Many of the second-wave Puerto Rican migrants joined relatives already living in a largely Puerto Rican and Spanish-speaking community in East Harlem. Parents arrived hoping that their young children would have a better quality of life than what had been available to them in Puerto Rico; they moved to East Harlem because family and extended family who lived there could help them find jobs. In the late 1950s, many Puerto Rican families who originally settled in El Barrio moved to the projects in Brooklyn. These "suburbs" of Brooklyn, as many referred to them, were a mix of mostly Puerto Ricans and blacks [14]

In the 1950s and 1960s, Brooklyn was also a destination for working-class African American migrants from the South, Afro-Panamanians (from the Canal Zone region of Panama City), Afro-Cubans (from Havana), and middle-class white Cubans (from provincial cities). "Just like in every other part of Latin America and many parts of the world, the dream [in Cuba] was to come to the United States," remembers Francisco Corona, a Cuban migrant. During the corrupt and repressive military dictatorship of General Fulgencio Batista y Zaldívar (1952–1959), members of six families in Guayos, Corona's birthplace, responded by immigrating to Brooklyn.[15] As life got tougher under Batista, Corona remembers, Cuban expatriates from Guayos would "sponsor friends and families who also wanted to come to New York." One of the first homes owned by a former Guayos resident on Henry Street in Brooklyn Heights became a receiving station for new arrivals. New migrants could go to Henry Street "to [share] news about family members back home and to learn about job [opportunities]," Corona says. Unlike earlier Afro-Cuban immigrants to New York City, the Guayos Cubans tended to be white and economically better off.[16]

Panamanian immigrants to Brooklyn in the 1960s arrived with much greater familiarity and comfort with American culture than did their

Cuban counterparts. George Priestly, an Afro-Panamanian sociologist who studied Panamanian immigrants to the United States, was himself born and raised in a working-class community in Panama City in the 1940s. His father was a native-born Afro-Panamanian, and his mother was a bilingual second-generation Afro-Panamanian of Caribbean descent who preferred to speak English. Most Afro-Panamanians of Priestly's generation attended a Spanish-speaking public school but spoke English in the home with at least one parent. There were also English-language schools in Panama City that many Afro-Panamanian children attended in evenings or during summer vacations. Many Afro-Panamanians were exposed to aspects of American culture through the African American GIs stationed in Panama. At the black bars in Panama City, "You would see black folks hanging out, some speaking English, some speaking Spanish, some speaking Spanglish," Priestly recalls. His older brother operated the first black-owned men's boutique in a working-class community of Panama City in the 1950s. "Eighty percent of his customers were African American GIs," Priestly recalls. His family, like many other Panamanian immigrants, was "pre-sensitized to African American culture" before migrating to New York.[17]

Afro-Panamanians began immigrating to Brooklyn in the early 1960s. Priestly moved there in 1961 at the age of twenty. The Panamanian community at the time was quite small, and most of the earliest arrivals were Afro-Panamanians of West Indian descent. Over time, Franklin Avenue in Bedford-Stuyvesant (Bed-Stuy) became the center of New York's Panamanian community. Due to their familiarity with English and their exposure to American culture, many members of this Panamanian community interacted with African Americans. "There were two or three Panamanian families in Bushwick who introduced me to their African American and Puerto Rican friends," Priestly recalls. "They would take me to clubs in Bed-Stuy and Crown Heights . . . [that] were largely African American clubs."[18]

Southern black migration to New York City had slowed considerably during the post–World War II era, but many southern blacks made their way to Brooklyn in the 1960s. In the 1950s and 1960s, New York City's African American population consisted largely of older residents who had moved from the South years earlier along with their children and grandchildren. The Latino community included old-timers who had arrived before World War II and who had rudimentary English-language skills, their bilingual children and grandchildren who were born in New York, and a much larger group of recent migrants from the circum-Caribbean basin who spoke only Spanish.

2

UPSETTING THE APPLE CART

BLACK AND PUERTO RICAN HOSPITAL WORKERS, 1959–1962

MORE THAN 2.5 million employees joined the nation's health-care work-force in the 1950s and 1960s, and there were more jobs in hospitals than in the steel and railroad industries combined. Many of these hospital service jobs—janitors, cooks, maintenance staff, and nurse's aides—were filled by the working poor, who earned some of the lowest wages in the country. It is no coincidence that between 1960 and 1970 the vast majority of these workers were black or Latino and constituted 80 percent of the hospital service and maintenance workforce in New York City. Their meager salaries even forced many hospital workers to seek public assistance.[1]

Efforts by the Service Employees International Union (SEIU), Local 1199, organized workers at New York's nonprofit hospitals. The campaign started in 1959 and culminated in 1962 when workers gained union recognition and collective bargaining rights. Victory did not come easily, and hospital work-ers went on strike more than once. These strikes built and strengthened interracial alliances as white labor leaders, Hispanic activists, unionists, and political leaders, black unionists, civil rights leaders, and black national-ists all played a role in the push to unionize. The most lasting relationships between blacks and Latinos were forged when these workers shared social identities and specific working conditions. In the hospitals, workers of dif-ferent races and ethnicities held similar positions and struggled together against often autocratic and disrespectful supervisors and hospital offi-cials. They talked and ate together in hospital cafeterias, and they vented grievances about hospital supervisors in hospital locker rooms. Solidarity increased as workers began meeting in union halls, at rallies, on picket lines, and in each other's homes. Speakers' platforms became important spaces for building alliances among the leaders of various black and brown communities. Between 1959 and 1962, hospital workers, regardless of whether they came from San Juan or Selma, developed a shared identity as workers of color.

WORKING CONDITIONS AND GRIEVANCES

Although workers in New York's nonprofit hospitals in the mid-twentieth century were an ethnically diverse group, they shared a universal motive for entering the hospital labor force: they all needed to pay their bills. For workers without college degrees, hospital service jobs were an alternative to working as live-in cooks, domestic servants, chauffeurs, or laundresses in the private homes of elite white families. For workers without proper immigration credentials or work visas, hospitals were often the only employment option. Hospitals were less concerned than other employers about new workers' immigration status because they had found it difficult to fill such low-paying jobs with meager rewards or opportunity for social mobility. For older workers who had to continue working after years of domestic service or physical labor, the hospital was a respectable choice.

Hospitals at that time were unusually intimate workplaces, environments where employees changed clothes together, ate together, and even boarded together. For example, Montefiore Hospital in the Bronx offered housing for some staff, and its workers ate for free or at vastly reduced cost in the hospital cafeteria. This intimacy helped foster solidarity among black and Latino workers even before the labor organizing began. In the cafeteria, service workers tended to sit in groups based on occupation and department rather than on nationality or language.

Ken Downs, a black kitchen worker at Montefiore, once got on his white supervisor's bad side for "not letting [a white kitchen supervisor] push the Puerto Ricans around." Similarly, the Puerto Ricans in the kitchen would "fight anybody" who tried to mess with him. "I got along with them well," Downs recalled. He had emigrated from Barbados to Trinidad as a young man and in 1950, at the age of forty-five, he immigrated to New York City "to better his conditions." He moved in with his older brother, a World War

I veteran who had settled in Harlem. Downs immediately got a job as a cook at Montefiore, cooking breakfast and lunch on the food line and grilling as many as "seventy-two eggs at once."[2]

Although the service workers tended to intermingle, ethnic and racial divisions remained pronounced between workers and managers. In most hospitals, registered nurses were predominantly white, middle-class women who supervised teams of black and Hispanic women working as nurse's aides, orderlies, and licensed practical nurses (LPNs). Registered nurses (RNs) had to go to school for four years and pass a state board examination, while LPNs needed but one year of vocational training to obtain their titles. However, RNs and LPNs did take many of the same classes together, such as anatomy and physiology, medication safety, medical terms, and the like. The historians Leon Fink and Brian Greenberg confirm that "the line separating licensed and unlicensed workers also demarcated ethnic and racial differences, as it did everywhere else in the hospitals."[3] At Montefiore, Mount Sinai, and Beth Israel hospitals, the hierarchy was the same: a small number of white registered nurses, doctors, and administrators supervised a majority black and Hispanic workforce.

In this racially segregated environment, New York hospital workers experienced maltreatment in the form of low wages, long hours, split shifts (8:00 A.M.–11:00 A.M. then 4:00 P.M.–11:00 P.M.), lack of benefits, and hostile supervisors.[4] Many workers received wages as low as between $26 and $47 for a forty-four-hour, six-day week. As a result, many full-time hospital workers had to "receive welfare aid from the city in order to feed and clothe their families," reported the *New York Amsterdam News* in January 1959.[5] In addition, hospital workers did not receive unemployment benefits. At Beth Israel, Hilda Joquin says that she and other dietary department workers put in forty-eight-hour weeks and earned just "fifty-seven dollars every two weeks."[6] Similarly, Julio Pagan, a Mount Sinai orderly, worked a forty-eight-hour week and earned "about seventeen dollars a week [after taxes]." By the time they paid their rent and grocery bills, Joquin says, "We had nothing at all."[7] In contrast, a unionized 1199 pharmacist earned $120 for a forty-hour, five-day week and unemployment benefits.[8] According to Nellie Morris, an African American nurse's aide at Maimonides Hospital in Brooklyn, workers sometimes had to work "four and five Sundays [in a row] and holidays. . . . And we didn't get paid for overtime."[9] In addition to earning no additional compensation for overtime hours, low-skilled workers received no benefits. Many workers at nonprofit hospitals did not have medical insurance themselves.

Even more than the inadequate compensation, black and Puerto Rican workers complained bitterly about the discrimination and disrespect routinely directed toward them by white supervisors and administrators. Workers described supervisors as hostile and threatening, often using the specter of termination to prod workers into harder and longer service.

Prior to 1959, there were no federal laws protecting workers, so if a supervisor wanted to fire a worker, he or she could do so without fear of recourse. Henry Nicholas, a Mount Sinai worker, says that his supervisor made it clear that her subordinates "had no rights" and that she could fire them at any time. The supervisor told Nicholas that if he crossed her, she could get him blackballed in the city so that he "would never get a job no place else."[10] Hilda Joquin had a similar experience with her supervisors at Mount Sinai. Born in Bermuda, Joquin moved to New York in the 1920s at the age of nineteen and began, in her late thirties, working at Beth Israel in the dietary department.[11] She soon became a critical labor leader from within the rank and file. "Joquin stood less than five feet tall," remembered 1199's former public-relations director Moe Foner, "but she packed a wallop."[12] According to Joquin, her supervisors "were not very friendly.... You couldn't ask them anything ... concerning you or your work—it was always brushed off." They provided neither the "help nor the time" necessary to do the job well, she says. "They treated us just like we were chattel, not human beings."[13]

HISTORY OF ORGANIZING

Before Local 1199 started its organizing campaign in 1959, workers at a few hospitals had made small strides toward improving working conditions. In 1953, workers at Montefiore successfully united to persuade management to implement an eight-hour day and to raise wages. "Everybody thought that we were working too [many] hours," says Salvadore Cordero, a Puerto Rican immigrant and one of the hospital's activists. "So, we [got] together." In a rare example of nonprofit hospital workers winning concessions from management, Cordero says that a committee of Puerto Rican workers and "a good many colored boys" went to the hospital president's office together and spoke with him directly about their demands. The workers came away with fewer hours and more pay.[14]

In general, three main issues stood in the way of efforts to organize hospital workers. Many workers did not dare voice their complaints about low wages, meager benefits, or oppressive working conditions for fear of getting fired.[15] Second, hospital workers' rights to union recognition and collective bargaining were not protected by the National Labor Relations Act of 1935, known as the Wagner Act.[16] This remained true until 1965 when some states, including New York, extended these rights to hospital workers. Nonetheless, federal legislation expanding the Wagner Act did not pass until 1974. The lack of protective labor laws made the prospect of organizing hospital workers even more daunting, and it is unclear why these laws did not extend to hospital workers. Third, union politics in the 1950s was itself an obstacle. The unions were controlled by whites during the late 1950s and early 1960s, and union leaders dedicated little effort to organizing workers in industries dominated by blacks and Latinos. Local 1199's Ted Mitchell, an African American, stated that white unions in the American Federation of Labor (AFL) had little interest in organizing blacks and Latinos, and thus focused primarily on skilled white workers. Born in Norfolk, Virginia, Mitchell had been active in unions in the South before migrating to New York, where he took a job as a Harlem pharmacist, joined 1199, and became its first full-time African American labor organizer. In 1957, 1199's founder and president, Leon Davis, charged Mitchell with partnering with Elliot Godoff, one of the pioneering hospital workers organizers, on SEIU's effort to unionize Montefiore workers.[17] According to Moe Foner, organizing the hospitals' low-wage, black and Hispanic, predominately female workforce "meant devoting vast resources to a risky effort that would, even if successful, mean a low return in dues and a new kind of [black and Latino] membership that most unions were unaccustomed—or even unwilling—to deal with."[18]

Despite these obstacles, some individuals in the labor movement had made attempts to organize hospital workers. Godoff's interest in organizing health-care workers dated back to 1935 when he first worked at Israel Zion Hospital in Brooklyn. He became a full-time organizer in 1938 and brought together several thousand workers in the city-run hospitals. Later on, his organizing became somewhat risky since he was also active in Communist circles during the McCarthy era and in 1957, Teamsters Local 237 laid him off. He then took a job as a pharmacy employee at Maimonides Hospital and joined Local 1199. Godoff and Davis already knew each other, and the two struck up a conversation when Godoff arrived at union headquarters in search of a job. Davis invited Godoff to join the staff and lead an effort to organize hospital workers.[19]

Foner describes Godoff as "one of the most skilled union organizers of his day," and a key strategist in organizing hospital workers:

> Godoff was a patient, gentle man who knew an enormous amount about organizing hospitals. He knew exactly what people did in the different jobs. He knew how to find the natural leaders in each department and get their help in organizing departmental committees. He knew how to listen and make suggestions without being overpowering. He knew how to inspire people and still not act like a know-it-all hotshot. He knew how to test workers to see what they were ready to do.[20]

ORGANIZING WORKERS, 1957–1959

Organizing workers at Montefiore Hospital was Elliot Godoff's first assignment. He and Ted Mitchell began in 1958 by handing out union leaflets between 5:00 A.M. and 10:00 A.M., again during the lunch break, and finally from 3:00 P.M. to 11:00 P.M. They established a headquarters in a rented storefront on Gun Hill Road near Montefiore in the Bronx. Because 1199's headquarters were in far-off Midtown Manhattan, Godoff and Mitchell practically lived at the Gun Hill Road location for a year. Mitchell remembers that "about six blacks and a couple of Puerto Ricans" attended their first meeting. But soon, word spread.[21]

After learning about the union, Thelma Bowles, who worked in the hospital's nursing department, would go to the Gun Hill Road office after her night shift to talk with Mitchell and Godoff about what she saw happening inside the hospital. Godoff and Mitchell gave Bowles advice and taught her how to sign up workers. "I knew nothing about unions," she says. "I had never been in a union before. [But] I wanted to see something worthwhile done. I've always been one for advancement, in anything. I can't stand anything

that moves backwards instead of forward." Once trained, Bowles was inde-
fatigable. After working the night shift, she would "come into the hospital
around lunch time [to] catch some of the girls," she recalls. In the women's
locker room during shift changes, she would talk with female workers from
all departments about the union, persuade them to circulate leaflets around
the hospital, and convince them to sign union commitment cards.[22]

Labor pioneers like Bowles, Downs, and Joseph Brown were the first to
start signing up black and Puerto Rican service workers in large numbers.
Brown had had some experience with labor organizing from his days in
Baltimore working in construction, where he became "union-minded." He
joined Local 240, an integrated union for mechanics, bricklayers, and carpenters, and eventually became a well-liked and well-respected shop steward. In 1948, he moved his family to the Bronx. His wife's sister worked for
the New York City Transit Authority, and another sister worked for a New
York hospital. Brown had visited them in New York several times. "I liked
it," he says, "and my mother-in-law liked it, too. So, I felt that coming to New
York, I could find a better job than what I had." He took a job as a meat cut-
ter in New Jersey and joined the amalgamated union, which was ethnically
diverse and included workers from Europe and Puerto Rico, again serving as a shop steward. He worked in the meat-packing industry for about
three years before an on-the-job injury laid him out for a year. In 1954, rest-
less and ready to get back to work, Brown walked the five blocks from his
home to Montefiore Hospital. Knowing something about maintenance and
engineering from his construction days, he got a job on the spot working
as a mason alongside mostly white immigrants from Germany, Yugoslavia,
Armenia, Poland, and Italy.

Brown proved a critical force in the early organizing efforts. Unlike his co-
workers, the threat of being fired for his organizing work did not intimidate
him. He believed he could return to his meat-packing job in New Jersey at
any point and had settled his worker's compensation claim for a large sum of
money. "I didn't pay that no mind," says Brown, " 'cause . . . I had nothing to
lose." When they first met, Brown told Mitchell and Godoff that he had been
"talking the union around here, but [the workers] seem to have a lot of fear."
Then Brown told them, "You give me a handful of cards, and I'll see what I
can do." Brown spoke to his fellow workers about their right to organize and
stated that no one "can stop a group of workers from organizing and making

a choice of a union." A pro-union boss, one of the chief engineers, facilitated Brown's organizing efforts by allowing him to go around the hospital to speak with other workers. Brown talked to the supervisors in other departments as well, gaining access to their employees, and he was able to organize thirty workers a day, including nurse's aides, orderlies, and dietary workers. With the help of a young colleague in his department, Bill Dallas, Brown organized close to 95 percent of the maintenance workers in less than two months.[23]

The first real break in the organizing drive came when the hospital administration decided to end a long-standing meal plan. Montefiore had traditionally allowed workers to eat in the cafeteria and then deducted the cost of these "free meals" from workers' paychecks. When the hospital hired Jacques Bloch, head of food and nutrition at Montefiore, to lead its new food-service department in 1954, he reorganized the department, opened a new cafeteria, and ended the free-food policy within three years. Fink and Greenberg argue that the decision "increased the amount of take-home pay for workers but still triggered resentments."[24] That may be true, but the real issue seems to have been that the quality and quantity of food provided by the hospital was greater than anything workers might be able to procure independently with their slightly increased take-home pay. In addition, the hospital cafeteria served as a de facto restaurant for many workers who could not afford to eat out, giving it cultural and social significance. Ken Downs, who worked on the lunch line, was the first to recognize that this change could be the thing to galvanize workers. He told Godoff to start an aggressive organizing movement.

Food played an important role in these first efforts to reach out to workers. "We had a party [at my apartment]," says Downs, "and I cooked chicken and rice and peas." The migration of large numbers of blacks from the South and the Caribbean during World War I and II contributed to the introduction of Caribbean and southern foods and dishes in New York City. Over the years, immigrants from these two regions have indeed made an indelible mark on New York culture, particularly in Harlem, Brooklyn, and the Bronx where jazz, reggae, and later hip-hop became popular forms of musical expression, and fried chicken, fried plantains, meat patties, jerked and curried meats and poultry, and rice-and-bean dishes became part of the local cuisine. In fact, every region of the American South and the Caribbean has had a different take on rice-and-bean dishes like Downs's Barbadian rice and peas.

BARBADIAN RICE AND PEAS

8 oz dried pigeon peas

3–4 dried bay leaves

3 garlic cloves, diced

Bajan spice mix*

4–5 whole peppercorns

¼–½ lb smoked turkey, salt beef, or salt pork
(or 1 cup vegetable broth for meatless rice)

1 cup rice

Small onion, peeled

2 celery stalks, diced

Oil

Cover peas with water, add seasoning, and bring to a boil. Reduce heat and simmer for approximately 45 minutes. Add meat, rice, onion, celery, and oil, stirring well. Cover and simmer until the water is absorbed or grains are soft and fluffy, approximately 20 minutes.
Serve hot.

▬

*Bajan seasoning is a blend of fresh herbs (thyme, marjoram, spring onions, onions, garlic, parsley, basil, and scotch bonnet pepper) and spices (such as clove, black pepper, paprika, and salt).

The workers met in one another's homes for a month—and Downs catered the food. Every day, he met more low-skilled workers and hospital lab technicians as they came through the food line in the cafeteria, and he convinced them to start attending the home meetings. He wore out his shoes going from floor to floor at night, signing up workers for the union. Downs gained a reputation not only as a great cook but also as a union man. He even won a union prize for the most new registrants. The catalyst for all this success, he argued, was the food. If the hospitals hadn't stopped giving free food in the cafeteria, he says, "I doubt a union would be in there today."[25]

Bowles and other organizers invited Montefiore workers to a union-sponsored lunch at the makeshift headquarters on Gun Hill Road sometime in 1958. Bowles and three other night shift workers went to her house the morning after their shifts to prepare sandwiches for the event. "We'd make the sandwiches and then I would pack them in a box and I would take them to the union headquarters for the luncheon," Bowles recalls. "I remember that Moe [Foner] was on the phone calling me, 'Bring more sandwiches, bring more sandwiches!'" Bowles says with laughter. "We were working like beavers trying to get these sandwiches" to all the workers who had heard about the free lunch and packed the union hall.

The Gun Hill Road headquarters became an important place for Montefiore workers to "drop in and talk to anyone if they wanted to," explains Bowles. It was within walking distance of the hospital, and workers could come by, "hear what the union organizers had to say," and ask questions. The Bronx union hall also played a crucial role in building solidarity among workers of different ethnic and racial backgrounds. In the hospital, workers often remained separated according to clearly established occupational hierarchies, but at the union hall, Bowles says, workers "began to know each other [as equals]. . . . By the time of the strike, everybody was like real brothers and sisters."[26]

Initially, few Puerto Ricans wanted to join the movement. "They wasn't accustomed to the big wages," Downs recalls, "they didn't have the experience" of how joining a union could improve working conditions. "But once they learned about the benefits, they started to join."[27] Roberto Gomez, an attendant in the physical therapy department, was the first Puerto Rican to participate. Salvadore Cordero, Bernardo Quinones, and Emerito Cruz soon joined Gomez in getting Puerto Rican workers to sign Local 1199 union cards. Cruz began working in Montefiore's nutrition department in 1952 when he was twenty-nine. Before following his sister to New York City in the early 1950s, Cruz had worked as an attendant in a psychiatric hospital in Puerto Rico. He had been a pioneer in organizing hospital workers back home, serving as vice president of a hospital workers' union and helping establish labor laws to protect the rights of hospital employees.[28]

In general, organizing Puerto Rican workers proved challenging, Cordero says, because of the cultural notion that having a job, regardless of the terms or conditions, was the most important thing. And, he says, Puerto

Ricans were "scared to join" a union for fear of being fired. To recruit them, Gomez explained that they had everything to gain and nothing to lose. They already had low wages and bad treatment, so how much worse could it get? Quinones used more pointed tactics. He was one of Montefiore's most popular Spanish-speaking workers, and was also the hospital's local loan shark and numbers runner, which meant that he lent money and placed illegal gambling bets on sporting events for many Hispanic workers. When Quinones asked Mitchell how he could help the union, Mitchell handed him twenty-five union application cards. Quinones went into the hospital and returned fifteen minutes later with all the cards signed. Thanks to Quinones's powers of persuasion, Hispanic workers became a large contingent of the organized workers at Montefiore.[29]

According to Mitchell, having bold, popular, and influential insiders willing to convince their peers to join a united struggle with other ethnic groups is the key to any successful multiethnic coalition. Mitchell and Godoff intentionally sought out workers like Brown and Quinones who could fill that role and mobilize the black and Puerto Rican populations at Montefiore. They knew workers in every department and had jobs that gave them mobility throughout the hospital. Brown signed up people for the union as he made his rounds as a plasterer while Cruz had daily contact with huge numbers of workers who passed through the cafeteria.[30] Organizers can't organize on their own, said Mitchell. "You gotta have the people on the inside."[31]

By the summer of 1958, a majority of the black and Puerto Rican workers at Montefiore carried 1199 membership cards. To test workers' strike readiness, Godoff and Leon Davis asked them to march with signs and pass out leaflets in front of hospital buildings.[32] They also organized a half-day work stoppage. During the first walkout, the technicians and maintenance workers proved the most disciplined and refused to let anybody go to work. During a subsequent cafeteria boycott, Mitchell reported, "The workers fell in line and nobody, including the doctors, ate."[33] Later that summer, Davis began talks with hospital administrators about formal union recognition and the right to collective bargaining. Montefiore officials refused. "Administrative intransigency stemmed at least in part from an awareness that the confrontation with 1199 involved more than local issues," explain Fink and Greenberg. "Recognition of the union at Montefiore would [have been] the first major breakthrough for hospital unionism citywide."[34]

In the fall, Davis took steps to formalize the union at Montefiore. Voluntary committees became official democratic structures and each department elected union stewards. On December 30, 1958, Local 1199 held a union election, and out of 900 workers eligible to vote, 628 said yes to union representation in collective bargaining talks and 31 said no.[35] Next, Davis reached out to Harry Van Arsdale, president of the AFL-CIO's Central Labor Council, which represented unions with a combined membership of more than 2 million workers. Van Arsdale liked the idea of uniting labor in a campaign focused on unionizing poor, non-white workers.[36] Van Arsdale later endorsed 1199's strike and represented the union in settlement talks with Mayor Robert F. Wagner Jr. Recognizing the demographic shift occurring in New York's workforce, Van Arsdale astutely realized the necessity of organizing blacks and Latinos in order for the labor movement to remain strong and relevant.[37]

Moe Foner, 1199's public-relations specialist, also waged a media campaign in support of the workers, establishing close working relationships with the staff at the *Amsterdam News*, a weekly African American newspaper, and *El Diario*, the Hispanic daily. He regularly sent news releases and once took a group of workers carrying their pay stubs to the Harlem offices of the *Amsterdam News*. In response, the paper published an article about the economic injustices facing workers at Montefiore, and *El Diario* followed with similar articles. "Coverage in the Hispanic and black press was extensive," observes Foner, while white-controlled papers like the *New York Times* and the *New York Post* took longer to get on board. Davis called a meeting of the workers and asked for a strike vote. At the last minute, however, the hospital agreed to enter into negotiations to avoid a strike.[38]

It's unclear if they negotiated before formalizing the union, but the two sides reached a settlement in December 1958 that provided a modicum of gains for the workers: a $30-per-month increase in pay, time-and-a-half pay for work beyond a forty-hour work week, establishment of grievance procedures, and the setting of minimum provisions for sick leave and vacation time. The settlement "electrified the strikers," says Foner. "The union became like a church to them. It was something they believed in deeply. It was theirs. It was their way to a better life." Foner recalls that "news about Montefiore spread around the city like wildfire."[39] Hospital workers citywide called 1199 headquarters and asked to join the union. "We distributed thousands of application cards and the postman was carrying in stacks and stacks of returns," Foner says.

As a result of its success at Montefiore, Local 1199 announced that it would try to organize all 35,000 employees in the city's voluntary hospitals and nursing homes. Godoff and Mitchell led the initial effort and were soon joined by Montefiore shop stewards.[40] Godoff developed a strategy that would allow 1199 organizers to identify potential pioneers at other hospitals and evaluate their strength and determination. "We didn't even know where some of the hospitals were," says Foner. "We sent Montefiore members all around the city to speak. Godoff charted the hospital departments where we had strength, and it was growing daily." They invited groups of workers to the 1199 headquarters to organize committees, plan meetings, and come up with strategies for signing up co-workers. "In different corners of our headquarters there would be meetings every night of workers from various hospitals," says Foner. Godoff opened union offices near each of the hospitals where workers could hold meetings with 1199 staffers.[41]

Julio Pagan, an orderly in the nursing department at Mount Sinai Hospital, was one the first pioneers Godoff recruited at Mount Sinai. Low wages and long hours as well as his desire that supervisors in the nursing department show workers some respect sparked Pagan's interest in union organizing. Originally from Ponce, Puerto Rico, Pagan attended an organizing meeting at 1199 headquarters in 1959. "That's when I got all the ideas," Pagan says. "How to have a union and how to organize the other workers—they taught us how to do it."[42]

Of the hundreds of workers Pagan brought into the union, Henry Nicholas, an African American from Mississippi, became one of the most influential. Nicholas was an unlikely crusader at first, hesitant even to sign his union card. Pagan "tried to get me to come to union meetings," Nicholas recalls, but "I was very afraid that I might get fired." When Nicholas, also an orderly, realized that black and Latino hospital workers faced the same problems he'd seen growing up black in the South—racist white supervisors, low wages, long hours—he was convinced to sign the card and start organizing alongside Pagan: "I saw . . . the blacks and Hispanics in the same kind of situation [as the black farmer in Mississippi].The hierarchical structure of the [hospital] administration was a carbon copy of the system used by wealthy white male land owners to control the South."[43]

When Leon Davis came to address workers at Beth Israel Medical Center in late 1958, he inspired a dietary worker, Hilda Joquin, to overcome her doubts that hospital workers could be unionized at all. Joquin contacted Davis and formed a group of thirteen Beth Israel workers. At meetings held at one another's homes, the group strategized about how to distribute information about the union to co-workers. As Joquin notes, black and Hispanic workers from the dietary, housekeeping, and laundry departments showed the most support for the union, and younger workers also tended to respond more favorably than older workers.[44] One Sinai employee, Olivia Barney, had belonged to a union as a clothing factory worker in Georgia; when Joquin and others began organizing at Mount Sinai Hospital, Barney recalls, "I was definitely for it."[45] The Sinai employees Pearl Jumack, Edith Garcia, Marjorie Phillips, Ramon Callone, Rose Coulter, and Joquin led the organizing discussions. Like the rest of the hospitals, black and Hispanic workers were the majority of Beth Israel's and Mount Sinai's workforce, and the emerging union leadership reflected that. Eventually, workers elected Garcia, Andrew Brown, and Cholla Simone to be shop stewards.

Similar organizing efforts spread to Lenox Hill Hospital, the Jewish Hospital of Brooklyn (now part of Interfaith Medical Center), Bronx Hospital (now part of the Bronx-Lebanon Hospital Center), Flower and Fifth Avenue Hospital (now Terence Cardinal Cooke Health Care Center), Beth-El Hospital (now the Brookdale Hospital Medical Center), and United Israel Zion Hospital (now Maimonides Medical Center). Things did not always go as smoothly in some other hospitals, however. It proved impossible, for example, for 1199 to organize the Cuban workers in Catholic hospitals such as St. Clare's Hospital and Health Center and St. Vincent's Hospital. The nuns who ran those Catholic hospitals hired many refugees who fled the 1959 Cuban Revolution, explains Mitchell. These relatively devout Catholic Cubans, who began migrating to Miami and New York in increasing numbers after Fidel Castro's consolidation of power, tended to side with the nuns' antiunion sentiments. The nuns also hired a large number of Catholic South American immigrants with conservative views on workers' rights. The nuns wielded significant power in the hospitals and held religious influence over their Catholic workforce, who viewed attacks on their employers as attacks on their religion.[46]

STRIKE, 1959

This flurry of union organizing was not ignored by hospital administrators. Under the auspices of its resolutely anti-union trade association, the Greater New York Hospital Association (GNYHA), hospital managers "launched a retaliation" that included firing workers who participated in union activities and requiring all employees speak English on the job in order to obstruct union business conducted in Spanish.

By early 1959, Local 1199 made a strategic decision to retrench and focus on organizing in the handful of hospitals where it had strong support: Mount Sinai, Beth Israel, Beth David, Lenox Hill, Bronx Hospital, and Brooklyn Jewish. Representatives of 1199 asked the management of those hospitals to hold elections so the workers could decide if they wanted formal union representation. Hospital officials, in Moe Foner's words, "stonewalled." The union responded by organizing a strike vote in May 1959 (figure 2.1). "We explained to the workers that a strike might be long and difficult," says Foner, "that the union had no money to pay strike benefits and that there might be injunctions and jail sentences. . . . But we said that if members went to jail, leaders would, too. The vote was 2,258 to 95 to strike."[47] Hospital officials obtained a temporary restraining order from the municipal court to prevent a strike. Meanwhile, Leon Davis and other 1199 officials went into hiding to avoid being served with the subpoenas. Davis appointed Ted Mitchell and Armando Ramirez, a Cuban, to be 1199 "area directors," which gave them the authority to negotiate on behalf of the workers in talks with hospital management while Davis and the others remained in hiding.[48]

The strike started on May 8, 1959, at 6:00 A.M. Except for a few workers who were afraid of losing their jobs, 3,500 workers from seven hospitals went out on strike in unison (figures 2.2–2.5).[49] "The spirit of the strikers was amazing," remembers Foner. "It was like they'd been freed after lifetimes of being bottled up."[50] At Mount Sinai, Julio Pagan was one of the first to walk out and went immediately to 1199's basement headquarters two blocks from the hospital. Hours later, he and several other Spanish-speaking workers hoisted placards on a picket line in front of the hospital. Henry Nicholas, who just months earlier had been afraid to sign his union card, marched with Pagan.[51] The two also organized the picket line

FIGURE 2.1 Members of Local 1199 voting to strike, 1959. (Courtesy of Kheel Center for Labor-Management Documentation and Archives, Cornell University, Ithaca, N.Y.)

together, splitting coverage so that they could take turns sleeping for a few hours at union headquarters. Nicholas recalls that Pagan "would come and wake me up and I would go out, come back and wake him up."[52] During the strike, the union hall provided a space where black and Latino workers could communicate openly. "I think the strike made us one big happy family, and everybody looked out for the other person," remembers Thelma Bowles.[53]

Multiracial coalitions worked together around the clock in support of the strike. Blacks and Latinos collaborated on contacting workers who had not supported the strike at the outset. They conducted home visits where they sat down, explained their rights as workers, and discussed what could be gained from joining the strike. In most cases, Pagan recalls, holdouts joined the picket line the next day. As the strike lingered, workers received various types of support from organized labor and civil rights groups.[54]

Shortly after the start of the strike, the labor leader Harry Van Arsdale called a meeting of all the unions in the city to develop a strategy for

FIGURE 2.2 Striking workers at Montefiore Hospital, 1959. (Courtesy of Kheel Center for Labor-Management Documentation and Archives, Cornell University, Ithaca, N.Y.)

FIGURE 2.3 Picket line at Lenox Hill Hospital, 1959. (Courtesy of Kheel Center for Labor-Management Documentation and Archives, Cornell University, Ithaca, N.Y.)

supporting the striking workers. Officials went back to their locals and asked their members to support everyone on the picket lines. "These strikers are *human beings,* no matter what their color or country of origin," the leaders from Local 585 stated in a letter sent to members on May 13, 1959:

FIGURE 2.4 Picket line at Brooklyn Jewish Hospital, 1959. (Courtesy of Kheel Center for Labor-Management Documentation and Archives, Cornell University, Ithaca, N.Y.)

Many of them are on WELFARE DEPARTMENT [capitals in the original] relief, so they can afford to buy just the food, clothing, and shelter to keep them and their families alive when they are working. The hospitals refuse to understand . . . and threaten the union with fines, jail, and the strikers [living in hospital-owned housing] with eviction notices and the threat of no jobs to return to. . . . YOU CAN HELP THEM WIN THIS STRIKE!"

FIGURE 2.5 Picket line at Brooklyn Jewish Hospital, 1959. (Courtesy of Kheel Center for Labor-Management Documentation and Archives, Cornell University, Ithaca, N.Y.)

Local 585 and many other unions encouraged their members to bring "canned food or [send] cash, check, or money order to us, to be given to Local 1199 FOOD FUND." They also asked members to send the striking workers "a note of support with your food or dollars to let them know that you believe in what they are doing." The letter ended: "This fight for rights is expected to continue for a lengthy period as more hospitals join in the strike. Give at least once, but please remember the need for food is three (3) times a day for these people, so keep the food and money coming in, and you will have the blessings of these unfortunate people."[55] In all, 175 unions responded to Van Arsdale's call for support, and contributions poured into 1199 headquarters.

The financial support from other unions allowed 1199's staff to distribute food, money for transportation, and free medical care to striking workers (figure 2.6). The brewery trade unions and the Service Employees

FIGURE 2.6 Members of Local 1199 preparing to distribute food donations for striking workers. (Courtesy of Kheel Center for Labor-Management Documentation and Archives, Cornell University, Ithaca, N.Y.)

International Union (SEUI) joined picket lines and brought food. The bakery workers brought fresh-baked breads, cakes, and rolls. The Amalgamated Meat Cutters and Butcher Workmen of North America (AMCBW) donated two weeks' worth of meat to every hospital worker out on strike and provided cold cuts to strike headquarters for sandwiches. Members of the Transport Workers Union (TWU) contributed thousands of cans of food and walked on picket lines. The International Brotherhood of Electrical Workers (IBEW) made the largest donation: $28,115, which paid for 48,000 eggs and 4,000 chickens.[56]

Eleven days into the strike, New York City mayor Robert Wagner tried to broker a settlement. The available documentary history does not provide details, but the members of 1199 voted overwhelmingly to reject the offer, and workers at nine additional hospitals voted to join the strike. The GNYHA went on the offensive. Their attorney filed legal injunctions against the unions for shutting down member hospitals, and a state court ordered

PUERTO RICAN ARROZ CON POLLO

In the 1950s, recently created public-housing projects in New York City had mostly Puerto Rican and black residents from the South and the Caribbean. Growing up in these ethnic borderlands meant having black and Latino people living on all sides of your family apartment. As a result, black youth grew up with the smells of southern dishes like chitlins, collard greens, and frying chicken; they also grew up smelling signature Puerto Rican dishes like *ropa vieja, mofongo* (a pounded plantain-based dish), *sancocho* (a vegetable-based broth/soup), *tostones* (deep-fried plantain chips), *moros y cristianos* ("Moors and Christians" [black beans and white rice]), and arroz con pollo (rice with chicken).

* * *

1 tbsp olive oil

4 chicken thighs

1 onion, diced

1 bell pepper, diced

1 cup white or brown rice

Salt and pepper to taste

1 tbsp cumin

1 tbsp oregano

Sazón (optional)*

2 cups chicken broth

Heat a drizzle of olive oil in a large pot. Heat chicken for five minutes a side and set aside in a container with a lid. Add onion and bell pepper to the pot, and cook until the onions are translucent and the peppers are softened. Pour in rice and let it cook for a few minutes. Stir ingredients (this part is essential for the smoky flavor of the meal). Add salt and pepper, cumin, oregano, and sazón. Pour in the broth and add the chicken. Bring to a boil. Put the lid on the pot and simmer for 15–20 minutes or until rice is soft.

---

*Sazón is a seasoned salt typically containing coriander, cilantro, achiote (a spice made from the red seed of the annatto tree), and garlic that is used to flavor meats, fish, poultry, soups, and stews (some brands include MSG).

Davis and 1199's business agent, George Goodman, to end the work stoppage at Brooklyn Jewish Hospital. When they refused, the presiding judge held the two men in contempt of court and sentenced them to fifteen days in jail and a $250 fine. Additional injunctions and fines followed, but they only hardened the resolve of the picketing workers and led to additional contributions from the labor community and minority-controlled Democratic political clubs.[57]

POLITICAL CLUBS

These minority-controlled Democratic political clubs have long played an important role in Progressive movements in New York City. Membership in political clubs was determined by party, ethnicity, and assembly district, and the clubs provided volunteers and support to candidates for office by distributing political patronage in the form of jobs, permits, and perks. If so inclined, political club bosses were able to help qualified people get appointed or elected to positions of power; they also held the ability to direct support toward favored causes. The hospital workers' strike was one such cause.[58]

In the 1950s, a Jamaican immigrant, Ed Stevenson Sr., founded the Jackson Democratic Club in the Morrisania section of the Bronx. The club not just became an important political institution for both southern blacks and black immigrants from the Caribbean but also carried on a protracted campaign to expand opportunities for minorities in the county Democratic Party. Out of that effort, the county's first African American assemblyman, Walter H. Gladwin, was elected.[59] There was also a thriving left-of-center club on 116th Street in Harlem called the Vito Marcantonio Democratic Club. Santos Crespo's father, a member of DC 37, belonged to that club and described Marcantonio as "very much to the left before [the] left was popular. And . . . although he was Italian, he represented a large constituency of Puerto Ricans and African Americans from Spanish Harlem to the tip of West Harlem. [He was] very progressive."[60] Thomas R. Fortune, a black political boss, controlled the Thomas R. Fortune Democratic Club (later the Unity Democratic Club) on Ralph Avenue and Decatur Street in Brooklyn's Bed-Stuy neighborhood. A native of Suffolk, Virginia, Fortune migrated to Brooklyn at nineteen and made his mark as a Bed-Stuy businessman. In 1969, he served the Fifty-fifth District as a member of the New York State Assembly and chaired the Black and Puerto Rican Legislative Caucus. He was also the chair of the New York Council of Elected Black Democratic Officials, which championed funding services for the poor. As a kingmaker in Bed-Stuy, Fortune launched the political careers of several well-known Democratic officials: the first black congresswoman and presidential candidate, Shirley Chisholm; the New York State assemblyman Al Vann; and Major Owens, who took over Chisholm's congressional seat when she retired.

During the strike, political clubs and ethnically based civic organizations provided support and financial assistance to the hospital workers. Thomas Russell Jones, vice president of a Brooklyn-based Democratic club, wrote:

> At the request of the members of the Bedford-Stuyvesant Political League, I have been directed to present to you the enclosed gift in the form of a check for $50 to assist you in your strike struggles. The Bedford-Stuyvesant Political League is largely composed of Negro people in Bedford-Stuyvesant who are engaged in a struggle on the political front for full citizenship rights and Negro representation in every phase of government. Our program is designed to protect our Negro citizens economically and in their civil rights. We will render every possible support to you and extend to you our sincere wholehearted best wishes for union recognition and decent wages.[61]

Similarly, the Gowanus Spanish American Club in Brooklyn sent a small contribution of $22.25 to 1199. Its members, all with Hispanic surnames, signed the cover letter "Your Fellow workers."[62] The Spanish Harlem–based Caribe Democratic Club made a $32 contribution to the food fund for striking hospital workers.[63]

Unions, political clubs, and individuals donated so much food that 1199 was able to create a makeshift grocery store for the striking workers. Ted Mitchell remembers distributing "bags of food" filled with fresh bread, poultry, meat, eggs, and canned foods to striking workers every week.[64] Olivia Barney recalls, "They gave us beans, peas, and sugar. We and the Puerto Ricans were bean people, so that was good."[65]

In the American South, African Americans, particularly country-store owners and family farmers, used a combination of cash, bartering, subsistence farming, canning, and the preparation of nitty-gritty, good-tasting, down-home food to survive hard times with dignity. They cooked garden-grown staples, herbs, and spices, such as greens (callaloo, collards, kale, mustard, and turnip greens), cornbread, molasses, and black-eyed peas or pinto beans seasoned with crushed red pepper, bay leaf, and sage. African American seasonings also make use of several fresh vegetables, including chopped scallions and/or onions and garlic. The final component that makes southern African American food unique is the addition of pork in dishes like greens, black-eyed peas, lima beans, and pinto beans. What's most southern about southern food is the inclusion of pork in some shape or fashion in just about every dish. Puerto Rican food has many similarities in terms of seasoning with distinctive variations, such as the use of the already mentioned sazón.

SOUTHERN PINTO BEAN SOUP

2 lbs dry pinto beans

2 clean pig's feet (or smoked turkey or vegan substitute)

1 tbsp salt

1 tbsp black pepper

1 tsp ground cayenne pepper

1 tsp onion powder

Check beans for rocks. Place pig's feet into a cheesecloth bag and make sure you have it tied so it cannot come loose in the pot. Put all the ingredients into a nonstick stock pot or a pot coated with cooking spray. Cover beans with water. Bring to a boil and reduce to simmer. Stir often and add water if necessary. Cook until soup is thick and brown. Remove cheesecloth and serve.

Source: http://www.soulfoodandsoutherncooking.com/how-to-cook-pinto-beans.html.

As the strike continued, 1199's Foner worked to gain support from prominent civil rights leaders. The New York attorney Stanley Levenson, who served as a close adviser to Martin Luther King Jr., organized a meeting between Foner and the young Atlanta-born pastor. Foner described the plight of the hospital workers to King, who responded, "Count me in . . . whatever I can do, call on me, deal through Stanley for anything you want from me."[66] Soon after, Foner got a statement from King saying, "The hospital struggle [is] against degradation, poverty, and misery" and that it is "against all the evils that afflict poor black people in this society."[67] King's endorsement of the hospital workers' cause persuaded a number of New York civil rights leaders and organizations to throw their support behind the strike. "Being able to say that Dr. King supported 1199 at such and such a hospital became a powerful tool," says Foner.[68]

Part of 1199's strategy was to link the hospital workers' strike with the larger labor and civil rights movements that were developing in the 1950s. Mitchell was a member of the labor committee of the National Association for the Advancement of Colored People (NAACP), and he spoke at NAACP meetings in support of 1199's efforts during the strike.[69] In press releases, 1199 stressed that black and Hispanic hospital workers went out on strike for "union and human rights."[70] According to Fink and Greenberg, the 1959 strike, composed of labor groups and a coalition of black and Hispanic organizations, was "one of the first northern struggles to directly tap a growing civil rights constituency."[71]

BLACK AND HISPANIC CIVIL RIGHTS COALITIONS

The human rights argument resonated with activists, and the demographics of the striking hospital workers challenged leaders to think beyond their own constituencies. L. Joseph Overton, president of the New York chapter of the NAACP, sent out a press release on May 17, 1959, calling on

all of those in the City of New York [in] all five boroughs who are of Latin-American descent or African descent to rise up in protest and demonstrate your objections to this type of injustice that is now being imposed on our brothers and sisters. We call on all of those who believe in justice and the right to freedom for all mankind to join this protest and demand that those who are desirous of having a collective bargaining agreement and a decent wage be granted.

At the end of Overton's press release, he pressured local politicians and members of the clergy to come out in support of the hospital workers as well. "I am sure that when brought to the attention of Congressman Adam Clayton Powell Jr. and the Baptist Ministers Association and the Methodist ministers as well, not forgetting, however, the Episcopal and Catholics, that they also will register their protest against any one refusing an individual the right to collective bargaining if they so desire."[72]

On May 19, 1959, Overton contacted Juan Sanchez, president of the Manhattan-based Federation of Hispanic Societies Incorporated (FHS), to ask that he encourage Hispanic groups to join the NAACP in support of the hospital workers. He was organizing "Operation Humanity," a series of mass demonstrations to take place on May 24, 1959, in front of several hospitals that were denying workers "their constitutional rights to bargain," and Overton wanted Sanchez to mobilize his constituency to take part in these events.[73] Sanchez sent a joint press release with Gilberto Gerena Valentín, chairman of FHS's labor relations committee and president of the Congress of Puerto Rican Municipalities, which stated, "Thousands of Puerto Ricans, Negroes, and other minorities are the victims of unbelievably bad working conditions. We ask and urge every citizen to file a strong protest with the proper authorities, so that the hospital workers are given decent salaries and working conditions, so that this shameful situation is corrected immediately." Sanchez and Valentín announced that Operation Humanity would launch the following week, and they asked "every Puerto Rican and other Spanish-speaking persons to march together with their citizens in this crusade, in this common fight of the Negro and the Puerto Rican community for a better life and a more compassionate attitude from their employers."[74] Sanchez and Valentín sent the press release to a wide variety of women's groups, civic and mutual aid organizations, councils and federations, labor unions, elected officials, and prominent lawyers. (Many of these organizations no longer exist.)

A number of prominent African American leaders and organizations also answered Overton's call, including delegations from local chapters of the NAACP, the Federation of Hispanic-American Societies, and the

Urban League. Adam Clayton Powell's participation was the most significant because his presence drew the media. To support Operation Humanity,
Powell came with several busloads of congregants from his Harlem church
and picketed outside Mount Sinai Hospital. Following the television coverage of Operation Humanity, political support and monetary contributions
poured into 1199 headquarters from national and local organizations.[75]

Fay Bennett, executive secretary of National Sharecroppers Fund, produced a press release in support of the striking workers: "We, the Board of
Directors of the National Sharecroppers, understand the problems of hospital workers particularly well because we find that they parallel the conditions
of hired farm and migrant workers with whom we are primarily concerned."
Puerto Rican agricultural workers represented a large segment of the people
whom National Sharecroppers worked with in the Hudson River Valley, just
north of the city. The press release, dated June 1, 1959, continued: "The average pay of hospital workers is $32.00 to $38.00 a week; this [is] not far from
the $5.90 a day which farm workers averaged in 1956 and 1957, and their pay
today is at approximately the same level. . . . The first and immediate answer
must be recognition of the hospital workers, like other workers, to the dignity of self organization in unions of their own choosing, and improvements
in their wage scale to allow for a decent standard of living."[76]

A number of new black and brown coalitions formed and sponsored
various events and demonstrations to aid the cause of the workers. One of
the most interesting examples of these was Local 32E and the Bronx chapter of the NAACP's creation of a black and Puerto Rican organization, the
Neighborhood Committee to Aid Bronx Hospital Strikers. In June 1959, the
coalition of activists organized an outdoor rally in support of the striking
hospital workers; it created bilingual flyers in Spanish and English to advertise the event, asking in large print, "WHO CAN LIVE ON $23 A WEEK?"
(figure 2.7)[77]

The impact of Operation Humanity and the subsequent rallies and demonstrations was enormous. These events drew sufficient media attention to
win endorsements from a number of high-profile people, including former
first lady Eleanor Roosevelt and former senator Herbert H. Lehman. They
also created enough political pressure to convince the mayor to intervene.
On June 22, 1959, after a forty-six-day strike, Mayor Robert Wagner forced
the two sides to an agreement. Hospital managers, a minority of workers

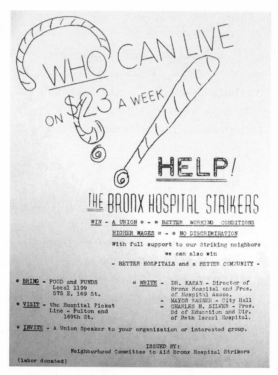

FIGURE 2.7 Flyer announcing a giant outdoor rally in the Bronx. (Courtesy of Kheel Center for Labor-Management Documentation and Archives, Cornell University, Ithaca, N.Y.)

who crossed picket lines, actually took over the work of those employees out on strike. Hospital mechanics and technicians receiving good salaries of as much as $80 per week insisted that they were not on strike, but they refused to cross the picket lines. In one instance, a plumber from one hospital told the *Amsterdam News* that one of the eight plumbers at the unnamed hospital where he worked had crossed the picket line. Hospital officials there increased the salary of the one plumber who did not go out on strike from $45 per week to $60 and hired a "scabbing Negro plumber" as a replacement worker.[78] In another example, Vera Green, a twenty-three-year-old clerk and typist from the Bronx, had earned $53 per week at an unnamed hospital. She went on strike in response to what she viewed as the hospital's unjust sick-leave policy. Green told the *Amsterdam News* that only three of the eight typists in her department went out on strike. The rest remained on the job but observed a work stoppage in which they refused to type. Hospital officials brought in a "scabbing typist" to do their work. The available sources do not indicate if the strategy of the hospital officials to replace the striking workers and those observing a work stoppage affected their abilities to care for patients or if any hospitals had to shut down or turn away patients. The agreement that Mayor Wagner worked out did not grant formal union recognition, but it did create the conditions for change. The settlement stated that a committee of twelve hospital representatives and six public representatives, to be appointed by the chief justice of the New York State Court of Appeals, would oversee hospital policy on labor relations. This committee would collect data, hear testimony, and make public recommendations to the hospitals based on its findings. It's not clear why the workers agreed to the committee structure; perhaps they interpreted its recommendations as nonbinding. It is also unclear whether the committee contained members of 1199's executive committee who are not mentioned in the available documented history.

The first state court hearing on the labor dispute began on May 31, 1960. Union representatives, who continued to organize workers behind the scenes, submitted proposals for improving wages and working conditions.[79] The union simultaneously began a legislative campaign in Albany to change state labor laws so that they would recognize hospital workers. Large delegations of workers went to Albany to lobby elected officials as part of this effort. "Our strategy after the 1959 strike," says Moe Foner, "was to achieve organized power in the workplace and enough political power to win passage in Albany of the collective bargaining rights."[80] Between 1959 and 1962, Local 1199 workers and organizers waged a protracted battle punctuated by long negotiations, legal fights, and occasional gains. They leveraged those small gains to organize workers at hospitals across the city.

In the spring of 1962, workers seeking union recognition at Beth-El Hospital in Brooklyn and Manhattan Eye, Ear, and Throat Institute went out on strike for fifty-six days. The courts again issued an injunction against 1199, and Leon Davis went to jail for thirty days. He refused to call off the strike after his release, so the judge sentenced him to six additional months in jail. A. Philip Randolph, the vice president of the AFL-CIO, put his substantial political capital and organizing skills toward assisting Davis and the striking

FIGURE 2.8 Baynard Rustin (*left*) and A. Philip Randolph (*second from left*) making a public statement. (Courtesy of Kheel Center for Labor-Management Documentation and Archives, Cornell University, Ithaca, N.Y.)

workers. Throughout his long career, Randolph, who was African American, put a premium on unity as a way to advance the labor movement's objectives. To that end, he reached out to civil rights leaders, ministers, bureaucrats, and elected officials—both black and brown—and asked for their help in battling what he called "the most dramatic form [of] second-class citizenship status and sweatshop wages of all minority group workers in our city."[81]

Bayard Rustin, Randolph's first lieutenant at the AFL-CIO, said that Randolph's charisma made him a favorite among unionists and Progressives (figure 2.8). Randolph had taken so much abuse from the government that "when he called [activists] to do anything, they turned out," Rustin recalls. "Many times up there we had Randolph's auditorium jammed with black trade unionists [and] church leaders in support of 1199. It was a kind of crusade." Randolph asked Rustin to draw up leaflets in English and Spanish aimed at winning support within the black and Hispanic communities for the striking hospital workers. While 1199 was mobilizing support for the hospital strike, Randolph's office was mobilizing hundreds of young people to go to the March on Washington the following year. "It was a very simple thing to put people on fire about one thing and to divert them to another thing where there was injustice and very obvious injustice to black people," Rustin says.[82] The NAACP, the Urban League, and the Congress of Racial

Equality (CORE) supplied additional ground troops to swell the ranks of 1199's picket lines. In fact, months before the 1963 March on Washington, Rustin had been mobilizing support for the 1962 strike at Beth-El Hospital in Brooklyn and Manhattan Eye, Ear, and Throat Institute.

Randolph also allied himself with Joseph Monserrat, a politician who had built a citywide multiethnic coalition of African Americans, West Indians, and Puerto Ricans. Born in Bayamón, Puerto Rico, Monserrat was a proxy leader for all Latinos, not just Puerto Ricans, and he held seats on multiple state committees related to labor exploitation and civil rights. By the time Randolph contacted him to help organize the hospital workers' conference, Monserrat was already an important power broker in the Hispanic community.[83]

EMERGENCY ACTION CONFERENCE, 1962

On June 29, 1962, approximately 150 people gathered in A. Philip Randolph's offices at 217 West 125th Street in Harlem to discuss the hospital workers' ongoing labor dispute. William K. De Fossett, an undercover FBI agent, attended the conference and wrote a detailed report describing the people who had attended the conference and what they had said. The FBI's surveillance records and 1199 correspondence show that a large number of the city's black and Hispanic leaders attended the conference, including noted intellectuals, performers, community activists, and unionists. Among those in attendance were James Baldwin, Ossie Davis, Gilberto Valentín, Cleveland Robinson (vice president of District 65 Distributive Workers of America, a labor adviser to Dr. King, and chairman of the 1963 March on Washington), and Cora Walker, the first African American female president of the Harlem Lawyers Association (figures 2.9 and 2.10).[84]

Above all else, De Fossett's report substantiates the claim that black and Hispanic leaders collaborated extensively to promote the civil rights and labor movements. In that regard, the participation of Malcolm X at the conference is particularly interesting. It was the first time that Malcolm X supported a labor union and the first time that he joined a multiethnic coalition as Elijah Muhammad's principal spokesman for the Nation of Islam. In 1962, Malcolm X was at the height of his popularity.[85] According to the FBI

FIGURE 2.9 Pete Seeger, Ossie Davis, and Ruby Dee singing at a Local 1199 event. (Courtesy of Kheel Center for Labor-Management Documentation and Archives, Cornell University, Ithaca, N.Y.)

FIGURE 2.10 Ricardo Montalban, Thurgood Marshall, and Local 1199 president Leon Davis presenting an award to Ossie Davis. (Courtesy of Kheel Center for Labor-Management Documentation and Archives, Cornell University, Ithaca, N.Y.)

report, Malcolm X sat quietly during much of the discussion and listened to the comments of other activists. Leon Davis said, "We talk so much about the conditions in the South . . . we forget about the conditions in our own backyard. It is no accident that 95 percent of the hospital workers were black and Puerto Rican—no one else would take such a low-paying and degrading job." Davis also criticized Congressman Powell for not taking a more active role in the labor dispute.[86] Percy Ellis Sutton, a prominent black activist and future Manhattan borough president, threw his support behind the hospital workers. Sutton suggested that the leaders of the various community organizations represented at the conference join the picket line: "We can't have civil rights until Negroes and Puerto Ricans have human rights." Joseph Monserrat argued a similar point. He thought that the city's white, privileged elites needed to learn that the city would not function "without the low-income workers. If all of these people would stop working for one day," he added, "the city would be at a standstill." When Malcolm X finally spoke, as De Fossett wrote in his FBI report, he "likened the problem of the Negroes and Puerto Ricans in New York City with the problems of the Negroes and Mexicans in Los Angeles. He severely criticized the Negro clergy and the Negro community leaders for failing the people they should be helping." Malcolm X offered all the community leaders and clergy the opportunity to speak at an upcoming Muslim rally in New York in July. "If the Negro and Puerto Rican are the balance of power in this city," he stated, "then they should use it and demand that the city government take action in this labor dispute." At the conclusion of the meeting, Bayard Rustin announced that a committee co-chaired by Randolph and Monserrat would be formed to strengthen community support for the hospital workers. This group was later named the Committee for Justice to Hospital Workers (CJHW) and Prayer Pilgrimage.[87]

This group set up a committee to raise money and collect foodstuffs for the strikers. The list of vice chairmen included Baldwin, Davis, James Farmer, Luis (Louis) Hernandez, Juan Mas, Frieda Montaldo, Cleveland Robinson, Sutton, Valentín, and Walker. Rustin served as the executive secretary. News of the creation of the CJHW had its intended effect. Just days later, Governor Nelson Rockefeller brought both sides to the bargaining table and publicly pledged to introduce legislation giving voluntary hospital workers coverage under the state Labor Relations Act and to back local legislation giving collective bargaining rights to workers at voluntary hospitals in the next legislative session. As a result, organizers suspended the second strike on July 18, 1962, and the CJHW planned a victory rally on July 22, 1962. The goals of the rally seemed to be to celebrate the end of the strike and apply political pressure on the governor so that he would keep his commitment in the months to come.[88]

We know that Malcolm X did show up at the rally (figure 2.11), but it's unclear whether others did not. A partial list of the planned speakers at the rally included Malcolm X; Martin Luther King Jr.; Roy Wilkins, the national executive secretary of the NAACP; Harry Van Arsdale; Davis; Monserrat Flores, president of the United Puerto Rican Organizations of the Bronx; Max Gonzalez, president of the Council of Puerto Rican and Spanish-American Organizations of New York; Robinson; Sutton; Valentín; Celia Vice, vice president of the Council of Puerto Rican Organizations of Brooklyn; and Monserrat. Police estimates put the crowd at more than 2,300 people—blacks, whites, and Hispanics.

FIGURE 2.11 Malcolm X speaking at a rally in support of black and Puerto Rican Local 1199 workers. (Courtesy of Kheel Center for Labor-Management Documentation and Archives, Cornell University, Ithaca, N.Y.)

Malcolm X addressed the crowd in his distinctively fast and force-ful tempo. His words reflected both his empathy with the workers and his respect for Davis:

> For the conditions that exist, it is important for our people, for the Puerto Ricans and the so-called Negroes . . . the masses of the people who are workers want a solution to their problems. Don't select anybody to speak for you who is compromising or who is afraid of upsetting the status quo or the apple cart of those people who are running City Hall or sitting in Albany or sitting in the White House. As Leon Davis has already proven, you don't get a job done unless you show the man that you're not afraid to go to jail. If you aren't willing to pay that price then you don't need the rewards or the benefits that go along with it.[89]

The CJHW had scheduled Dr. King to follow Malcolm X, but "conditions in Albany, Georgia made it impossible" for him to attend. In his absence, he sent an audiotape message of support that CJHW played to the crowd:

> It was my sincere hope to be able to address the prayer pilgrimage because of my deep conviction that the struggle for justice, freedom, and dignity in New York City is part and parcel of the fight we are waging today in Albany, Georgia. . . . The full implications of Local 1199's historic vic-tory will have a profound effect upon millions of unorganized workers throughout the nation. . . . I want to extend my very hearty congratula-tions to Mr. Randolph and Mr. Monserrat for their effective leadership of the Committee for Justice to Hospital Workers. Your demonstration of unity of all sections of the Negro and Puerto Rican communities was decisive in achieving a victorious settlement. That unity spells even greater victories in the immediate future. . . . I am convinced that what-ever differences we have in approaching [problems] should be and can be clarified within our community, and that regardless of our differences we must present a show of unity in regard to the solution of these vital prob-lems. If this cannot be achieved, it is clear to me that the opposition will utilize our inability to cooperate to divide us and to weaken that degree of unity which is imperative if we are to achieve justice and freedom in our in our time.[90]

In the end, the organizing efforts of 1199, the resolve of the workers, and the creation of the CJHW compelled Governor Rockefeller's intervention and the eventual settlement of the strike. The CJHW kept up the pressure until the state legislature passed laws in 1965 granting unions the right to represent hospital workers throughout the state. By 1968, it had negotiated a doubling of the minimum weekly salary for hospital workers.[91] Randolph and Monserrat, like King, saw the hospital workers' strike as part of the larger struggle of blacks and Latinos in the city. "The unshakeable unity of the Negro and Puerto Rican communities, forged in the struggle for justice for the hospital workers, must be continued and expanded," said one CJHW resolution. "This fight involves more than the hospital workers. It is part of the larger fight in our city against discrimination and exploitation, against slums, against juvenile delinquency, against drug addiction, against all forms of degradation that result from poverty and human misery."

After the conclusion of the strike, the leadership of the CJHW wrote, "Our united effort in the interests of the hospital workers has taught us an old but decisive lesson—that in unity there is strength. We hereby pledge to continue the work of our committee to win first-class citizenship rights, human dignity and human rights—right here and right now."[92]

3

DEVELOPING THEIR MINDS WITHOUT LOSING THEIR SOULS

BLACK AND LATINO STUDENT COALITION BUILDING, 1965–1969

WHILE BLACK AND LATINO STUDENTS had markedly different cultural backgrounds, they shared a broader class-based and ethnic identity, which served as the foundation for the diverse and influential student coalitions of the late 1960s. Moreover, both groups shared a history of marginalization and deep frustration with the institutional racism rampant at educational institutions.[1]

The rise in the number of black and Latino students on college campuses during this period led to demands for more black and brown faculty, and provoked demonstrations calling for programs in Black and Latino Studies. Students of color became radicalized by and created alliances with the Black Power, Brown Power, and a variety of international liberation movements. As much as the Black Power ideology informed the growth of black and Latino student movements on campus, it also contained limitations. Black Power excluded Latino voices and perspectives, so Latino students formed distinct organizations designed to advocate for their unique interests. Remarkably, even as Latino students begin to develop their own power centers, they continued to work in close collaboration with black student organizations in pursuit of their common goals.

BLACK AND BROWN STUDENT MOVEMENTS

Black and Latino student movements in the 1960s had many antecedents, including the civil rights movement, Black and Brown Power movements, and the growing anti–Vietnam War movement. They were also influenced by the militant independence movements across Africa and student anti-apartheid efforts in South Africa in the 1950s and 1960s. These forerunners had produced a "brilliant" new generation of angry black intellectuals that rivaled that of the Harlem Renaissance.[2] The civil rights activist Bayard Rustin observed in his book *Report from Black America* that African American students "began to get blackenized" in the 1960s. Black Power proponents such as Stokely Carmichael (who later changed his name to Kwame Ture), H. Rap Brown, and Amiri Baraka (LeRoi Jones) advocated "thinking black" and moving beyond the double consciousness that W. E. B. Du Bois outlined in his classic work *The Souls of Black Folk*. They proposed moving toward a truly independent and proud black identity.[3]

The phrase "Black Power" is associated with many goals, from defense against racial oppression to development of institutions to support black collective interests to the militant promotion of black separatism. Elements of a Black Power ideology were at once espoused by Malcolm X, direct action protesters, the pacifist Student Nonviolent Coordinating Committee (SNCC), and the Black Panther Party for Self-Defense. Scholars correctly note that Black Power ideology influenced an ethos that rejected white student participation, favored separatism, and championed black agency in achieving desired goals. What scholars often fail to recognize is that although black students barred whites from participating in their movement, they often worked in solidarity with Latinos. Those who write about the Black Power movement commonly overlook the agency and participation of Latino brothers and sisters in separatist black movements.[4]

The joint efforts of black and Latino students at Lehman College, City College of New York, and Columbia University challenged the racist status quo and advocated for Black Power scholarship to stop treating Latino activists like Ralph Ellison's invisible man.[5] Stefan Bradley's article in the *Journal of African American History*, "'Gym Crow Must Go!' Black Student Activism at Columbia University, 1967–1968," explained that the students and residents around Columbia University—the "black community"—made race a key factor in the 1968 movement to stop the school from developing deeper into Harlem.[6] In fact, it was black and Latino Columbia students working alongside black and Puerto Rican residents in Harlem who successfully blocked development. Historically, both Harlem and the Bronx since the 1930s were largely populated by blacks, Puerto Ricans, and Cubans. In the same issue of the *Journal of African American History*, the historian Peniel Joseph focused almost exclusively on black agency and black institutions in his discussion of the radicalization of black students. While he acknowledges that some black intellectuals were influenced by their travels to Cuba in the early 1960s, Joseph ignores the important legacy of the Chicano movement in California and Texas, and the influence these movements had on black and brown students nationwide. Almost as much as the Black Power movement, the Chicano movement helped radicalize brown and black students in the late 1960s.[7]

In 1927, Chicanos in Texas organized the League of United Latin American Citizens (LULAC), which led the first organized struggles by Mexican Americans to obtain civil rights. By the mid-twentieth century, however, Mexican Americans were in "a situation similar to blacks in the United States," writes historian Edward Escobar. "In California, for example, blacks had a higher unemployment rate, lower income, and faced greater housing discrimination than Mexican Americans. Mexican Americans, on the other hand, had lower levels of educational attainment and experienced more rigid occupational stratification and more dilapidated housing. In addition, Mexican Americans had even less political representation than African Americans."[8] And in 1960, Chicanos in California formed the Mexican American Political Association (MAPA), which also led campaigns to gain equal rights for Chicanos.

By the late 1960s, both of these organizations were controlled by the older Chicanos, a conservative generation committed to "gradual acculturation, integration, [and] individual mobility" as solutions to the social and political challenges they were facing. However, the generation of Chicanos coming of age in the late 1960s was frustrated by the perceived acquiescence of their parents and grandparents to a rigged system. Similar to the African American youth in the Black Power movement, young Chicanos viewed American culture as "inherently racist and corrupt," according to Escobar. They rejected demands for assimilation and "declared themselves a non-white minority in solidarity with other oppressed racial groups throughout the world."

The Chicano movement of the late 1960s had four goals: (1) inculcating cultural pride; (2) raising the general consciousness of Chicanos to their repression; (3) building an ethnically based political movement; and (4) ending the white racial discrimination that limited opportunities for Chicanos. Those in the movement saw themselves as victims of white racism and championed direct action and civil disobedience to achieve their goals. In 1962, César Chávez, Philip Vera Cruz, and Dolores Huerta founded the National Farmworkers Association (NFA), later renamed the United Farm Workers (UFW), which was the prototype for other militant Chicano organizations that emerged in those years. Following the example of the UFW and its strike against white farmers in California, in 1967 Chicano youth organized the Brown Berets, "a community-based military youth group similar to the Black Panthers, [which] also concentrated on issues of education, health care, and police brutality," and in 1968 they banded together in the United Mexican American Students (UMAS). In March 1968, just months before the eruption of student demonstrations in New York, UMAS organized a walkout by more than 10,000 East Los Angeles Chicano high school students to protest the L.A. school board's policy of tracking Mexican American students into vocational training and refusing to include Latin American/Chicano history in the curriculum. Students in Denver, Phoenix, and San Antonio soon organized similar demonstrations and walkouts.[9]

BLACK AND LATINO STUDENT ENROLLMENT

New York colleges began actively recruiting black and Latino students in the mid-1960s with the largest increases in minority-student enrollment taking place between 1967 and 1971. A number of programs were designed to attract minority students to public and private colleges and universities. Among the most successful were the City University of New York's (CUNY) Search for Education, Elevation, and Knowledge (SEEK), the State University of New York's (SUNY) Educational Opportunity Program (EOP), and the New York State's Higher Education Opportunity Program (HEOP). Local organizations were also formed to help prepare minority students for college. Antonia Pantoja, an Afro-Puerto Rican activist, started the group ASPIRA (Spanish for "aspire") in 1961 as a youth group for Latino youth to learn about their cultures and histories. The group targeted college-bound

Latinos in high school and provided guidance through the college admissions process.[10]

At that time, David Dinkins was serving in the New York Assembly when the SEEK program was founded. It was 1966, and there was a fight brewing among the Democrats in Albany over whom to nominate for Assembly Speaker: Anthony Travia or Stanley Steingut, both from Brooklyn. The previous year, the Republican governor Nelson Rockefeller had thrown some GOP votes to Travia, helping him narrowly win the post. This time around, Percy Sutton, the Harlem state senator, decided to visit Travia before the vote with a delegation of leftist, black Democratic assembly people—David Dinkins, Basil Patterson, Charles Rangel, and Shirley Chisholm. During a meeting in Travia's hotel room, Sutton said, "Without our black votes, you're not going to have a majority and you'll be facing an embarrassing situation, as you did last year." He told Travia that if he wanted to remain Speaker, he was going to have to give the black members something they could take to their districts. "Among the things we got that night [was] the SEEK program," said Dinkins in an interview in 2011.

In 1967, CUNY contained nine senior colleges, six community colleges, and one graduate school with degree-granting programs. An ethnic census conducted in December of that year showed that the City College of New York (CCNY) had the highest percentage of black and Puerto Rican students of all CUNY institutions. Although the total matriculated student body at CCNY in 1967 could not be documented, a CCNY school newspaper (*Campus*), provided an ethnic breakdown of the student population by percentages: 87.3 percent white, 4.9 percent Puerto Rican, 4.2 percent African American, and 3.6 percent "other." Of CCNY's non-matriculated students, 55 percent were white, 28 percent were African American, 8.4 percent were Puerto Rican, 7.4 percent were "other," and 1.2 percent gave no response.[11] It is not clear why so many black students were non-matriculated. Basilio Serrano, a Puerto Rican student at CCNY in the late 1960s, recalls that the number of Puerto Rican students in the CUNY system had grown sufficiently large that by 1969, he and other student activists were able to start the Puerto Rican Student Union (PRSU).

Obdulia and Migdalia Pérez, sisters from a poor Puerto Rican family of nine children from Brownsville in east Brooklyn, were members of the first group of Latinas to attend CCNY as part of the new SEEK program. With such a large family, there was never enough food at home, so they started school at CCNY underweight and hungry. After paying for the ferry and the subway to reach campus, they would have only enough money left for coffee and a bagel with cream cheese. The cafeteria workers warmly greeted the girls in Spanish and then would "put like a pound of cream cheese on our bagel," says Obdulia. It was from them that they received help and support, not from faculty and other students, recalls Obdulia.[12]

Lehman College, which was founded as the Bronx campus of Hunter College in 1931, became an independent institution within the CUNY system in 1968. In the spring of 1968, 96 SEEK students enrolled at Lehman, 15 of them as part-timers. An ethnic breakdown of that class shows 73 African Americans, 13 Puerto Ricans, and 10 whites. The group included 55 females and 41 males, the average age of which was twenty-two. In the fall of 1968, 58 more students entered the program and, in spring of 1969, 77 additional students came on board. Thus by the spring of 1969, students under the SEEK program made up about 8 percent of the college's student population: 153 African American students, 39 Puerto Rican students, 19 white students, and 1 Cuban student.[13]

Victor Manuel Quintana enrolled as a first-year student at Hunter in the fall of 1966 and witnessed the demographic changes to the student body as a result of SEEK. In 1966, when he left to join the Marines, Quintana recalls, "I left a campus that was predominantly white." But when he returned from Vietnam in 1969 to complete his undergraduate degree, he noted that the SEEK program "brought . . . a lot more black and Latino [students] onto the campus."[14] The on-campus SEEK director, Dr. Benjamin Lapkin, called it a "revolutionary program, one whose effect will ultimately shift the structure of our society."[15]

Changes were taking place at New York's other private colleges and universities as well. Mark Naison, a Brooklyn native, entered Columbia University as an undergraduate in 1962. After graduation, he stayed at Columbia to complete a doctorate in history, and he served as a CORE leader during the student takeover of university administration buildings in 1968. "In my entering class in Columbia in 1962, there were six black students out of six hundred and sixty. . . . In the entering class of 1967, there were forty," says Naison, who is now a professor of history, urban studies, and African American Studies at Fordham University.[16]

Although these programs were relatively successful at bringing minority students to college campuses, little was done for the students once they arrived. "Few white institutions had taken positive action toward the elimination of racism, either in the country at large or in the institutions in particular," wrote Allen Ballard, a former CCNY professor.[17] Few had any black or Latino faculty or administrators, saw any value in creating Black Studies or Latino Studies programs, or understood the difficulties and challenges confronted by black and Latino students. Colleges operated on the assumption that they were doing black and Latino students a favor by granting them admission. And, according to Ballard, they "felt no particular pressure to make special arrangements for . . . youth who not only had experienced deprivation and white scorn but were also sensitive to every conscious or unconscious manifestation of racism."[18]

Campuses now became more racially diverse, and student activism against the Vietnam War reached new levels of intensity during the late 1960s. On campuses across the country, teach-ins escalated into sit-ins, which escalated into violence among administrators, faculty, and students over the presence of military recruiters on campuses. Civil rights activists and leaders of the Black and Brown Power movements began coming to campuses to speak, and students started forming their own organizations with ties to national antiracism organizations. In this roiling political environment, newly enrolled black and Latino students rapidly became radicalized. Ballard wrote, "If the sheer whiteness of most campuses had not been stimulus enough to explosive action," then the assassination of Martin Luther King Jr. on April 4, 1968, and the rhetoric of the Black and Brown Power movements, "would have triggered the difficulties experienced on most campuses."[19]

From the moment of their radicalization in the late 1960s, black and Latino students worked collaboratively to hold these all-white institutions of higher learning to account and, by so doing, shift the racial consciousness of the entire nation. But by the time Victor Quintana returned from Vietnam in 1969, Kubanbanya, the first African American student organization established at Lehman, had begun to lose Latino members who wanted to start their own organization, one that worked separately to bring about progressive change at Lehman.[20]

KUBANBANYA

Kubanbanya, "those who are seeking" in Swahili, was established at Hunter College, later Lehman College, in 1965. Its original membership was both African American and Puerto Rican.[21] Black and Latino Lehman student organizing—including members of the Onyx Society, Kubanbanya, and other groups—took place at the Alamac Hotel on Seventy-first Street and Broadway, where CUNY officials set up SEEK housing for some two hundred to three hundred students.[22] Archived copies of Lehman's campus newspaper, the *Meridian*, offer the best record of Kubanbanya's founding, and activities and early coverage about it show that African American and Puerto Rican students were universally considered to be "black."[23]

Students viewed Kubanbanya's Puerto Rican members as black, partly because of their appearance. A vignette from the 1967 autobiography of the Puerto Rican activist Piri Thomas provides an excellent example of the way dark Puerto Ricans, like Thomas, were viewed in the 1950s and 1960s. In the sketch, Thomas is seventeen and playing "the dozens" (a tradition with West African origins in which people trade verbal insults, particularly about one's family, until an opponent is speechless or provoked to anger) on the street with his African American friend, Brew:

> I looked at Brew, who was as black as God is supposed to be white.
> "Man, Brew . . . you sure an ugly spook."
> Brew smiled. "Dig this Negro calling out 'spook,'" he said.
> I smiled and said, "I'm a Porty Rican."
> "Ah only sees another Negro in fron' of me," said Brew. . . . "If you white, tha's all right. If you black, da's dat."
> "Yeah, Brew," I said, "it must be tough on you Negroes."
> "Wha' yuh mean, us Negroes? Ain't yuh includin' yourself? Hell, you ain't but a coupla shades lighter'n me, and even if yuh was even lighter'n that, you'd still be a Negro."[24]

Kubanbanya's alignment with the Black Power ideology of the late 1960s also led to its being labeled as such. In most instances, Black Power groups and their leading intellectuals remained largely disconnected from Spanish-speaking segments of the African diaspora in the Americas: Puerto Rico, the Dominican Republic, Panama, Nicaragua, Cuba, Brazil, Colombia, and Ecuador. Participants in the Black Power movement juxtaposed black activist organizations against majority-white organizations such as the Students for a Democratic Society (SDS) and set themselves apart by using Afrocentric terminology like "black" or "Kubanbanya."

From 1959 to the late 1960s, much of the country morphed from a civil rights movement into a Black Power movement, and this can best be described as a youth and/or young adult movement. The intellectual architects of Black Power came from some of the most prestigious public high schools on the East and West Coasts of the country and thereafter earned undergraduate and graduate degrees at equally impressive public and private colleges and universities. Stokely Carmichael (Kwame Ture) graduated from the prestigious Bronx High School of Science in 1960 and attended Howard University, a historically black university in Washington, D.C. The famed anthropologist and author Zora Neale Hurston had briefly attended the university decades earlier. She had this to say about Howard in her autobiography: "Now as everyone knows, Howard University is the capstone of Negro education in the world. There gather Negro money, beauty, and prestige. It is to the Negro what Harvard is to the whites. They say the same thing about a Howard man that they do about Harvard—you can tell a Howard man as far as you can see him, but you can't tell him much."[25]

Carmichael, considered by many the father of the Black Power movement, called for community control of neighborhoods with black majorities from the school-board level up to the city mayor. In contrast to the mainstream civil rights movement, he and other leading figures in the movement advocated a revolutionary ideological shift to a distinctly North American ethnocentric interpretation of Africa and African culture. He encouraged radical changes, such as learning an African language, changing one's name, and adopting an affinity for African music, food, hairstyle, and clothing. And this created hierarchies within certain communities that bestowed privilege upon people with darker complexions and kinky hair over lighter ones and straight hair. The cultural productions of the Black Power movement included soul music, soul food, Kwanzaa, and the arts that featured African dance, plays, and poetry such as that of poet Gil Scott-Heron. Finally, like the Marcus Garvey movement of the 1920s, Black Power inspired a vibrant black entrepreneurial spirit, which encouraged a number of black-owned businesses, including several restaurants and jazz clubs in the 1960s such as Sylvia's, the Lenox Lounge, and Showman's Café.[26]

The black nationalist rhetoric of the movement masked a more complex, multiethnic reality in New York City, where black and brown youth lived in the same public-housing complexes and attended the same schools in the South Bronx, Harlem, and sections of Brooklyn. Born in 1951, José Candelario grew up in Williamsburg, Brooklyn, during the Black Power movement: "[D]espite the fact that [some like him had] very light skin and green eyes," Black Power "had a great influence" on young Puerto Ricans because they "were so closely aligned and living with African Americans" in housing projects and schools in Brooklyn. Candelario recalled that the antiwar movement and the militant philosophy of Malcolm X resonated with young African Americans and Puerto Ricans in Brooklyn.[27] Edwin Cruz, a Puerto Rican, describes a similar collaboration between black and Latino youth during the Black Power era while he was growing up in the East New York section of Brooklyn where black and Latino youth "lived in the same neighborhoods and emulat[ed] each other." He continues, "There were some kids that became [bilingual]; I had a very good friend of mine named Sally. And Sally was from the South, but she lived in the projects around all the Spanish [speaking] kids and she was just as fluent as we were. I hear of other stories of kids who lived in the same building and they would visit each other and have rice and beans." Over time, they would become bilingual from the constant contact with Hispanic friends and their families. Similar collaboration occurred between black and Latino students who shared campus spaces at Hunter College in the Bronx and CCNY in Harlem.[28]

African-influenced organizations that proliferated in the late 1960s in New York, particularly those on college campuses, tended to take a more inclusive, diasporic view of black urban identity when it came to matters of membership and partnership. Noelle Douglass wrote in the *Meridian* that Kubanbanya was seeking to organize "black (including Puerto Rican) students" on the campus of Hunter College in the Bronx.[29] Likewise, groups like Kubanbanya stood in solidarity with Latino organizations such as PRSU and the Young Lords as Latino groups tended to include African American members and supported the various political demonstrations by groups like the Black Panthers and Kubanbanya.[30]

THE ONYX SOCIETY

Shortly after students at the Bronx campus of Hunter College formed Kubanbanya, African American students at CCNY in 1966 approached Dr. Allen Ballard, an African American professor and head of the college's SEEK program, to serve as faculty adviser for a new black student organization to be called the Onyx Society. Ballard recalled that the first Onyx members were "comparatively conservative students, all admitted under regular City College standards." (The school's regular admissions policy called for assessing students based on their composite high school grades; once admitted, students could take up to eighteen credit hours per semester. In contrast, SEEK students, who often came from poorly performing high schools, entered under a dual score admissions policy—one part using their academic potential as a criterion and a second part assessing their combined high school grades. SEEK students could take only a maximum of twelve credit hours, the minimum necessary to qualify as a full-time student.) The Onyx members felt the need to relate to one another socially and to do service in the community.[31] Soon after its founding, however, Onyx became a more radical organization that aligned itself with the community control movement in Harlem and international liberation movements. In Ballard's words, "The leadership of the society had passed to more militant students, still regularly admitted, [but] who began to draw for membership on the students specially recruited under City College's SEEK program."[32]

In the 1966 fall semester, Onyx began holding a weekly forum, open to the community, where people could come and learn about or debate issues related to the civil rights and black liberation movements. Some Onyx members already held militant views and advocated for direct action after the race riots in Brooklyn. These disturbances had taken place in the summer of 1966 in the wake of white residents' attacks on black and Puerto Rican newcomers in white, ethnically controlled neighborhoods in East New York.[33] Onyx's president, Edwin Fabre, reported to the *Campus*:

If you see a white man being beat up by forty blacks, you don't go help that white man. You become the forty-first black beating up that white man. . . . This is the reaction of the black man who sees his brothers shot down in the streets. This is the reaction of the black man being subjected to a racist war against non-white peoples in Vietnam. This is the reaction of the black people whose very existence is being threatened. To some it's a question of whether we'll accept an inevitable American Auschwitz.[34]

By the fall of 1967, Onyx was a Black Power–oriented society with a distinctive African consciousness. Fabre described Onyx as an unabashedly black student organization rooted in a strong sense of its African origins: "The word black refers to people who were brought from Africa, who recognize their origins and appreciate them. Members of the Onyx Society are black—not Negro." Fabre continued, "We concern ourselves with the members of the black community. They are our concern because we are a part of them. And this is Onyx's business." Fabre described the organization's goals as providing for the "cultural, educational, and social well-being and advancement of all black people." Onyx wanted to spearhead the "necessary changes on campus and off" to improve the conditions for black people. "For example, there is a lack of curriculum here at the college which has real relevance for black students. There have also been no meaningful attempts to secure black professors for teaching here. There are very few black teachers here. Just think, if you did have such educators, you'd be able to plan courses which would study intelligently black culture. This is what the black community needs."

As part of its community outreach program, Onyx members ran a tutoring service for children who lived in the neighborhood around CCNY's Harlem neighborhood. As Fabre explained, "The main purpose of the program . . . is to bring those students who are behind up to grade level. In the process, we try to give the children a realistic sense of identification with their black heritage." Gail Powell (class of 1970), Onyx's correspondence secretary, said, "You can't just have theory. You've got to get right down to the community level if you want to teach. . . . The community must take part in the programming. What is taught must be relevant to the community." Fabre argued that black and Puerto Rican people didn't have any control over resources or decision making in New York City: "We don't have any piece of the pie. We want our share. In a city that is 50 percent Negro and Puerto Rican we deserve half and we are going to get it."[35]

To meet their goals, organizations like the Onyx Society and Kubanbanya joined and created a critical mass of students who belonged to student fee-supported organizations like the Student Government Association (SGA) and campus newspapers. They gained leadership positions in these student organizations and, over time, turned them into critical components of the black and brown liberation movement infrastructure. Using SGA funds, the groups organized teach-ins and brought activists to campus, thus providing a critical space for the formation of a collective black and brown movement against institutional racism on New York City college campuses. By 1967, the black student movements at Lehman and CCNY had just about taken over their student newspapers as well. The pages of *Tech News* were full of black liberation rhetoric and notices of Onyx-sponsored activities. The same was true with the *Meridian*, which increasingly wrote about a black and brown urban political identity. The news reports they published provided detailed accounts of militant activism around the world, student activism around the country, and speeches by various leaders of the Black and Brown Power movements. In the New York City schools, college newspapers helped students form an interconnected movement across numerous campuses. Newspaper accounts provide evidence that Kubanbanya and Onyx members knew one another and attended one another's events. The Lehman and CCNY campuses were geographically close, so students could get back and forth easily using the mass transit system. They studied each other's demands and political strategy, and built on each other's momentum.

GROWTH IN STUDENT MILITANCY

On October 3, 1967, Paul Simms published an interview with William Wright, president of the United African American Association (UAAA), a Black Power organization based in Newark, New Jersey. The UAAA was dedicated to uniting black Americans, improving conditions, and raising their political consciousness. But Wright insisted that the same racist, white-controlled political parties and structures that had "enslaved the black man will try to enslave the Puerto Rican."[36] Wright's solution to the political oppression facing both blacks and Puerto Ricans was to prepare "all the necessary tactics for fighting on a battlefield." He said it was time to begin communicating with other oppressed peoples of the world and to seek their aid in the struggle.[37]

Later that month, Simms reported on a lecture by H. Rap Brown to a standing-room-only crowd in the grand ballroom of CCNY's Finley Student Center, the outspoken chairman of SNCC. The Onyx Society, which had organized the event and partially paid for it with SGA funding, denied white people entrance. During his lecture, Brown insisted that "America is practicing a genocidal war against black people now. Thirty percent of the casualties in Vietnam are black; they got rid of Adam Clayton Powell Jr. Muhammad Ali received the maximum sentence and the maximum fine." Programs like SEEK "will not save you," he said. "You saw that in Detroit— the honky beat the middle-class niggers with middle-class sticks. . . . In order to alleviate this condition we must move as a common force. . . . Power, as Chairman Mao says, comes from the barrel of a gun."[38]

Brown, who would leave SNCC in 1968 to become the justice minister for the Black Panther Party, told his audience that the "Black Revolution will go on wantonly until you [educated] brothers and sisters give it some direction." He wanted college-educated blacks to radically revise the history then being taught in American classrooms. He challenged the CCNY students to learn "the little facts" in history that most "educated people don't know" and to get engaged in rewriting the history books and teaching history.[39] There is evidence that the Black Power message spread quickly to college campuses throughout metropolitan New York and as far north as Ithaca. Shortly after his speech, black and Latino students did indeed rise up—first at Columbia, then at Lehman, CCNY, and Cornell—and they issued lists of demands intended to radically change their respective colleges.[40]

STUDENT TAKEOVER AT COLUMBIA, 1968

On April 23, 1968, just two and a half weeks after Martin Luther King Jr. was gunned down in Memphis, two groups of student protesters shut down Columbia University. During the infamous six-day siege at Columbia, student activists barricaded themselves inside several university administration buildings. Members of the predominately white SDS wanted the university to formally end its affiliation with the Institute for Defense Analyses, a think tank dedicated to weapons research that had ties to the U.S. Department of Defense. Members of Columbia's Black Power–inspired

Student Afro-American Society (SAS) wanted to stop Columbia from building a new gymnasium in Morningside Park, the one natural barrier between the university and the surrounding black and brown working-class neighborhood.[41]

SAS's outrage wasn't unfounded. Elite urban universities have had a long history of physically expanding in the name of public and educational progress without giving much, if any, thought to the impact further development would have on the surrounding communities. Gentrification, dislocation of longtime residents, and destruction of important institutions and historic sites were some of the consequences of development by such institutions as Johns Hopkins University in Baltimore, the University of Pennsylvania in Philadelphia, Yale University in New Haven, Harvard University in Cambridge, and historically black colleges such as Howard University in Washington, D.C., and the Atlanta University Center Consortium in Atlanta.[42] Columbia's plans to demolish valuable open space in Harlem appeared to the students to be another landgrab by a rich institution at the expense of a poor black and brown neighborhood. Harlem residents saw the white men who ran Columbia University as callous and arrogant people who threw their weight around for selfish ends and formed a number of organizations to resist the university's attempt to expand the campus, thereby dislocating Harlem residents. The East Harlem Tenants Council tried to organize around the threat of gentrification. Arnie Segarra, a Puerto Rican, already a Harlem mainstay as a former star basketball player and now a manager of one of the top Latin nightclubs in Harlem, worked as an organizer for the council. Segarra knew people and had a gift for reaching out and bringing diverse groups together regardless of class or ethnicity. When the unrest in Harlem began in 1968, Mayor John Lindsay hired Segarra to serve as the community liaison between his office and East Harlem. As part of his job, Segarra built coalitions between the blacks and Latinos by reaching out to Charles Rangel, Percy Sutton, and City Clerk David Dinkins. Segarra and Dinkins formed a close personal relationship, and Segarra ultimately became a Dinkins aide and an organizer with Latinos for Dinkins.

The SAS and other Columbia students worked closely with local Harlem organizations as student tutors and community organizers. Juan González—a Brooklyn native, Puerto Rican, and former Columbia student—volunteered at a student tutorial program in Harlem. Mark Naison joined CORE's

Columbia chapter and participated in tenant organizing in East Harlem; that group focused on uncovering housing discrimination and organizing tenant organizations, rent strikes, and working with local tenant organizations fighting against the displacement of low-income residents as part of the state's urban-renewal program.[43] In January 1968, González's community group participated in a protest against the construction of a new Columbia University gym at the designated site "so I went, because it was our community group that was involved."[44] At the protest, an anonymous, young, militant African American minister made it very clear that Gonzáles, Naison, and another student CORE organizer from Columbia should follow him. Out of respect for the minister's position (this almost sounds like they did this grudgingly), González and the two CORE members staged a sit-in in front of bulldozers. They were soon arrested along with other protesters and spent the day in the Tombs, the old and infamous New York City jail. In the meantime, SAS students had met with community organizers and were now convinced that Columbia's landgrab was indeed a white supremacist attempt for local control over a black and brown community that they had to resist even if it meant harassment or expulsion. This type of militant stance was common for the era. A month before the takeover of Columbia, SAS members at Howard University participated in a building occupation there, which inspired SAS members at Columbia to take over Hamilton Hall on the Harlem campus.[45]

Prior to the campus takeover on April 23, SAS and SDS had collaborated as well, and during the takeover SAS received support from SDS students, the Barnard Organization of Soul Sisters, and Latin American and Asian students.[46] Black students from CCNY and other campuses, along with activists such as SNCC leaders, supported Columbia's SAS members. Harlem residents brought in home-cooked food, which fed the student protesters who were locked in Hamilton Hall. Vertamae Smart-Grosvenor, a native South Carolinian—a culinary writer, activist, and, anthropologist—lived in Harlem at this time. In addition to her other activities, cooked "neck bones, chicken feet stew, biscuits, greens, and grits" and "batches of fried chicken, cornbread and potato salad" for SNCC fundraisers. She played an important part in literally feeding civil rights activists in New York thereby feeding the civil rights revolution itself. Fried chicken recipes from all over made important contributions to the Black Power, community control, and student movements as

FRIED CHICKEN

1 chicken, cut into pieces

2–3 cups buttermilk

Poultry seasoning*

2 cups flour

2 cups milk, as needed

Enough canola oil to deep-fry the chicken

For best results, marinade chicken overnight in mixture of buttermilk and poultry seasoning. Combine another batch of poultry seasoning and flour in a mixing bowl and then pour it into a brown paper bag. Put half of the pieces of chicken into the bag and shake well; remove and deep-fry until golden brown and/or floating in a cast-iron skillet filled with hot canola oil. When the chicken floats, it is completely cooked. Repeat the same process with the second half of the chicken pieces.

For a healthier version, bake it in the oven at 450 degrees, turning every 10 minutes, until golden brown.

▬

*Poultry seasoning is sage, season salt, pepper, paprika, black pepper, garlic powder, and Adobo seasoning.

CORNBREAD

2 large eggs

2 cups buttermilk (or 2 cups vanilla soymilk)

2 cups cornmeal

1 tsp salt

2 tsp baking powder

½ tsp baking soda dissolved in 1 tbsp hot water

¾ cup corn, canola, or vegetable oil

Mix eggs and buttermilk. Sift in cornmeal with salt, baking powder, and dissolved baking soda or use self-rising cornmeal. (I add just a little high-ground flax seed as fiber.) Mix ingredients and, if you are a northerner like me, add ¼ cup sugar. Spray hot cast-iron skillet with nonstick cooking spray. Preheat oven to 425 degrees, then turn down to 375 and bake for 30–40 minutes or until golden brown. Brush with melted butter when done.

one of many signature soul foods that became fashionable, popular, and gave black people a sense of pride in regard to their food.[47]

At this point, however, many SAS members thought it might be time to separate from SDS and other groups. Thus days into the standoff, the student forces began to fracture along racial lines. Naison wrote, "What started out as a united protest had turned into a tension-filled standoff, with black students in one side the building and white students in the other."[48] While members of SDS were opposed to the gym, they were primarily concerned with staging an antiwar demonstration. But members of SAS were centrally focused on protesting racial injustice. In addition to blocking additional development in Harlem, the SAS student mobilization was aimed at forcing Columbia's administrators to hire more black faculty, offer more Black Studies courses, and admit greater numbers of black students.[49] One of the SAS leaders, William Sales, gave a speech during the occupation that went even deeper, linking the local fight in Harlem to the broader movement for self-determination and to the struggles of freedom fighters in Vietnam, Angola, Mozambique, Guinea-Bissau, Zimbabwe, and South Africa.[50] Differences in priorities and ideology led to a bitter confrontation between white and black students, and the SAS members asked the SDS members to leave. The SAS retained control of Hamilton Hall, renaming it Nat Turner Hall of Malcolm X University (figure 3.1), and the white members of the SDS moved into Low Library, which housed the president's office.[51]

The SAS side of the demonstration was not made up of only Columbia students but included students from New York University (NYU) and CCNY, black and Puerto Rican residents of East and West Harlem, CORE members, and activists involved in a nascent school-board struggle in Ocean Hill, Brooklyn. "In addition to students who had Columbia IDs, there were at least an equal number of these community forces who stayed with us throughout the demonstration," said Sales in Tech News, the CCNY newspaper. Notably, when the white and black students parted ways, Harlem's Puerto Rican community closed ranks with its black neighbors. Stokely Carmichael and H. Rap Brown, heavy hitters from the national Black Power movement, also visited the campus during the standoff to show solidarity and attract greater press coverage for the demonstrators.[52]

The protests ended after six days when police stormed both buildings. One hundred and fifty students were injured and at least thirty were

FIGURE 3.1 Students picketing at Columbia University, 1968. (Private Collection of Photographer Nancy Shia)

suspended, but both the SAS and SDS achieved their immediate central goals: Columbia ended its affiliation with the weapons firm and scrapped its plans to build a gymnasium on Morningside Park. Harlem residents said they felt as if they had gained a new level of control over their community and their future.[53]

OCEAN HILL PEOPLE'S BOARD OF EDUCATION

Soon enough, a new front in the battle for racial equity in the educational system opened up in the Ocean Hill section of Brooklyn in East New York. It was part of a nationwide movement by blacks and Latinos to reform school curricula, introduce black history, boost black and Latino parent participation, and win greater control for local communities over the operations in their school districts. "Across the city, schools with black and Latino majorities received fewer resources, were overcrowded, and were often saddled with teachers who failed to perform adequately in other schools," according to the historian Wendell Pritchett. "The situation for blacks and Latinos deteriorated throughout the 1960s as more whites left the school system."[54]

The demand for community control in Ocean Hill developed from a two-decade-long struggle to improve and desegregate New York schools. Progressive black and brown activists along with educators who often worked for the New York City public school system viewed community control as a cure for these ills. For more than two decades, they had demanded change from the highly centralized public school system, which had shown a track record of neglect and apathy in its supervision of schools in poor, black, and brown neighborhoods. In the activists' view, community control would end that systematic neglect.[55] Progressives called for the establishment of local school boards via local elections that were empowered to make decisions on budgets, staffing, student-to-teacher ratios, and the daily operational policies within their local school districts. In short, advocates of community control viewed the entrenched white elites who controlled the city's educational bureaucracy as an obstacle to the education of black and Latino children who were now the majority in the public school system. They argued for a radical change: redistributing the decision-making power to the hands of locally elected school boards in poor black and brown communities.

Al Vann was one of the leaders of the struggle for community control of the Ocean Hill public school district, with its approximately 9,000 students.[56] Born and raised in Brooklyn's Bedford-Stuyvesant neighborhood, Vann had been a public school teacher and then an assistant principal in Ocean Hill. He helped found the Negro Teachers Association (NTA) in 1964 along with Les Campbell (who later changed his name to Jitu Weusi), a fellow former teacher at Junior High School 35, now Marcus Garvey Junior High School, in Bed-Stuy. Vann served as the organization's first and only chairperson during its existence from 1964 to 1973 and helped to spearhead the push for greater community control of the school district. Vann increasingly identified with the emerging Black Power movement, and as the spokesman of the NTA he championed incorporating African American history into the public school curriculum.

Weusi was the more radical of the two, due in large part to his regular attendance at the meetings of Brooklyn chapters of CORE and the Black Panther Party. He later became an active member of the now defunct East, an Afrocentric cultural organization in Central Brooklyn that became an important space for radical black nationalists, many of whom remained outside electoral politics until the candidacy of David Dinkins for mayor in the late 1980s. In the early 1960s, Weusi joined CORE and was impressed by its series of lectures by prominent Progressives. He introduced the concept to the NTA, and the organization started a monthly speakers series, which included noted black intellectuals such as the psychologist Alvin Poussaint, who was on the faculty of Tufts University at the time, and Basil Paterson (a CORE activist and president of the Harlem NAACP), who represented the Upper West Side and Harlem in the New York State Senate. These events attracted several hundred teachers, and in conjunction with a citywide newsletter started by the NTA the organization grew from one Brooklyn chapter to twenty-five across the city. It gained a solid reputation as the voice of black teachers in New York City. In 1966 the organization changed its name to the African American Teachers Association (AATA). In the same year, Vann presented a number of demands to Albert Shanker, head of the United Federation of Teachers (UFT), the city's teachers' union. These injunctions included adding African American history to the curriculum, increasing the number of African American teachers and administrators, and increasing tutorial support for at-risk African American students. Shanker and his executive board found these demands outrageous and adamantly opposed them. There is, however, no mention of equal treatment for Latino students, teachers, and administrators, proof that they were considered invisible by AATA's black nationalists. This is notable considering that AATA's members taught in schools located in black and brown neighborhoods.[57]

In 1967, the AATA and the union clashed again over the union's attempt to get the Board of Education to allow teachers and administrators to relocate those children who were labeled as "disruptive" to alternative schools. The AATA viewed the move as an attempt to criminalize black children and affix a label that would impair their educational and employment opportunities. The UFT wanted the school board to accept the label as part of its new contract negotiations, which the AATA publically opposed. In a 2006 interview, Weusi described the disruptive child clause as a critical but not commonly known element of the 1967 contract negotiations between the UFT and the Board of Education. The AATA publicized the issue and mobilized its supporters against it, which infuriated Shanker. Nonetheless, for many years after the event, scholars have overlooked this part of the 1967 contract.[58]

The AATA had some powerful friends in New York politics, including Basil Patterson, Charles Rangel (founder of the Harlem-based Martin Luther King Jr. Democratic Club), David Dinkins (leader of the Carver Democratic Club), the Progressive Harlem political operative Carl McCall (head of the city's Commission Against Poverty), and Percy Sutton (former legal counsel for SNCC). These politicians held considerable power in New York City and Albany, and they were able to pressure Mayor John Lindsay to implement greater community control. In the spring of 1967, in response to grassroots community organizing around the city in support of community control, Mayor Lindsay announced a trial decentralization programs in three communities: Harlem, the Lower East Side, and Ocean Hill.[59]

Prior to the 1960s, Ocean Hill had been a white, predominately Jewish neighborhood with a long history of support for leftist-socialist politicians and ardent unionism. Then the population changed dramatically as whites moved out and blacks moved in. By 1968, the student population in the Ocean Hill district was 29 percent black and 21 percent Puerto Rican. The teacher population, however, remained at 65 percent white and Jewish. The community established the Ocean Hill People's Board of Education (OPBE) in 1967 with a $44,000 grant from the Ford Foundation and the support of Vann and the AATA.[60] The OPBE quickly formed a governing board that consisted of five community representatives (four African Americans and one Hispanic) empowered to hire administrators and principals for the schools in the district, set educational goals, develop curricula, and hire or fire teachers. Rifts emerged almost immediately between the governing board and white teachers. Blacks and Latinos saw decentralization as a form of empowerment that would finally give parents and residents some influence over their children's education. The teachers (and other white unionists) saw it as a form of backdoor union busting because the unions would have to engage in collective bargaining with potentially dozens of local boards rather than a central administrative body.

The OPBE hired Rhody McCoy, an African American, to serve as the superintendent of schools. Born and raised in Washington, D.C., McCoy had served as a teacher in New York City public schools for eighteen years before becoming an acting principal. He soon found himself at the center of a growing conflict between the new black and Latino board and the predominately white UFT. Shanker and many union activists in the Ocean Hill school district did not agree with the selection of McCoy because he had not been on the board's approved list of applicants for the position. This flouting of union rules was seen as a first step down the slippery slope toward union irrelevance and black domination.[61]

The board appointed McCoy over union objections and went on to accept his recommendation that five white principals be removed and replaced by new staff—one white, two black, one Chinese American, and one Puerto Rican (the first in the city's history). McCoy also removed nineteen white teachers and lower-level administrators, and advocated that the board hire African American and Puerto Rican teachers who would be able to work more effectively with the district's black and Latino students. The OPBE introduced bilingual reading programs, trained three hundred parents to work as classroom aides, created a student-run community newspaper, and initiated new after-school programs. As a result of these initiatives, student and parent participation and support in the school district increased drastically.[62]

The teacher dismissals, however, provoked Shanker and the UFT to organize a teachers strike. The ensuing protests and counterprotests sparked intense racial acrimony, with enraged white and Jewish UFT members directly confronting black and Puerto Rican supporters of the OPBE and McCoy. The strike closed almost all of New York City's schools for thirty-six days in the fall of 1968, affecting just about every aspect of city life. The conflict then escalated when black and Puerto Rican community-control supporters attempted to reopen the school but the striking white workers fought to keep them closed.[63]

Across the city, citizens and activists mobilized in support of either the OPBE (and the AATA) or the UFT. In October 1968, Dr. John Hatchett, the director of NYU's newly established Martin Luther King Jr. Afro-American Student Center, gave a speech at the school's Bronx campus in front of seven hundred students in which he called Vice President Hubert Humphrey, President Richard Nixon, and Al Shanker "racist bastards." New York University fired Hatchett. Student groups, including the Black Allied Student Association, Katara (a Kubanbanya-like organization), the Peace and

Freedom Party, SDS, and the Independent Socialist Club protested Hatchett's firing by occupying the Bronx campus library and student center for five days. When NYU administrators assured the students that they would reinstate Hatchett, the students left the occupied buildings chanting, "WE won! WE WON! Yes! Yes! Beep Beep, Bang Bang. Um-gowa, Um-gowa, Black Power!"[64]

In terms of the larger strike, though, the city was forced to accede to UFT demands. Seventy-nine teachers who had been removed from the district or walked out during the strike were reinstated, and an agreement was signed regarding teachers' rights in community-control districts. In October 1968, the New York State education commissioner, James E. Allen, suspended the OPBE and put the Ocean Hill district under state control trusteeship, which reinstated teachers, transferred a number of principals, and ran the district for four months. It then reinstated the OPBE, and shortly thereafter the New York State legislature implemented a school decentralization plan that created thirty districts across the city with 20,000 students in each. The UFT supported the initiative, but the AATA and the majority of community control activists did not, arguing that the increased size of the districts would not facilitate community control initiatives and experiments.[65]

In the case of the community-control movement in Ocean Hill, African American activists can at best be described as advancing a black nationalist agenda that failed to incorporate the needs of the various sectors of their Latino coalition partners (parents, students, teachers, and administrators). For example, at no time did they make the suggestion of incorporating both African American and Latin American history into school curriculums. Instead, they demanded only African American history. Moreover, African Americans created and maintained decision-making bodies in which they dominated and in which Latinos served as junior partners instead of equals, seen in the imbalance of appointments of school administrators. Black activists filled all but one position with male African Americans and made what seems like one token appointment of a Puerto Rican. Ultimately, African Americans failed to develop an egalitarian agenda, which might have expanded their political base and given them a better chance of advancing the goal of community control. Vann continued on a similar black nationalist path in coalitions with Latinos as he made the transition from Brooklyn activist to Brooklyn elected official after the failure of the movement in 1968.

Vann eventually resigned from his position in the school system and took an administrative role at Long Island University in Brooklyn, where he headed a federally funded college-placement program for minority students. He would go on to create the Fulton Street, Bedford-Stuyvesant Vanguard Civic Association (FBCA), complete with pictures of Malcolm X and Marcus Garvey on the walls of the front office. He broke with the political and cultural center called the East (whose members labeled him a liberal sellout) and used the FBCA to advance his commitment to teaching black history in black communities and thus, over time, created a political base from which he launched a career in electoral politics. In 1972, Vann shed his revolutionary African clothing and started campaigning as a registered Independent for an open seat in the New York Assembly representing the largely African American and black Caribbean Bedford-Stuyvesant district. He lost. He ran again in 1974 as a registered Democrat and won. Vann would spend the rest of his career in electoral politics building Progressive black and Latino coalitions, using them to elect and appoint people in support of community control initiatives. However, he never seemed to Latinos as an equal partner, but rather appeared to consider them as political pawns for advancing a black nationalist agenda.[66]

UNICA AND PRISA

While the battle for community control raged in Brooklyn, Kubanbanya announced its organizational agenda for the 1968/1969 school year. Specifically, Kubanbanya intended to launch "Project Confrontation," an agenda modeled on the curriculum and community engagement initiatives that the Onyx Society had developed at CCNY.[67] Beginning in September 1968, Kubanbanya started working closely with the growing black and Puerto Rican community around Lehman College in the Bronx. The club sought to radically change the college's teacher training curriculum in order to better meet the surrounding community's needs. The demand for black and Latino public school teachers was growing as a result of the city's move toward decentralization, and Kubanbanya wanted student teachers to be trained to "introduce into the school curriculum a course on Afro-American history and literature and African art" and to help spearhead the community's "fight for black administrators on the junior and senior high school levels."[68]

"We will need the cooperation of the administration and faculty members," wrote Kubanbanya's Frank Critton in the *Meridian*. "We seek the cooperation of the white students on campus also. We feel they can help their race overcome their subconscious racism, by (a) organizing poor whites around their own self-interest, and (b) educating the middle class to its need to understand Black Power and to understand its own racist attitudes."[69] In late October, Kubanbanya's new president, James Harris, presented the group's demands to Rita O'Hare, the acting dean of Lehman's Education Department, which included the immediate adoption of four courses: (1) The Afro American and the American Education System, (2) The Puerto Rican in the New York City Public School System, (3) Human Relations, and (4) Third World Groups in the American Education System. Kubanbanya also demanded the right to decide how the new courses would be taught and who would teach them. O'Hare responded by inviting student representatives from Kubanbanya, SEEK, and others organizations to discuss their requests with her department's faculty.[70]

As these established groups mobilized, two Lehman Latinas, Hildamar Ortiz and Myrna Martínez, decided to form their own student organization called UNICA in 1969.[71] Ortiz and Martínez and other Latina leaders created UNICA to respond to the barriers and injustices confronting Latina and Latino students at Lehman College.[72] Puerto Rican women made up the leadership of UNICA, and the Puerto Rican and Dominican female students held more militant and radical worldviews than their Latino male counterparts at Lehman. This happened in part because Lehman College evolved out of the former all-female Hunter College, and the Latina students had a longer history with the Eurocentric orientation and campus culture of the college and its administrators. In addition, the majority of UNICA members (and SEEK students attending CUNY schools) were described as the best and brightest Puerto Rican and Dominican Bronx natives who had belonged to ASPIRA programs in high school and had a historical memory of black and brown organizing from exposure to Black Power. UNICA students acknowledged that some of their parents had gone to the March on Washington and that the civil rights movement had played a role in radicalizing their parents. They also insisted that the Black Power movement had awakened their political consciousness to white supremacy, race, and class in New York City and on the island of Puerto Rico, and their recognition of the African roots in Puerto Rican culture and society.[73]

At Lehman, UNICA called for a revised School of Education curriculum—one that would focus even more on "Puerto Rican culture and heritage and the failure of the educational system to respond to the needs of the half million Puerto Rican children in the public school system."[74] Like Kubanbanya's demands for black faculty, UNICA wanted Puerto Rican faculty teaching education courses. UNICA also asked that the Education Department "allocate funds for the translation and distribution of materials from Puerto Rico [that] would be relevant to the need of giving the [Puerto Rican] school child a sense of pride in his bilingualism and heritage." UNICA wanted a representative from its delegation to be part of the body that would make decisions about curriculum changes. UNICA argued that the "educational sequences of Lehman College, which produces a sizable number of teachers, is inadequate because it leaves prospective teachers culturally starved." Teachers graduating from Lehman, they worried, "lack an awareness of the culture, heritage, language, and philosophical outlook of the Spanish-speaking community."[75]

From the beginning, Progressive faculty members, including the dean of the Education Department, called UNICA and Kubanbanya's demands "reasonable."[76] But white administrators within Lehman, CUNY, and the state's education department hindered the speedy implementation of these changes. They claimed that there was a "shortage of qualified faculty" and cited restrictive state regulations that prevented certain changes to the curriculum. According to a former Black Studies professor at Lehman, Charlotte Morgan-Cato, "foot dragging" by "entrenched" administrators stymied student efforts.[77]

While UNICA, Kubanbanya, and SEEK were forming a new black and brown student coalition at Lehman, a fight was unfolding on CCNY's campus in Harlem between white students and administrators. Two hundred and fifty white students, mostly members of the SGA and SDS, were protesting a New York Police Department raid on CCNY's campus. Two weeks earlier, 170 students had taken over the school's ballroom, using an expired permit, and assured an AWOL Vietnam veteran that he could have sanctuary there. The students refused staff requests to leave the facility, so CCNY's president, Dr. Buell Gallagher, called in the police to force them out. Students were incensed that Gallagher had invited the police onto the campus, in violation of an earlier pledge not to do so "without prior consultation with the faculty."[78] In the aftermath, student protestors issued a list of demands to Gallagher to end the tumultuous demonstrations. They wanted promises from the CCNY administration college that there would be no police interference in peaceful student political activity, CCNY would end its Reserve Officers' Training Corps (ROTC) program and affiliation with the military, and CCNY would give the ROTC space to SEEK.

Illustrative of the split between black and white student activists on New York campuses, Onyx's president, Tom Shick, reported in the campus newspaper that "Black students had not been involved in any planning of the demonstration and therefore could not pledge allegiance." Shick added that Onyx was "preparing for a confrontation which will be directly relevant to black students."[79] More specifically, the Onyx Society was beginning to work with a new Puerto Rican student group at CCNY, and together they were about to lay out a set of demands similar to those issued by Kubanbanya and UNICA at Lehman.

In November 1968, one week after the antiwar event, Puerto Rican students at CCNY launched a new group, Puerto Rican Student Activities (PRISA), which was dedicated to Puerto Rican self-determination. "There are Puerto Rican necessities that have to be taken care of on campus," said the group's first president, Henry Arce.[80] Many of the original members of PRISA had actively participated in the Onyx Society but started PRISA out of a desire for a uniquely Puerto Rican student organization. Approximately 125 Latino students, mostly Puerto Ricans, attended the organization's first meeting. Like members of UNICA, they embraced and incorporated the philosophy of the civil rights and Black Power movements, and as ASPIRA alumni they had studied Puerto Rican leaders. However, Puerto Ricans at CCNY were particularly influenced by two New York–based Boricuas (a Taíno Indian term for Puerto Ricans): Evelina López Antonetty, the founder and director of United Bronx Parents, an organization dedicated to improving educational opportunities for black and brown students in some of the poorest sections of the South Bronx; and the self-proclaimed Puerto Rican socialist and activist Gilberto Gerena Valentín, who represented the Upper West Side and the South Bronx on the New York City Council. Antonetty inspired the founding members of PRISA to give back to the community, and Valentín used his political capital to support PRISA's community work.

At the time of the student takeovers at CCNY, Valentín and Antonetty belonged to the secret Wednesday Night Club, which regularly held meetings in New York City from 1967 to 1972. This had been an informal underground group of twenty to thirty left-of-center Puerto Ricans encompassing grassroots organizers, political operatives engaged in national initiatives, and others interested in coalition building. If anyone outside of the group asked a member about it, they would deny that it existed. Valentín and Antonetty can best be described as two of the more radical members of the club that organized and/or supported protests (such as the campus takeover) that were taking place across the city.[81]

PRISA's founding members also created an organization at CCNY for Puerto Rican students and the struggling communities from which they came: the South Bronx, East Harlem, the Lower East Side, and Brownsville. They envisioned an organization that would "funnel" CCNY graduates back into their communities "to assess and help our people," said Eduardo "Pancho" Cruz, a former PRISA member.[82] Members of Onyx and PRISA had some cultural differences but they shared an identity as SEEK students confronting discrimination at CCNY. Cruz remembers, "If you were part of the SEEK program, they [racist members of the faculty] would sit you on one side of the classroom, and the regular students would sit on the other. We were excluded from basketball; we were excluded from almost everything. As SEEK students, we were being rejected."[83] Ultimately, PRISA and Onyx Society members formed the Black and Puerto Rican Student Community (BPRSC) in order to coordinate their activities to promote black and Latino admissions and the creation of programs in Black and Puerto Rican Studies. Similar coalitions formed between black and Latino student groups at Lehman, CCNY, Bronx Community College, Brooklyn College, and Queens College.[84]

CONTINUING STUDENT RADICALIZATION

The impetus for these new organizations and their bolder claims lay in the continued radicalization of black and Latino college students throughout the tumultuous year of 1968. In quick succession, the country witnessed the assassination of Martin Luther King Jr. in April, the violent suppression of student protests in Paris in May, the murder of Robert F. Kennedy in June, the brutal police action against demonstrators at the Democratic National Convention in Chicago in August, and the massacre of hundreds of students in the Tlatelolco section of Mexico City by the Mexican government just weeks before Mexico was due to host the Olympic Games in October.[85]

At those Olympics, two black athletes, John Carlos and Tommie Smith, gave the Black Power salute from the podium during an award ceremony, which was transmitted live around the world and helped to further galvanize black and brown student militancy. In November 1968, CCNY's Onyx Society sponsored a rally in support of Carlos and Smith. Tom Shick stated in the *Campus*, "We want to give black students a chance to express their support for these men, who are our heroes." When Carlos came to the microphone to speak, a huge crowd of largely black students greeted him with a "wave of cheers and shouts of 'Black Power' and 'Peace Brother.'" Carlos, speaking of his decision to give the Black Power salute at the Olympics, told the crowd, "I had to find some way to help black people." Accompanying Carlos on his visit to CCNY was Harry Edwards, who had earned a Ph.D. in sociology from Cornell University in 1967 and had, in the fall of 1967, organized the Olympic Project for Human Rights, which had inspired Carlos and Smith to give the Black Power salute in Mexico City. Teachers from neighboring P.S. 175 brought 150 elementary school children to the rally. After thirty minutes of speeches, Carlos ended the event by proclaiming, "All right now, are you ready? Say it loud." And the crowd roared back instantly, "I'm black, I'm proud."[86]

Stokely Carmichael, the radical "Black Panther Prime Minister," spoke at CCNY on December 3, 1968, shortly after the formation of PRISA and its coalition with the Onyx Society. CCNY's Great Hall was packed with students and activists from all over the city. During his hour-long speech, Carmichael lectured on what he called a "blueprint for 'armed struggle' against American racism and capitalism." He directed some of his remarks specifically to the CCNY students, saying, "The best black students can do inside a white university is . . . politically educate the masses of our people who are being prepared for the confrontation." The confrontation would happen in the future, he said, after blacks and Puerto Ricans had united to use "revolutionary violence" to "destroy the status quo and to implement a new system that speaks to the desires of the masses of our people." Carmichael defined "revolution" as that period after you have taken power and have the ability to make revolutionary changes. He drew a distinction between black militants and black revolutionaries. A militant, he said, is "angry at white folks for keeping him out of the system. . . . A black revolutionary wants to overturn, destroy, wipe out, and completely and thoroughly and resolutely destroy the system and start all over again."[87]

Two weeks later, CCNY students heard another similarly fiery address, this time from a Latino. The Du Bois Club hosted the Puerto Rican anti-war activist Dennis Mora on December 12, 1968. Mora was a member of the "Fort Hood Three." In 1966, he and two other draftees (the African American James Johnson and the Lithuanian Italian American David Samas) had been sentenced to twenty-eight months at Fort Leavenworth Garrison in Kansas for refusing to serve in the Vietnam War. Speaking at CCNY, Mora emphasized the necessity of unity, organization, and sound ideology. He particularly praised Black Panther socialism, with its emphasis on community control, armed confrontation against violent racist systems, and depiction of North American capitalism as violent, exploitative, and imperialistic. On the question of alliances between white and black activists, Mora said that white leftists had been "historically untrustworthy" with regard to black people. He used the 1968 New York City teachers' strike as an example, saying, "You don't see them involved in the school strike issue, but the blacks and Puerto Ricans united to fight the racist structure and left the [L]eft behind." In an interview with a *Tech News* reporter, Mora advised all radical and revolutionary groups to read the works of Che Guevara and Franz Fanon and to "begin to apply them to [the] everyday situations" of working-class blacks and Puerto Ricans. "The question," he said, "is how to make these black and Puerto Rican brothers realize what's happening to them, given the situation in which they live."[88]

THE COMMITTEE OF TEN—AND THE FIVE DEMANDS

One month after the start of the spring semester, on February 6, 1969, black and Puerto Rican members of Onyx and PRISA mobilized in full force and developed demands to present to the CCNY administration and President

Buell Gallagher.[89] The Committee of Ten issued a set of five demands: (1) a separate school for Black and Puerto Rican Studies, (2) a separate orientation program for incoming black and Puerto Rican students, (3) a role for SEEK students in determining guidelines and staffing for the SEEK program, (4) a racial composition for entering classes that reflects the black and Puerto Rican populations in New York City high schools, and (5) a requirement that all education majors be proficient in Spanish and able to teach black and Puerto Rican history.[90]

The students left their demands with the president, who agreed that he would answer within one week. On February 13, the students mobilized outside the president's office to hear his response. Gallagher stonewalled, and the students moved en masse to occupy the administration building. The president told his administrative staff to "utilize their well-known good discretion and to vacate the premises."[91] In the days following the brief occupation, the faculty unanimously approved the implementation of the coalition's five demands, but the administration of CCNY still refused. In response, members of the BPRSC organized a black and brown slate to run for SGA offices as a way to expand the political base of the Committee of Ten. The strategy worked to mobilize the most progressive sectors of the CCNY student body to join PRISA and Onyx, and to implement their demands. Members of BPRSC, along with white members of SDS who had held rallies in support of the five demands, organized a campus-wide rally. At the same time, BPRSC members met and secretly organized into cells for a planned occupation and lockdown of CCNY, the goal of which was to turn it into "University of Harlem" unless their demands were met.[92]

On the morning of April 23, 1969, BPRSC cells went into action clearing the campus of people not involved in the takeover and permitting only those members of the takeover team and its supporters to remain on campus. The takeover essentially shut the campus down for the entire summer of 1969. Susan Polirstok, a CCNY student, recalls the takeover: "I remember being in the cafeteria early one morning in a study group having breakfast. Some African American young men came into the cafeteria and told us that the campus was being taken over and that we had to leave. At first we really didn't believe them and we said, 'Come on, you kidding?'" Using "strong language," Polirstok continued, "they said no and added in a militant tone, 'You will leave the campus.'" Polirstok and her study group were escorted to the front gate of the south campus where they walked through what she described as an intimidating "gauntlet" of the takeover movement. The campus gates were locked behind them.[93]

At 11:00 A.M. that day, a multiracial assembly of 1,500 striking students marched toward Wagner Hall. Rally leaders from the BPRSC "carried the red, black, and green flag of the Third World and a dummy labeled 'racism.'"[94] The students marched through the campus calling for others to join in a strike and general shutdown of the university. Eventually, black and Puerto Rican students occupied CCNY's south campus. One of the first things the students did was raise the Puerto Rican flag at a location normally reserved for the American flag. They renamed the campus University of Harlem, and several buildings were renamed in honor of black and Latino leaders (figures 3.2 and 3.3). Making the campus accessible to the working-class black and Latino residents around CCNY represented an important part of the campus takeover. From its inception, the students of the University of Harlem kept the community involved and informed by passing out leaflets about the campus takeover.[95]

Like the Black Panthers and Young Lords, they set up a free breakfast program for community residents. They also organized a free child-care program, fairs, and political education classes with the support and participation of Kathleen Cleaver (a member of the Black Panthers), the Harlem activist "Queen Mother" Audley E. Moore, Dixie Bayo (an activist from the Puerto Rican movement), and the Lower East Side activist Julio Rosado. Henry Arce was president of PRISA in 1969. At the time of the takeover, his mother worked as a family assistant in the Head Start program. She organized a group of twenty-five parents who would prepare and deliver "big pots of rice and beans and pork and *pasteles* [Puerto Rican-style tamales]."[96] In Spanish Harlem, musicians and clubbers ordered tons of *pasteles* made from stuffed mashed green plantains, poultry, meat, and vegetables such as peppers, olives, and capers served with rice and beans. "Everywhere slave traders imported Africans in large numbers—Cuba, Brazil, [Puerto Rico, the Dominican Republic], and South Carolina—the African developed regionally distinctive rice and beans dishes," similar to what they ate in West Africa, says the food historian Karen Hess.[97] Rice and beans provided people with an inexpensive, nutritious, and easy-to-make food combination.

FIGURE 3.2 The Puerto Rican flag (*left*) and Black Liberation flag (*right*) hanging outside the newly renamed University of Harlem, formerly CCNY. (Private Collection of Photographer Nancy Shia)

FIGURE 3.3 The newly renamed Huey Newton Hall on the campus of the University of Harlem, 1969. (Private Collection of Photographer Nancy Shia)

Arce served as one of the movement's spokespersons and ambassadors, meeting with different community organizations and Puerto Rican educational leaders and visiting college campuses to increase the movement's political base. The strategy of engaging with other organizations worked to increase support for the University of Harlem among students at Manhattan College, who were in the midst of their own campus takeover, and other schools across the city. Arce also spoke to student groups at Brooklyn College and Bronx Community College. Shortly thereafter students at Bronx Community College participated in a campus takeover, as did SEEK students at Queens College.[98]

PUERTO RICAN RICE AND BEANS

2 tbsp oil

2 tbsp sofrito

4 oz tomato sauce

1 packet sazón con culantro y achiote

1 can *gandules verdes* (green pigeon peas)

1 small green pepper, chopped

Olives, to taste

Ham, to taste

1 cup brown or white rice

1 cup water

Heat the pan over high and add oil. Add sofrito and stir for a minute. Add tomato sauce and stir again. Toss in sazón, beans, and green pepper. Add olives, ham, or vegan substitute in the desired amount. Stir in rice and water. Cook, stirring frequently, until the water has nearly evaporated.

When the rice is adequately dry, mound it all in the center of the pot. Turn the heat down as low as possible and put the lid on firmly. Let the rice set with the lid firmly in place so that heat remains inside until it's done, roughly 20 minutes. The rice is prepared al dente style and may come out sticky, requiring you to scrape it out of the pot when serving.

As a result of the months-long CCNY campus takeover, the Education Department faculty invited "student participation in curriculum planning," and a committee was formed to "report on a Black and Puerto Rican Studies Program." In addition, moves were made to address the demand for a separate orientation program and to give SEEK students more "voice in curriculum and personnel" decisions.[99] Ultimately, CCNY officials met the students' demands for hiring more Puerto Rican staff to run the SEEK program, diversifying the faculty and staff, and establishing Black and Puerto Rican Studies. It did not, however, permit student participation in the hiring and firing process. Those who participated in the takeover believed that their actions had moved the administration to meet the majority of its demands, and they expressed a pride in serving as catalysts to similar changes in higher education nationally. Following the shutdown, in 1970 CUNY introduced an open admissions policy four years in advance of its original rollout date. The new policy called for (1) offering admission to all high school graduates in the city, depending on their high school transcripts, to some two-year community colleges or four-year university programs; (2) providing remedial courses and support services for students who needed them; (3) maintaining and enhancing the standards of academic excellence at CUNY schools; (4) advancing the ethnic integration of CUNY schools and providing for increased student mobility among the various CUNY programs and units; and (5) ensuring that all admitted to specific CUNY colleges under the previous admissions criteria would continue to be so admitted.[100] There is a consensus that those who participated in the takeover never wanted an open admissions policy. They argued that it undermined the quality of the education received at CCNY and other CUNY institutions.[101]

LEHMAN AND THE BLACK STUDENT ASSOCIATION

A similar, albeit smaller, confrontation took place between students and administrators on Lehman's campus. Kubanbanya had presented its demands to the president of the college in October 1968. They wanted black- and Latino-focused courses that had been approved by the Education Department to be made a mandatory part of the teacher-training curriculum. (Frank Critton of Kubanbanya said that the faculty council had "shown nothing but opposition in attempts to make the courses mandatory.") They demanded the establishment of a Black Studies Department that "would serve in the interests of black students at Lehman." And they wanted a black administrator hired in the registrar's office who would be empowered to increase the number of "minority students" on Lehman's campus.[102] In November, the Kubanbanya president, James Harris, wrote an editorial in the student newspaper stating, "There is a dire need for more black educators on this campus and the black students emphatically stress that there be provisions made immediately for the fulfillment of this need."[103]

After several months of administrative delays, Kubanbanya went on the offensive at the start of the spring 1969 semester. They staged a series of "mini-demonstrations" intended to show the administration that black students were serious and united.[104] On January 28, Kubanbanya staged a protest during the half-time break of a Lehman and Southern Connecticut State basketball game. Two Kubanbanya members flanked by roughly thirty black students took control of the microphone on the gym floor. They passed out flyers listing their demands. Shortly after the game, Kubanbanya sent a letter of "Grievances from Kubanbanya" to the college president, Dr. Leonard Lief, and two of the college's deans. The letter reiterated the previous set of demands and called for the creation of a "Black Associate Dean of Admissions position."[105]

By March 1969, SEEK and Kubanbanya had merged to form the Black Student Association (BSA). They met with President Lief and personally presented him with the demands of this growing student movement. The BSA sought a 10 percent increase in the number of black and Puerto Rican students on the grounds that, in the face of looming budget cuts from Albany, "it is imperative that the administration act immediately to insure the admission of a significant number of black students to Lehman." The group again expressed its desire for a black dean to deal exclusively with the admission of black students.[106]

In response to student demands, the faculty called an emergency meeting. They voted in favor of establishing new majors in Black Studies, Puerto Rican Studies, and other ethnic group studies. In addition, the faculty directed Lief to appoint a special student–faculty committee to develop a Black Studies major. The faculty refused to support a motion stipulating that the student body must be 10 percent black, however, arguing that such an act might be unconstitutional.[107] The student groups were not satisfied with this outcome. Professor Charlotte Morgan-Cato, whom Lehman officials hired as a result of the student protest, said that Lehman's black and brown student organizers were following the events at CCNY, knew about the enormous changes "sweeping the country, and were fully conscious of their participation in this movement." They had a sense of momentum and righteousness that drove them to push for more. The students held a series of off-campus meetings to decide how to force university administrators to capitulate. On the afternoon of March 19, 1969, a majority of the black and Latino students on campus walked out at the same time and "chain-lock[ed] building entrances." All the faculty members were "in a lecture hall where they were debating the establishment of Black Studies and Puerto Rican Studies" when approximately one hundred members of the BSA and a newly formed Latino student group called the Puerto Rican Students' Movement (PRSM) disrupted the meeting. The students surrounded the faculty council, including President Lief, sealed off all the exits, and presented demands for immediate consideration.[108]

Lief, who was chairman of the faculty council, informed the students that normal procedure allowed for only two representatives of the student body to be present at council meetings. But, he said, the faculty could vote on a motion to allow all the students to stay. A black student called out, "You might as well vote because we're not leaving." A substitute motion calling for the adjournment of the council until the students removed themselves was passed by a vote of 47 to 11. The council took a fifteen-minute recess as the students held their ground. James Harris, the president of Kubanbanya, and William Patterson, the president of SEEK, reiterated the coalition's demands to the assembled faculty in the crowded lounge. The faculty members refused to take a vote on the substantive issues under pressure, so they voted to adjourn the meeting "with provisions made for another meeting with ten representatives of the black students."[109] In an emergency session in April 1969, the faculty council overwhelmingly endorsed a resolution urging the president to take "immediate action" on the latest "reasonable" demands of the BSA.[110] Lehman administrators approved the new programs and departments within six months. It was a victory to be sure, although Morgan-Cato questioned whether the changes had their desired effect, saying, "The students failed to realize . . . that traditional solutions—new departments, new courses, new teachers—would not guarantee that their goals would be achieved . . . [what we need are] empathetic, committed teachers for their children."[111]

4

YOUNG TURKS

PROGRESSIVE ACTIVISTS AND ORGANIZATIONS, 1970–1985

T HE 1970S AND EARLY 1980S represented a transitional time in which left-of-center Latino organizations such as El Comité, Young Lords, Puerto Rican Socialist Party (PSP), and later the New York Committee in Support of Vieques (NYCSV), and the National Congress for Puerto Rican Rights (NCPRR) proliferated throughout different Hispanic communities in New York City. These organizations, as well as organized labor, served as important training grounds where future Latino Progressives learned political strategy and how to run a grassroots campaigns. In addition, African American Progressives, who later became noted local operatives, gained similar knowledge as members of unions and civil rights organizations such as the NAACP and CORE.

But the 1970s and early 1980s also represented a tumultuous period in black and Latino relations, particularly during Democratic primaries in newly created districts, struggles over access to political patronage in Albany, and conflicts over federal antipoverty funds. Orientation politics over where to focus one's energy—whether on the political struggle on the island of Puerto Rico for independence or on civil rights issues and the need for progressive changes in New York City—began to divide and implode those Latino movements. COINTELPRO also contributed to the demise of radical Latino and black organizations such as the Young Lords and the Black Panthers. As a result, by the early 1980s Progressive organizations that had started up in the 1970s no longer existed, and the radical leaders from them decided to trade their bullhorns and/or bullets for ballots. Many of them first took on Democratic Party regulars in local races for district leaders and in primary elections for openings on school boards, the City Council, or seats in newly created congressional districts such as the Eleventh and Twelfth in Brooklyn.

Coming out of the radical protest movements of the late 1960s, there was uncertainty and disagreement on the Left about how to proceed. Some activists continued to work primarily through grassroots organizations that aimed to alter the social and economic status quo through external pressure and direct action. "Most of us stayed far away from electoral politics," says Frank Espada, the former Puerto Rican civil rights activist from East Harlem. He explains that for the most part Latinos had seen too many candidates who, after being elected repeatedly, failed to keep their campaign promises. As a result, few participated in local elections, although candidates running for office "often" approached us "for one thing or the other."[1] Others began to focus increasingly on breaking into electoral politics and making reforms from within the system. During this period, a wide array of new organizations tried in various ways to direct public attention to issues of social and economic justice for blacks and Latinos.

This was also a period of personal and political development for the people who formed these new grassroots organizations. Activists such as Zenaida Mendez, Bill Lynch, Zoilo Torres, Sandy Trujillo, Luis Garden Acosta, José Candelario, Ramon Jimenez, Hector W. Soto, and others who would later play important roles in black and Latino coalitions in the 1980s were now learning how to find supporters, how to network, and how to mobilize. Many Progressives who walked door-to-door in the 1970s in Williamsburg, Hell's Kitchen, Spanish Harlem, and Bushwick would later hold leadership positions in Progressive politics in the 1980s and 1990s. According to Bill Lynch, a notable political strategist who came of age at this time, they were a bunch of "Young Turks" trying to make their communities better.[2] They represented insurgents seeking to remove obstacles to progressive change in their communities created by conservative politicians.

As stimulating as this period was for blacks and Latinos, it was also a time of inconsistent engagement between the two groups. These activists came together in tenant, block, and parent-teacher associations as well as coalitions of construction workers. But in black communities and Latino communities, each created separate organizations and political clubs that fought for specific ethnic neighborhoods. At times, they did come together to support candidates for school boards and superintendents of schools. However, Democratic primaries involving elites from both communities vying for more high-profile and powerful positions on city councils, state assemblies, the U.S. House or Senate, or in the mayor's office proved more divisive as differences became more pronounced in the electoral arena.

As minority candidates became more common and more competitive, the black and Latino coalitions themselves became more fractured. With rare exceptions, until the early 1970s the Democratic Party machine in New York City had shut out African Americans and Latinos. Starting in the 1940s, the machine blocked the attempts of black and Latino politicians from gaining Democratic Party nominations. The enormous war chest of the machine outspent and crushed Democratic independents in primary elections. The machine tried to befriend those Independents who rarely won primaries by co-opting them with the promise of support in general elections against wealthier Republican candidates.[3] When Latinos started stumping for seats of their own in the 1970s, black political leaders saw the newcomers as a threat. Blacks were concerned that Latino candidates would split that base and lead to fewer minority representatives overall. In fact, there were elections in the 1970s, such as in the Eleventh Congressional District in Brooklyn, when Edolphus Towns, an African American, ran against Jack John Olivero and Luis Hernandez, both Puerto Ricans, in which blacks and Latinos actually worked against one another. This strategy resulted in the reelection of white incumbents in districts with increasing numbers of black and Latino voters. This trend was halted somewhat when a new common enemy arose: Ronald Reagan. Opposition to the Reagan administration's foreign and domestic policies reunited blacks and Latinos, at least in the New York City labor movement.[4]

EL COMITÉ

El Comité had its roots on the Upper West Side, a largely working-class Puerto Rican neighborhood from the 1950s to the late 1960s.[5] The group was born in response to Mayor Robert Wagner's urban-renewal policies, which were an effort in the late 1950s to relocate Puerto Rican residents from Lincoln Square to the Bronx so that the Upper West Side could be redeveloped.

Wagner promised that the residents would be allowed to return. That promise proved empty. "It didn't happen," says El Comité member Sandy Trujillo. "Some of the people who were directly involved were activists who lost their homes. It became a good example of what urban renewal meant, and it led to the fight for housing and . . . the squatters movement in that area."[6] The forced relocation became a galvanizing moment for Latino activism.

With some of its most active members attending college and universities in the city, El Comité developed a vibrant political education program that included showing political films and organizing community events around issues of education, housing, and jobs for young people. Hector Soto was a member of El Comité in the 1970s; he later became an important advocate for black and Latino candidates for city, state, and national offices. He was also an attorney who focused on issues surrounding community policing and was one of the architects of the New York City Civilian Complaint Review Board, which was established after the election of the city's first black mayor, David Dinkins, in 1989. El Comité spoke to Soto's philosophical commitment to universal freedom and equality. While the organization championed Puerto Rican independence, many members came to the conclusion that the future of the Puerto Rican diaspora in the United States had similar political interest to that of African Americans and other minorities struggling to have a voice. Soto recalls, "Although we supported and collaborated with the [Puerto Rican Socialist Party] and the Lords, we were very much involved" in the broader political struggle across New York.[7]

ORGANIZING CONSTRUCTION WORKERS: THE COALITIONS

Construction trade unions endured fluctuating periods of success and failure until the economic boom during the late 1940s and 1950s. After that period, developers' profits declined and economic pressures triggered the end of favorable concessions to the construction trade unions. Opportunists also began to monopolize leadership positions within unions. In many instances, they marginalized the most radical elements within the movement. Similarly, union purists lost ground to self-aggrandizing union leaders, and professional officers focused more on building the financial strength of the unions than protecting the rights of their members. Up through the

1960s, construction union leaders routinely capitulated to the demands of contractors and defended a system rife with racism, nepotism, and gangsterism. The leading construction unions barred membership by African Americans and Latinos. The Negro-American Labor Council of the 1950s, founded by civil rights leader A. Philip Randolph, served as a response to the lack of opportunity for African Americans in the trade union movement during the post–World War II boom.[8]

The first protests against corrupt unionism occurred in Brooklyn in 1963 where loosely affiliated members of black churches and CORE rallied against segregated construction sites. Later, in 1969, left-of-center African American labor organizers launched a major effort to reclaim the unions and integrate the construction trades in New York. James Haughton (who had served as an aid to Randolph) and William Epton Jr. (a firebrand who served jail time in 1964 for his political activism) teamed up to start Harlem Fight Back, a radical group of unemployed workers determined to integrate the construction industry in Harlem.[9]

Armed with bats, chains, and guns, members conducted militant protests against Jim Crow construction sites. They demanded that contractors hire non-white workers and threatened to shut down the job site. Since work stoppages could cost a contractor thousands of dollars a day in late fees, coalition members often got immediate results. "This militant armed struggle went on," says trade unionist and author Gregory Butler. It "forced the doors of the unions open to minority workers."[10]

Because it was the first group to use these tactics, Harlem Fight Back served as a model for other such groups as the Black and Puerto Rican Coalition of Construction Workers and Black Economic Survival (BES) that formed in other parts of New York City and around the country. These groups came to be known generically as "The Coalitions," because they often brought together African American and Latino workers.[11] "Construction coalitions were huge things in New York in the 1960s, '70s, and '80s," notable for the fact that they were made up entirely of black and brown members, says Mark Naison, a historian and former student activist.[12]

Moses Harris, an activist with a reputation for turning down bribes in a construction industry controlled by organized crime, founded the Brooklyn-based group BES. Following in Harris's footsteps, James T. Sims started a chapter of BES in the Bronx, which by the early 1980s had approximately eight hundred members. BES would force its way onto a construction site and shut it down, recalls Sims's contemporary Leroy Archibald, and would sometimes even use dynamite to destroy scaffolding to force a closure. It was "a little too radical for me," remembers Archibald. "It was a dangerous bunch of guys."[13]

José Rivera, a Puerto Rican immigrant who became an assemblyman in the New York State Legislature, was one of the men Sims pulled into the movement. As organizers with BES and other working-class movements in the South Bronx, Sims and Rivera gained a reputation as men who could get good-paying jobs for black and Latino construction workers. Over time, however, questions began to be raised about Sims's and Rivera's tactics and personal conduct.[14] Some street-level activists wondered whether the BES and similar groups were "legitimate organizations or rackets," says Naison. Rumors were rampant: Had these groups been corrupted by payoffs from contractors and organized crime? Did payments go to benefit workers or the organizers? Were these shakedown shops or legitimate operations?[15] The suspicion was there, but there was no proof. We do know that Rivera broke from Sims in 1975 and, with the help of coalition activists Julio Munoz and Jacob Ross, founded a new coalition in the South Bronx called United Tremont Trade (UTT).

In 1978, Mayor Ed Koch approved the creation of an eleven-member special investigation team called Dolphin within the New York Police Department to monitor coalition activities and apparently help build cases against them for the city's district attorneys (who, like the mayor, are elected officials) (figure 4.1). In 1979, the Bronx district attorney, Mario Merola, charged the thirty-one-year-old Sims and the twenty-five-year-old Puerto Rican José Roman with extortion related to their work with BES.[16] Sims's attorney, Murray Richman, told reporters that in the last three to four years his client "secured" more jobs for black and Latino workers in the Bronx then "anyone else," between "two thousand to three thousand jobs for minority workers."[17]

Like BES, UTT focused on obtaining employment for black and Latino workers in union-supported development projects and job sites that historically did not hire minority workers without union membership, and as stated earlier unions cleverly obstructed them from gaining membership in the first place to the construction trade unions. In contrast to Sims, Rivera would join an almost all-white carpenters' union and eventually get a

FIGURE 4.1 Ed Koch (mayor of New York, 1978–1989) and David Dinkins (mayor of New York, 1989–1993). (Courtesy NYC Municipal Archives)

leadership position. Thereafter, he used his role to sponsor and facilitate the entrance of new black and Latino members. He remained staunchly independent of left-of-center Puerto Rican organizations until he became interested in running for office.[18]

As the head of the UTT, Rivera played an important role as a Progressive organizer and spokesperson during the 1980 People's Convention movement. In June 1980, members of the Coalition for a People's Alternative and the South Bronx Convention Coalition made preparations for a festival to be held on August 8–9 in a "tent city" on the Charlotte Street site that President Jimmy Carter had visited on his tour of the South Bronx in 1977. Convention organizers chose the space because it illustrated how out of touch elected officials had become with the housing, employment, and public services needed in the community. They occupied, cleaned, and built a convention infrastructure in an area where apartment buildings had been leveled, leaving empty lots that had become unsanctioned dumping grounds. Rivera told reporters that the groups expected some 2,000 people and a hundred groups from around the country and the world for its convention. Once the festival got under way in August, a diverse coalition of groups—including African Americans, Native Americans, Latinos, gays, lesbians, Communists, anti-Castro groups, and representatives from Latin America—occupied the makeshift convention space. The groups pitched tents at designated locations and sat down to discuss how to revitalize U.S. politics and revamp American foreign policy in Central America, South Africa, and elsewhere. Participants also discussed the needs of citizens and the broken promises of the Carter administration regarding poverty programs, health care, jobs, and welfare. Some called it a counter-convention of the unrepresented people within the Democratic Party and an opposition movement to big business in America. The People's Convention agenda in the South Bronx called for a day of picketing at the 1980 Democratic national convention on August 10, at Madison Square Garden.[19] The group wanted the Democratic Party to stop "their phony promises . . . and meet with the basic demands of people, and put people to work. We have enough people willing and able to rebuild our own community," Rivera stated.[20]

Like the recent Occupy Wall Street movement, the 1980 People's Convention sought to expose the neglect and disregard of government officials for black and brown poor people in the Bronx. But unlike Occupy Wall Street, it went farther and sought to provide a third-party alternative to the Republican and Democratic parties. During the Democratic Party convention, Rivera led a large People's Party–sponsored protest march through the streets of Manhattan to the steps of Madison Square Garden. Rivera's work with the UTT and its participation in the 1980s People's Convention helped him develop a political base that launched his career in electoral politics.[21]

YOUNG LORDS AND LATIN JUSTICE

In May 1969, Fred Hampton, the leader of the Chicago chapter of the Black Panther Party, brokered a truce among warring ethnic groups in his city. Coining the term "Rainbow Coalition," he argued that poor people must unite and that violence among them would only perpetuate the cycle of poverty. (Jesse Jackson would later famously use the same moniker to describe his unrelated coalition.) Hampton helped create a national multiparty alliance among the Black Panthers, Young Lords, Brown Berets, American Indian Movement, the Young Patriots (unemployed white Appalachian youth), the Chinese American Red Guard Party, Asian American I Wor Kuen, and other radical organizations.[22]

Back in New York, the East Harlem native Miguel "Mickey" Melendez, an undergraduate student at SUNY College at Old Westbury on Long Island, had just formed a study group with a few friends called the Sociedad de Albizu Campos (SAC), which drew inspiration from Fred Hampton and the Black Panther Party in Chicago. Melendez also helped recruit Latino students for SUNY Old Westbury as part of his work-study job in the admissions office. In February 1969, he and a member of the admissions department traveled to Chicago to recruit Latino students. During that trip, he met with José (Cha Cha) Jimenez, the founder of the Young Lords Organization (YLO, later the Young Lords Party), a Chicago youth gang, at the office of the Latin American Defense Organization. Jimenez recommended a Chicago high school student, David Pérez, and he enrolled in the fall of 1969 and became an active member of SAC. That fall, Paul Guzman, a former Puerto Rican SAC member, returned to the SUNY campus. He was newly radicalized, thanks to time spent in a Spanish-language immersion program in Mexico, as Pablo "Yoruba" Guzmán.[23]

SAC members closely followed the emergence of Hampton and the Chicago Rainbow Coalition alliance. Guzmán—along with Juan González, a Columbia University student activist (later a journalist and co-host of the Pacifica Radio show *Democracy Now!* with Amy Goodman), Felipe Luciano (later a television personality and news anchor), and Mickey Melendez—jumped in a Volkswagen and headed for Chicago to see for themselves how Progressive minority groups had begun to move from organized gangs to political organizations.

David Pérez helped facilitate a meeting between the national leaders of the Young Lords in Chicago and the New York student activists. At the meeting, the New York contingent formally requested and received permission from the national office to establish a chapter of the YLO in New York City. The national office had already granted similar requests to a group of Puerto Rican activists from East Harlem and asked Melendez and his colleagues to join forces with them, which they did. At the same time, a YLO chapter in Boston emerged.[24]

In 1972, reflecting on its genesis, members of the New York chapter of the YLO wrote in a joint New York resolution that their group, "ideologically as well as organizationally, was the Black Panther Party. Of all the organizations in the U.S., the Panthers had the major leading role from the time they began in 1966 until the split in 1971."[25] While originally focused on the issues of gentrification and Puerto Rican displacement, the mission of the YLO soon broadened to include police misconduct, health care, tenants' rights, education, and nutrition. New York chapters included Puerto Rican, African American, Dominican, Mexican, Cuban, and Panamanian members. It is important to note that the YLO also included street-educated members such as Vincente "Panama" Alba, but perhaps a larger percentage of its members came out of the campus takeover movements in New York City.[26] Alba was born in Panama City in 1951, joined the YLO on the day that it took over Lincoln Hospital in 1970, and started a substance abuse program there. And in 1989, he ran the "Latinos for Dinkins" campaign headquarters in the Bronx.

The YLO played a pivotal role in the transition to electoral politics that occurred in Latino communities in New York in the 1970s. Alba insists that

CARNE GUISADA

Food played a pivotal role in the YLO's work in the South Bronx. "The free breakfast program was a cornerstone of the community work done by the Young Lords," Vincente Alba said. "It was actually something that was inspired and something that we emulated from the Black Panther Party. It was a means of providing something to the community's children that many of them would not get any other way" and made a day in school bearable. Obtaining sufficient food remained a constant challenge for members of the organization in the South Bronx. Members sold copies of the Young Lords's newspaper *Palante* (*Advance*) to purchase food and other necessities. "We sold a hell of a lot of *Palantes*," which served as "the primary income of the organization" and paid for rent, the phone bill, and food.* Sympathetic Latino seniors near the organization's Longwood Avenue office also donated sweaters and delicious homemade Puerto Rican food like *carne guisada* (beef stew).

★★★

2 lbs boneless stewing beef

2 cloves garlic

¼ tsp dry oregano

½ tsp black pepper

2 tsp salt

1 tbsp white vinegar

1 tbsp vegetable oil

3 tbsp achiote tinted oil

½ cup prepared sofrito

1 tsp chopped capers

12 stuffed olives, sliced

½ cup tomato sauce

2½ cups very hot water

4 medium potatoes, peeled and cut

Wash and remove the fat from the beef and cut into 2-inch cubes. Using a mortar and pestle, crush together the garlic, oregano, and black pepper. Add the salt, vinegar, and vegetable oil to this mixture, mix well, and rub thoroughly onto the cubes of meat. Allow to sit for ½ hour before beginning to cook the stew.

Heat the achiote oil on medium-high heat and sauté the beef pieces on all sides until the pink is gone. Add the sofrito, capers, olives, and tomato sauce. Lower the heat to medium and continue sautéing for another 3 or 4 minutes. Add the hot water and raise the heat to high until the pot begins to boil. Quickly reduce the heat to low, place a lid on the pot (making sure to leave a space for the vapor to escape), and cook for 1½ hours. After the first 5 minutes, check and adjust the heat to maintain a steady simmer. Add the potato pieces and your vegetable of choice, if desired, and continue cooking for an additional ½ hour until the meat and potatoes are tender and the sauce thickens. Season to taste.

———

*Young Lords Party, Resolutions & Speeches: Puerto Rican Revolutionary Workers Organization (November 1972), Box 11, Folder 11, Lourdes Torres Papers, Archives of the Puerto Rican Diaspora, Centro de Estudios Puertorriqueños, Hunter College, CUNY, New York, N.Y.

prior to the Young Lords arrival in New York, Democratic and Republican Party regulars had ignored Puerto Ricans because of their lack of political organization and their failure to mobilize members of their community on behalf of an issue, cause, or candidate. "When the Young Lords began doing community organizing in the community, we always pointed to colonialism as the root cause for our political problems," says Alba. And that was in sharp contrast to the antipoverty movement that "pretended that Puerto Ricans were Americans and the streets of New York were really paved with gold." He adds, "Our community began to see itself differently as a result of the presence of the Young Lords. Now, we could actually conceive change as a community."[27]

The Young Lords had a profound impact on Julio Pabon, one of the student leaders advocating for a Puerto Rican Studies program at Lehman College in the 1970s. "I came in [to the student movement at Lehman] when [the Puerto Rican Studies Program] was already established," Pabon says. "But then we had to fight to sustain it because they wanted to cut it, and they also wanted to cut a lot of the African American professors and Latino professors. They were very, very progressive. These were the people who were really teaching us."[28]

Born in Guayama, Puerto Rico, in 1952, Pabon moved to the South Bronx with his family when he was five years old. "I was always on my block helping somebody," remembers Pabon of his Caldwell Avenue roots. "I was one of the few who was actually going to school. So if somebody needed help with something they would say, 'Oh, go to don Julio's son' . . . because I was always going to school." Pabon became a bookworm and a savvy street kid.[29] Even though Pabon lived in the Bronx, he attended Aviation High School in Queens. One day while waiting for the bus to go back to the Bronx, he saw members of the Young Lords distributing "Free Puerto Rico" handouts and copies of their newspaper, *Palante*. "I read the paper and it was like, 'Wow!'"

At the time, Pabon was working for Evelina López Antonetty, a member of the left-of-center Wednesday Night Club, a founder of United Bronx Parents, and an outspoken community control advocate, who would later play a significant role in Progressive politics in the city.[30] The Young Lords already had an office on Longwood Avenue in the Bronx, and they soon began to organize young Puerto Ricans, like Pabon, on Caldwell Avenue. Pabon also attended a demonstration at Plaza Boricua on a 138th Street in the South Bronx where he learned about the Manhattan-based Puerto Rican Progressive group El Comité.[31] Interactions with Antonetty and these various Puerto Rican activists primed Pabon for a true political awakening during his undergraduate years at Lehman College regarding institutionalized oppression and "national liberation movements taking place in Africa, Latin America, [and] Vietnam."[32] In 1974, Pabon decided to start his own group called Justicia Latina (Latin Justice). "We got a storefront and we began to work with the Young Lords and El Comité," Pabon explains. "El Comité would send somebody up with literature for us to read and the Young Lords [would show] us new ways to serve our community like arranging free anemia tests and other public programs." Latin Justice broke up sometime in 1977, and Pabon then joined El Comité.[33]

PUERTO RICAN SOCIALIST PARTY

Political repression in Puerto Rico (along with economic hardships) led activists to relocate to mainland cities such as New York City and Chicago, and thus PSP began to grow there. The transition began in the late 1960s when the University of Puerto Rico became the center of the island's Pro Independence Party (PIP), which had its roots in the Movement for Independence (Movimiento Pro Independencia, MPI), a group started in Puerto Rico in 1959. Puerto Rican exiles in East Harlem in 1964 re-formed the party in the United States. The East Harlem–based MPI consisted of mostly first-generation Puerto Ricans, many of them with ties to the national independence movements of the 1950s. By the late 1960s, MPI had become largely a Marxist-Leninist party that backed movements such as the student takeover at CCNY in 1969. The organization's leadership hesitated to recruit second-generation Puerto Ricans born on the mainland because they questioned their political orientation and receptivity to Progressive politics. In 1971, the MPI changed its name to the Puerto Rican Socialist Party (PSP).[34] (It is unclear what the ideological and strategic rationale for the name had been.)

In New York, the PSP worked closely with Puerto Rico's labor movement and often shared members. As the FBI and Puerto Rican police officials investigated the PIP and PSP during the late 1960s and early 1970s, they discovered that University of Puerto Rico (UPR) students and faculty had become some of these political movements' most active members. As a result, state officials took steps to monitor and repress their campus activities using informants, violence, mass arrest, and, in some instances, the assassination of activists and protestors. The researcher Ramón Bosque-Pérez along with the political scientist José Javier Colón-Morera documented COINTELPRO operations in Puerto Rico in their book *Las carpetas: Persecución política y derechos civiles en Puerto Rico*, published in 1997. *Las Carpetas* is a collection of reprinted FBI memorandums, which documents the bureau's COINTELPRO operations in Puerto Rico and their surveillance of exiles who came to New York City after repression on the island became intolerable in the 1970s. The documents place the political repression and assassinations in the context of the broader culture of surveillance during the Cold War years and the fear of the spread of communism in United States and its colonies.[35]

COINTELPRO wreaked havoc on left-of-center organizations like the Puerto Rican–based FALN (Fuerzas Armadas de Liberación Nacional [Armed Forces of National Liberation]) and Los Macheteros, and in the United States, the Black Panthers and the Young Lords.[36] "To my mind, PSP was always more of a danger to the status quo in Puerto Rico than anywhere in the United States," says former PSP member Zoilo Torres. The leadership of the PSP affirmed the right to armed struggle against colonial domination, but internally the organization remained "engulfed in a vigorous debate as to its timing." That debate continued until its demise. While U.S.-based PSP chapters participated in local civil rights struggles, including electoral politics, more of its members remained dedicated to supporting the independence movement in Puerto Rico via fund-raisers, mass education, media relations, and political organizing. As a result, violent state repression focused on groups united and committed to armed struggle like the Black Panthers, the Young Lords, FALN, and Los Macheteros. *Las carpetas* shows that COINTELPRO agents did, however, infiltrate PSP chapters in the United States, as it had done in Puerto Rico.[37]

On September 26, 1969, in response to the imprisonment of a fellow student for resisting the draft, seven UPR students were suspended after burning and ransacking the school's ROTC building. On October 7, 1969, forty UPR students started a hunger strike held in the rotunda of the school's administration building, vowing to consume only water with lemon and sugar until the school ended its ROTC program and the suspension of the seven students. The fasting students attracted widespread sympathy and support for their protest on the campus. Rubén Berríos, a Yale-educated UPR Law School professor, became president of the PIP in 1970 and active in the student protest. Violence occurred on March 5, 1970, as pro- and anti-ROTC supporters had a fistfight and threw chairs at one another in the student center's cafeteria. The all-out brawl increased as more people took sides. Some ROTC members took up positions at the training facility; their opponents positioned themselves just opposite in a space located in the student center. The fight escalated from rocks thrown from rooftops to shots fired as the island's riot police commandeered the campus. The fight spilled onto the streets of San Juan, resulting in looting businesses and burning a local supermarket. In the end, sixty-two people were injured; the police killed two people and arrested about twelve.[38] Berríos was subsequently sentenced to three months in prison that year for trespassing on a U.S. naval base on the island. University officials fired him, arguing that he spent more time on Progressive causes than on his duties as a law professor. His supporters created an iconic poster, Desde la Cárcel (From the Prison), with a photo of him raising a clenched fist. "The food, bad; but the majority of Puerto Ricans eat worse [but] here, no one dies of hunger," Berríos said in one of several phrases on the poster.[39] In the early 1970s, reports of increasing layoffs and deteriorating living conditions came from the island. In November 1974, residents started paying more for food on the island than did those on the mainland.[40] As it did with African American activists and organizers, COINTELPRO subjected an entire generation of Puerto Rican Progressives to a systematic repression rooted in Cold War politics.

At this time, activists began a large-scale exodus from Puerto Rico to the mainland. Some of the newly settled activists set up study circles in Los Angeles, Chicago, Boston, and New York. They shared their historical memory of the PSP and provided Puerto Rican youth in those cities with a theoretical and political framework for creating their own movements as well as starting up PSP chapters within the U.S./Puerto Rican diaspora. There were PSP supporters in the Bronx, Harlem, and Westchester County, but the PSP's largest and most influential New York chapter was in Brooklyn. Founded in November 1971, the Brooklyn branch of the PSP gained more than eight hundred members and affiliates in its first months. At its peak in the 1970s, the PSP in Brooklyn represented the largest Progressive organization in the

city and one of the best organized. It lasted until 1993 when internal disagreement about whether to focus on Puerto Rican independence or Puerto
Rican rights on the mainland eventually led to a major split.[41]

The PSP gave young Puerto Ricans in Williamsburg, Brooklyn, a clear
ideological framework for their political activism. "We were reading Malcolm X, Marx, Engels, that kind of literature," remembers PSP member
José Candelario. The group's study leaders taught about socialism, class
consciousness, and Puerto Rican history, but creating a respect for Africa
and their African roots was, perhaps, the greatest contribution of the PSP
study leaders. Candelario says, "We were more closely identified with African Americans and the fact that we ourselves had African in us, in our
culture. . . . The dominant Eurocentric view did not fit who we were."[42]

Torres, who later did extensive organizing in Williamsburg, traveled to
California in 1973 and joined the Los Angeles chapter of the PSP. "It was sup-
posed to be a three-week trip, and it turned out to be a four-year visit," says
Torres, who rose to hold a leadership position in the Los Angeles chapter of
the PSP.[43] In 1978, Torres returned to New York, where he became active in
the PSP chapter in Sunset Park, Brooklyn, while also working for the DC 37
union. Candelario returned to New York from Los Angeles, joining the Williamsburg chapter of the PSP and becoming involved in the local tenants'
rights movements.[44] Torres earned a reputation as a gifted political strategist with a remarkable talent for theoretical and conceptual thinking. Early
on, he made his mark as a leader who refused to engage in dirty politics
or questionable behavior. Williamsburg's great tenants' rights leader, David
Santiago, once joked that Torres's problem was that he was "not conniving
enough."[45]

Access to public housing was another major issue for Puerto Rican activists during this time. In the late 1970s, Santiago helped build a black and
Latino coalition called the Williamsburg Fair Housing Committee, which
later became the Southside Fair Housing Committee. By the 1970s, Williamsburg had become a mix of Jews, African Americans, and Latinos, but
in the coalition's opinion many government officials gave the Jewish community preferential treatment. The coalition fought to end what members
saw as the city's practice of favoring white Hasidic Jews over black and
Latino applicants for apartments in the three city-owned public-housing
complexes in Williamsburg. In 1978, a consent decree issued by the city

mandated that 51 percent of the apartments had to go to black and Latino applicants, and approved the construction of Roberto Clemente Plaza. As the construction of the plaza came to an end, the percentages changed. Seventy-five percent of the apartments were slated for black and Latino residents, and the remainder to white, and more than likely Hasidic, residents.[46]

According to Candelario, Santiago's ability to immediately "understand how to take an idea from the conceptual to the structural and programmatic," along with his skill as a fund-raiser, made Santiago an invaluable player in the tenants' rights movement in Brooklyn.[47] Saul Nieves, another longtime friend and colleague of Santiago, describes him as Machiavellian—someone who would do whatever he deemed most politically expedient and apologize for any harm done later.[48] Candelario agrees that Santiago could be overzealous, but he also marvels at the fact that Santiago remained "a true left-wing ideologue. [He] fashioned all the aspects of his life around serving our community. . . . David gave a million times more than he ever took. He didn't keep anything for himself."[49] Santiago did not become entrenched in one organization and remained independent by continually founding new groups and forming alliances with new partners and coalitions. He is best described as a leftist seed-planter, explains Candelario. "Once he laid the agenda and the vision," other people were able to step in and help it grow.[50] This signaled a new stage in activism in which Puerto Ricans moved from changing policies at the city schools to finding ways to pressure the city into responding to their interests.

The PSP in Williamsburg operated like a family in those years. The former PSP member Jaime Estades argues that the organization functioned as a "very cohesive" kinship network.[51] In an apartment building in the community, half of the residents were PSP members living and working together.[52] Most members of the PSP in New York also belonged to unions and participated in labor organizing. Torres was working as an associate editor for District Council 65's newspaper where he met Estades.[53] District Council 65 was a trade union representing retail, wholesale, and department store workers, and later the United Auto Workers. The union had 30,000 members, including 5,000 Puerto Ricans, before it became defunct.[54] "There were so many needs that Latino workers had inside the union," remembers Estades, "and they did not have enough bilingual workers. I ended up doing social work in the members' assistance program and also helping with organizing and helping Latino workers on immigration issues." In addition to Estades and Torres, the Puerto Rican immigrant Dennis Rivera worked his way up the ladder in Local 1199, the health-care workers union.[55]

ELECTORAL POLITICS

During the 1970s, there was a slow but noticeable shift in the orientation of many black and Latino activists away from direct action and toward working within the political process. Where they once refused to be co-opted by a corrupt political system, activists now came to believe that their goals could not be achieved through outside agitation alone. Increasingly, leaders of black and Latino organizations began to focus on electoral politics and mobilizing political constituencies. But the few black and Latino political elites who existed in the Democratic Party in New York had a notoriously difficult time working together effectively to elect more minority candidates. Thus, the decision to embrace the potential power of elected office opened up both new opportunities and challenges for the Left.

Scholars and reporters have described attempts by black and Latino political elites to forge electoral alliances in 1970s New York City as elusive, unsuccessful, contentious, and short-lived. Competition over limited funding and patronage for their constituencies was a powerful obstacle to unity. The civil rights and Black Power movements forced some openings in the city's Democratic Party machine, first for African Americans in sections of Manhattan, Brooklyn, and Queens, and to a much lesser extent for Latinos in East Harlem and the South Bronx. Meanwhile, the Democratic Party made room for a small cadre of Latino elected officials such as Herman Badillo, the first native-born Puerto Rican elected to the U.S. Congress; Representative Robert Garcia; Angelo Falcon, president of the National Institute for Latino Policy; and Senator Olga Mendez, the first Puerto Rican woman elected to a state legislature in the United States. The slow but steady shifts in New York City mirrored changes in the national scene with the election of black officials like Carl Stokes as mayor of Cleveland in 1968 and, perhaps more important, Atlanta's Maynard Jackson, who in 1974 became the first African American elected mayor of a large southern city and led a number of civil rights and Black Power activists to redirect their energies into becoming Democratic Party activists. Manhattan Borough President Percy Sutton, the labor negotiator and lawyer Basil Paterson, Representative Charles Rangel in Harlem, and New York City Councilman Al Vann in Brooklyn are examples of former civil rights and Black Power 1960s activists who energetically advocated voter-registration drives and electoral politics as a strategy for black Progressives. Thus by the 1970s, a gradual transition had occurred in the Black Power movement as the emphasis shifted from cultural nationalism to include politics and gaining access to and control of decision-making positions within government institutions.[56]

Percy Sutton would go on to become one of a handful of black kingmakers as leader of the Harlem Clubhouse, a close-knit group of Harlem politicians that included Rangel, David Dinkins, Paterson, and Leon Bogues. This group of politicians controlled the Martin Luther King Jr. Democratic Club, the George Washington Carver Democratic Club, and the Young Democratic Independent Citizens Club. They supported one another's campaigns and shared political resources.[57]

During the 1970s, tension—if not outright contempt—grew between the city's larger, more influential black delegation of elected officials and its smaller, less powerful Latino counterpart. These two groups waged battles together against white, racist, elected officials for state's resources and patronage, but these coalitions often resulted in a disproportionate amount of the spoils going to African Americans communities. By the end of the decade, however, an ethnocentric political culture blocked the development of vibrant, mutually beneficial political alliances between the groups. Fed up with what some viewed as winner-take-all alliances with black politicians in New York, Latino politicians and leaders occasionally obstructed development projects in places like Harlem, and withheld or gave insincere symbolic support to black candidates running for office.[58]

Exceptions to this ethnocentric divide did exist. For example, African American elected officials such as Adam Clayton Powell Jr. and Charles Rangel, who defeated him for his seat in the U.S. House of Representatives in 1971, depended on Latino votes in their Harlem Fifteenth Congressional District to remain in office. By the 1950s, more than 40 percent of the district was Latino, with Puerto Ricans in East Harlem and, later on, Dominicans in Washington Heights making up the largest population of Latinos in the Fifteenth Congressional District. Throughout his long tenure, Rangel, who is part Puerto Rican and part African American, benefited from the unwavering support from East Harlem's state senator, Olga Mendez.[59]

Similarly, Herman D. (Denny) Farrell Jr. has since 1975 represented the Seventy-first District in the New York State Assembly, which encompasses the Manhattan neighborhoods of West Harlem, Washington Heights (a historically Dominican neighborhood), and Inwood. As a county leader, Farrell says, he had the ear of the heads of the different ethnic constituencies that made up his district (in which Dominicans made up 50 percent of the residents). He also insisted that he had always made low-key coalitions with Latino leaders in his district and kept his promises to them. Therefore, no one ever "mess[ed] with me" and "I've gotten reelected." Farrell also used his political capital to put Dominicans in positions of power, and he played an important role in creating a position for the city's first Dominican and Mexican judges and the first Dominican district leader on the Democratic National Committee. Moreover, by supporting and attending important community initiatives and events of his constituents, Latino voters developed a historical memory of the significant events that included Farrell. These combined strategies have served him well over his thirty-nine years in office despite some rough patches in his relations with Latino voters.[60]

There have also been differences between black and Latino leaders on issues such as immigration policy, undocumented workers, bilingual education, the English-only movement, extending the Voting Rights Act to Latinos, and broadening tuition tax credits to parochial schools.[61] In some instances, African Americans simply disagreed with their Latino colleagues on these issues. In other cases, they had different priorities on education, policing, economic development, and access to state and federal funding for poverty programs. They disagreed over support for Spanish-language initiatives, parochial schools, and policies that would put African American workers in competition with immigrants from Latin America. When disagreements occurred among black and Latino political elites, African Americans leveraged the larger size of their political base and political capital compared with their Latino colleagues in order to advance a black agenda. Thus some black politicians, often those without a large Hispanic population among their constituents, showed an inability to work beyond a winner-take-all negotiating tactic and were thus unwilling to compromise and work together with Latinos. Some Latino elected officials developed

FIGURE 4.2 David Dinkins (Manhattan borough president, 1986–1989), Representative Charles Rangel, Shirley Chisholm (congresswoman, 1969–1983), and Hugh Carey (governor of New York, 1975–1982). (Courtesy NYC Municipal Archives)

the perception that this had occurred too many times in the state's black and Puerto Rican caucus in Albany during the administration of Governor Hugh Carey (figure 4.2).[62]

Finally, black and Latino political alliances were stymied by divide-and-conquer strategies effectively employed by white-controlled political machines. When Progressive black or Latino challengers entered Democratic primaries, party bosses flush with money and a well-established infrastructure would often back a Latino candidate to siphon votes away from an insurgent African American candidate. The tactic worked effectively to split black and Latino political alliances and allow the party favorite (most often an entrenched incumbent) to cruise to victory in a primary. Ultimately, this allowed the Democratic political machines to employ an effective strategy of divide-and-conquer ethnic politics to win in Latino/black and Latino districts where registered Democrats outnumbered registered Republicans. The 1985 Democratic primary for borough president in the Bronx and Brooklyn illustrate this point. These strategies created internal conflicts among black politicians and Latino politicians, as well as divisions between campaign managers and activists. However, one does not see these tensions spilling over to the voters.[63]

In other parts of the country, even when blacks and Latinos occasionally formed successful electoral coalitions, the partnership did not often survive much past a candidate's swearing-in ceremony. Tom Bradley became the first African American mayor of Los Angeles in 1973 with 40 percent of the Latino vote, mostly from Latinos in poor neighborhoods who thought he would serve their interests better than the incumbent, a white conservative Democrat. Nonetheless, Bradley alienated his Latino base during his twenty years as mayor. He quickly estranged Latino voters by supporting an all-black slate to occupy three vacant seats, leaving Latinos without a seat on the City Council. Black candidates held on to those three seats for the next thirty years, completely shutting Latinos out of the process. Los Angeles's Latinos came to distrust the Bradley machine and African American politicians in general.[64]

The history of black and Latino coalition building around elections in New York is similarly fraught. The Puerto Rican nationalist Ramon Santiago Velez became one of the most powerful Latino political bosses in New York City. Not a radical or a social activist, Velez built a political machine that successfully vaulted Latinos into the world of New York politics. Velez grew up on a farm in Hormigueros, Puerto Rico, where his father grew plantains and citrus fruits and raised cows. After completing his undergraduate degree at the Inter-American University of Puerto Rico, Velez attended law school at the University of Salamanca in Spain and then served in the U.S. Army. In 1963, when he was twenty-eight, Velez settled in New York City. His first exposure to New York City political life was as a welfare coordinator and part-time radio commentator. With a $50,000 grant through Lyndon Johnson's War on Poverty and Great Society programs, Velez created the Hunts Point Multi-Service Center, which ran programs focused on the elderly, housing, health care, and substance abuse.[65]

The center was just the beginning. By some estimates, between 1965 and 2005, Velez won $300 million in largely government health-care grants.[66] With these funds, he operated a number of institutions that gave him a political base and the ability to mobilize votes for Democratic and Republican candidates and various ballot initiatives. Velez organized a voter-registration drive in the South Bronx as part of a Puerto Rican community empowerment project, and he led the movement to eliminate English-language qualifications for Spanish-speaking citizens. He helped create and run the Puerto Rican Day Parade and ran the South Bronx Democratic Club, which launched the political careers of numerous Puerto Rican officials including Representative José Serrano. Velez unsuccessfully ran for U.S. Congress twice and served one term on the New York City Council. "El Jefe," "king-maker," "the baron of poverty programs," "a poverty pimp," "emperor of the South Bronx," and "godfather" were just some the titles given to Velez over the course of his long career.[67] Julio Pabon remembers, "Being in the South Bronx, every program I worked in [during high school and college], had something to do with Velez. Whether you [saw] him or not, [with] every poverty program in the South Bronx, Velez or his people had input."[68]

Unlike young radicals in the Fred Hampton mold, who saw power in unity, Velez did not try to form coalitions with African American leaders. Instead, in the late 1970s, Velez became involved in some nasty turf battles with certain African American organizations in the Bronx that tried to claim their share of government funding for poverty programs.[69] Leroy Archibald, a well-known black Democrat activist from the Bronx, said Velez reached out to him a few times but insisted that he fall in line with his goals and objectives. Archibald recalls, "I told him that I was [pro] black" and would sell out his people for personal gain.[70] An old-school, Eurocentric-thinking Puerto Rican, Velez focused on providing patronage jobs to Latinos in the Bronx, at the expense of other ethnic groups, particularly U.S.-born blacks whom he viewed negatively.

During the summer when Pabon was working as a program supervisor for high school kids in the South Bronx, he met Serrano, one of Velez's young lieutenants. Velez wanted all of the high school students in the program to participate in a massive voter-registration drive. Pabon and another supervisor, Confessor Cruz, refused. Young activists like Pabon and Cruz—who were aligned with groups like El Comité, the PSP, YLO, and the Black Panthers—wanted nothing to do with electoral politics because they viewed politicians as part of an unethical power structure. Serrano and Francisco Lugovina, Velez's right-hand man, invited Pabon and Cruz to lunch to try to convince them to participate in the voter-registration program.[71] The two young radicals met Velez's representatives at a diner on Third Avenue in the Bronx. Pabon was a broke Lehman College student at the time, so once Serrano and Lugovina indicated that they were paying, "I went all out, ordering the cheeseburger, fries, and a malted," he recalls. "I ate the whole thing while Lugovina and Serrano talked to us." Pabon and Cruz articulated their objections to buying into traditional electoral politics and questioned the legality of using city summer program funds to bankroll a voter-registration drive. Lugovina and Serrano responded by explaining that Velez intended to empower the entire Puerto Rican community in the South Bronx through electoral politics and that voter registration was the basis of all political power. Even though Cruz and Pabon didn't change their minds, Pabon, in reflection, believes that the registration drive proved effective. It became an important strategy that helped lay the groundwork for Serrano's future run for congress.[72]

Voter-registration drives were also crucial to the career of Herman Badillo. He was one of the first Puerto Ricans to achieve success in electoral politics. Born in 1929 in Caguas, Puerto Rico, Badillo came to live with his aunt in the Bronx at the age of eleven. In 1951, he graduated from CCNY and was first in his class at Brooklyn Law School in 1954.[73]

Badillo was not a radical. In fact, his loyalty to his superiors and acceptance of the status quo helps explain why he was able to win office before other Latinos were able to do so. He served as Mayor Robert Wagner's housing commissioner during the Lincoln Square urban-renewal project and mass relocations in the late 1950s. Having earned the support of Wagner and the Democratic Party machine, Badillo won the election for Bronx borough president. He served in that position from 1966 to 1970, and then won election to the U.S. House of Representatives in 1971. In 1973, he entered the Democratic primary for mayor against Abraham Beame, a Jew who had served as the city's budget director and comptroller. Instead of supporting Badillo, Percy Sutton, the highest-ranking African American in New York City as Manhattan borough president, endorsed Beame. Sutton planned to put in a bid to become the city's first black mayor in 1977, and he wanted to ensure that he would get Beame's endorsement. The strategy outraged Badillo and other Latinos across the city.[74] A serial candidate for one public office after another, Badillo had a short career as a borough president and a congressman. As a result, it is difficult to tell how his political career affected the Latino community or how he balanced the interests of Latino and African American communities. The fallout from Sutton's endorsement created tensions between black and Latino community leaders, making future political coalitions between them difficult.

Badillo came in second to Beame in a field of four in the primary, but Beame did not receive the necessary plurality of 40 percent, resulting in a runoff. Badillo lost to Beame by 2 or 3 percentage points, due to strong support among African American voters after Sutton endorsed Beame in exchange for the promise of future support and political patronage. The same black voters propelled Beame to victory in a close general election against the Republican John Marchi.[75]

To repay the debt he owed the black community, mayor-elect Beame announced that he would select David Dinkins to serve as a deputy mayor. "In those days, the mayor had only two deputies," recalls Dinkins. "Now he's going to have a third one, and he's going to be black. So, it was a very, very big deal." But then it was revealed that Dinkins hadn't filed income tax returns for three years. A team of lawyers and accountants worked around the clock to help clear up the situation. In the end, Beame decided to distance himself from what looked like a possible scandal and asked Dinkins to withdraw his name. The tax problem would come back to haunt Dinkins when he ran for mayor in 1989.[76]

When Beame took control in 1974, the city was in a deep financial crisis, and he spent most of his term simply trying to keep New York out of bankruptcy. But his strategy, which included shrinking the city's workforce and imposing deep cuts on citywide programs, did not sit well with many black and Latino activists who felt that their communities were bearing the brunt of the city's woes. Ramon Jimenez, a Harvard Law School graduate, helped lead the fight against spending cuts in education and remembers, "It was a time when coalitions were developing trying to save major institutions in our community."

Jimenez grew up in Brooklyn and Queens and lived on the same block as Malcolm X and his family. When Beame started his budget-cutting campaign, Jimenez was on the faculty at CUNY's Hostos Community College, which had a predominately black and Latino student population and, along with Brooklyn's Medgar Evers College, was threatened with closure. To protest the cuts, in 1976 Jimenez helped lead a coalition of African American,

Jamaican, Puerto Rican, and Dominican students, teachers, and staff in a takeover of Hostos Community College's campus. The takeover lasted about twenty days and included demonstrations, classes, and the transformation of the president's office into a day-care center. Students at Medgar Evers took over their campus as well; that ordeal ended with of the arrest of forty black and Latino protesters, including Jimenez. But the movement was a success—city officials saved Hostos and Medgar Evers.[77]

In 1978, Jimenez moved away from protest politics toward electoral politics by running for a New York State Assembly seat in the Bronx with the backing of the black and Latino coalition that had formed during the Hostos protests.[78] He lost in large part because he was unable to get the support of organized labor and other Progressive organizations to defeat an opponent who was backed by the powerful Democratic machine.[79] The Bronx Democratic machine's unwillingness to support Jimenez was consistent with its resistance toward independent Democrats who challenged their political power.

José Rivera, the Bronx-based labor organizer, suffered a similar fate when he first ran for New York City Council in 1981. He lost to Sean Walsh in a district that used to be heavily Irish but was slowly becoming more black and Latino.[80] These are examples of united black and Latino coalitions that almost defeated machine candidates. They stand in contrast to the Democratic primary for borough president in the Bronx and Brooklyn in 1985, when a black and Latino coalition failed to form and support José Serrano and Al Vann.

In 1977, Percy Sutton entered the crowded Democratic primary for mayor. In addition to Sutton, the incumbent mayor, Abe Beame; Congressman Ed Koch; New York's secretary of state, Mario Cuomo; Representative Bella Abzug; and the previously spurned Herman Badillo entered the race. Sutton was furious that Badillo decided to join at the last minute, splitting the black and Latino vote, and in all likelihood propelling Koch to victory. "I had commitments from a number of Puerto Rican leaders before Badillo came into the campaign," remembers Sutton. "That support was wiped out as soon as he entered the race."[81] Badillo won a majority of Latino votes, Sutton won a majority of black votes, and Ed Koch won just enough of each, in addition to his majority white base, to finish first in the primary. After defeating Cuomo in the runoff for the Democratic nomination, Koch won the general election easily. Koch began building affordable housing for the middle class. At the same time, the housing stock for the poor drastically decreased during his first term in office, leading those on the Left to protest his housing policy. Like Beame, Koch also proposed making severe budget cuts that would disproportionately impact the city's poor. These moves quickly led to a rise in tenant activism and budget protests across the city.[82]

Around this time, the civil rights worker Bill Lynch returned to Harlem. He joined a group of other Young Turks who belonged to El Comité and various tenant organizations to fight for improved housing conditions. He met Diane Lacey Winley, a local activist, who encouraged Lynch to enter politics. "I said, 'Why would I want to get into [politics]?'" Lynch recalls. "Then it dawned on all of us: If you want something to happen, [politics] is the place to make it happen."[83] Over time, Lynch gained a reputation as a brilliant Progressive political strategist who was closely aligned with Local 1199 and labor trade unions in the city. He would later played a key role in the campaigns of Representative Major Owens, Jesse Jackson, and David Dinkins.

Lynch was born and raised on Long Island and attended the historically black Virginia Union College in Richmond, Virginia, where he became involved in the civil rights movement and joined student demonstrations to integrate the stores in downtown Richmond. After two years, he dropped out of school to devote himself to the movement. "That's how it started," says Lynch. "I got so caught up in that that I did not go back to school."

His break into politics came in 1975, when Winley decided to run for Democratic district leader in Central Harlem and the Upper West Side. Lynch was her campaign manager, a position of high esteem in the local political circuit, and helped her successfully defeat the incumbent. Lynch came away from the experience with a passion for campaign work. He also became a founding member of the New Amsterdam Democratic Club, along with Winley and state senator Carl McCall. In 1976, Lynch again served as Winley's campaign manager, this time in her effort to win an empty New York State Assembly seat representing Harlem. Winley faced four other candidates in the Democratic primary. With such a crowded field, one key to winning the nomination was to get the support of the Harlem Clubhouse. Winley attended the Harlem Clubhouse candidates' forum and distinguished herself from her peers during the question-and-answer period.[84] Even still, the Harlem Clubhouse endorsed the Democratic Party activist Innis Francis, a former president of the Harlem Council, a group that evolved out of efforts to organize unemployed workers during the Great Depression.[85] Lynch insists that Francis "didn't have a snowball's chance in hell to win" the general election. "It dawned on me a while later," he recalls. "Innis was loyal to the [clubhouse]. She had been district leader herself; they could go to her when they needed petitions; when they needed volunteers, she would provide for them. That's what it was all about." This instance points to the theme that in the old minority political clubhouse system, bosses, like regular Democratic machine bosses, supported incumbents, more experienced candidates, and those who had demonstrated loyalty to them.

Without the clubhouse endorsement, Winley came in second in the primary, but Lynch learned an important lesson: loyalty is more important than talent when comes to gaining an endorsement. Lynch's campaign savvy also caught the attention of some in New York political circles. Lynch insisted that from the beginning of his participation in electoral politics he believed in creating a black and Latino coalition, and he had done that in Winley's campaign gaining support from activist in the Upper West Side.[86]

Lynch made his first mark as a political strategist during the 1982 Democratic primary for the newly created Twelfth Congressional District in Brooklyn. The primary in the neighboring Eleventh District, also newly created in Brooklyn and comprising Williamsburg and parts of Bed-Stuy, provides insight into black and Latino coalition building before the "Latinos for Jackson" groups that formed during the 1984 Democratic presidential primary. In the Eleventh, the federal courts drew a mostly Democratic district that would guarantee the election of a black or Latino candidate to the U.S. House of Representatives. The district incorporated parts of the former Fourteenth Congressional District of Representative Frederick W. Richmond, who had resigned in disgrace after a criminal investigation.[87]

As mentioned earlier, Edolphus Towns, a black migrant from North Carolina and an ordained minister, ran against Puerto Ricans Jack John Olivero and Luis Hernandez in the Eleventh Congressional District. Towns had a solid political base from his twenty-year tenure as district leader in the mostly black and smaller Latino communities in East New York and his six years as deputy borough president in Brooklyn. The two positions gave Towns access to political patronage, including appointing members of community boards and distributing funds for local programs and organizations. As a result, Towns had the support of the Brooklyn assemblyman Al Vann, then chairman of the state legislature's black and Puerto Rican caucus, and other insurgents who opposed candidates that regulars in the Brooklyn Democratic Party supported. Vann and others like him had formed an all-black Coalition for Community Empowerment. The Hispanic elected officials—councilman Luis A. Olmedo and Assemblyman Victor L. Robles—also endorsed Towns. It is unclear why they supported Towns.[88]

One of Towns's opponents, Olivero, had the support of Latino Progressives in the Eleventh Congressional District. Olivero had grown up in the Latino section of Bedford-Stuyvesant, which shared a border with the Latino neighborhood of Williamsburg. Some Puerto Ricans viewed him as a "kind of dashing" community role model after graduating from their streets to Fordham Law School and passing the New York State bar exam. Olivero got a job with AT&T and became one of few Latinos in corporate America.[89] Despite his corporate connections, he had deep roots in the 1960s Puerto Rican Progressive movement. Olivero had been a member of the left-of-center Wednesday Night Club, which met between 1967 and 1972, and was a founding member of the Puerto Rican Legal Defense and Education Fund. In addition, he had public-sector experience serving as the regional director of the Equal Employment Opportunity Commission and deputy director of the commission's Washington office. In 1982, Olivero returned to Williamsburg from Manhattan to run for the open seat in the Eleventh District. However, he faced obstacles to winning the primary. No African American leader would endorse him over Towns, and some Latino voters, including his other opponent in the primary, Luis Hernandez, viewed him as an outsider. [90]

Olivero did get the support of Latino Progressives in Brooklyn, including Luis Garden Acosta's Educational and Community Center from the Fort Greene section. Acosta saw the much older Olivero as a better alternative to Hernandez, whom he described as one of the deans of Latino politics in Brooklyn and a Democratic Party regular in the county dating back to the 1960s. Some Latino voters called Hernandez a reformer because during the 1960s and 1970s, he and other Latinos had struggled to keep Democratic regulars from completely ignoring the demands of Latino residents in Brooklyn. But by 1982, he had become for many an obstacle to the political objectives of Latino Progressives in the county.[91] Like Olivero, Hernandez ran in the 1982 primary without African American support, and the two of them split the Latino vote. Puerto Ricans of all political stripes in Brooklyn believed that the time had come for increased Puerto Rican representation in the U.S. Congress, but they also held no illusions that Al Vann or other African American leaders in Brooklyn would endorse Olivero or Hernandez in the Democratic primary against Towns. Instead, Acosta and others who backed Olivero, including Badillo and Cesar Perales, the executive director of the Puerto Rican Legal Defense Fund, pursued a strategy that called for mobilizing as many Latino and white votes as possible in the Eleventh Congressional District to defeat Towns and Hernandez.[92] They failed to build a coalition with Progressive African Americans willing to oppose Towns and Latino Democratic regulars willing to oppose Hernandez. In addition, Olivero had the challenge of appearing as an outsider. But Towns won in the Eleventh District because Olivero and Hernandez split the Hispanic vote. Towns received some 14,600 votes; Olivero, 7,900 votes; and Hernandez 7,570 votes.[93] Combined, Olivero and Hernandez had enough votes to beat Towns. Hernandez and Olivero failed to attract sufficient number of African American votes. The challenges of ethnic politics, candidates learned, are maintaining communication and trust between ethnic groups and unity within each ethnic group.

In the Twelfth Congressional District, the insurgent Major Owens ran against Vander L. Beatty, an African American state senator supported by the Brooklyn Democratic machine. The Twelfth District included a large section of Shirley Chisholm's former district and sections of Crown Heights, Bed-Stuy, Brownsville, and Flatbush. Approximately 400,000 of its 500,000 residents in the newly formed district were black, most of them from the Caribbean, with whites and Latinos making up the rest of the population. In 1982, Towns and Owens went on to win the Democratic primaries and the general election in the Eleventh and Twelfth Districts. Owens won the Democratic primary, beating the machine-backed opponent because he had the support of a black and Latino Progressive coalition.[94] The newly elected Bronx assemblyman, José Rivera, supported Owens as the Coalition for Community Empowerment candidate. However, it is unclear who, if anyone, he endorsed in the primary race in the Eleventh District that pitted Towns against Olivero and Hernandez.

As blacks and Latinos moved into electoral politics in the 1970 and 1980s, problems between the two groups persisted, and new tensions emerged. Many black leaders assumed that few differences existed between blacks and Latinos in terms of their community needs and goals. The communities shared a need for better jobs, affordable housing, and safer neighborhoods. But they competed for patronage jobs, appointments, and training programs, and disagreed on bilingual education and immigration policy. African American leaders also excluded Latino leaders from such groups as the Coalition for Community Empowerment.[95] Until Jesse Jackson ran for the Democratic nomination for president in 1984, African American candidates (with the exception of Adam Clayton Powell Jr., Charles Rangel, and Denny Farrell) had no apparent need to reach out and mobilize Latino voters in the city, causing another gulf between the two groups.

DENNIS RIVERA AND THE LATINO SHIFT

Dennis Rivera, a Puerto Rican immigrant who would become Bill Lynch's co-campaign manager in several high-profile elections, arrived in New York in 1977 shortly before the 1982 election.[96] In 1969, while studying political science and sociology at the UPR, he became involved in leftist causes and joined the PSP. He actively protested the Vietnam War both in his hometown, Aibonito, and on UPR's campus. He ultimately dropped out of school, just one class short of earning his degree, to pursue a career as a trade union activist.

When Rivera got to New York in 1977, he joined the staff of Local 1199 and started organizing workers at the Albert Einstein College of Medicine in the Bronx. At the same time, Rivera made regular runs to LaGuardia Airport to pick up *Claridad*, the Puerto Rican Socialist Party newspaper, for distribution throughout the metropolitan area.

Rivera's views of working with African Americans in political coalitions were shaped as a labor organizer in New York. At the time, Einstein College of Medicine had 1,500 workers, including researchers, administrative assistants, and those in the service and maintenance departments. Jews and Italians made up the professional positions in the staff, and African Americans and Latinos held the majority of the positions in the service and maintenance departments and accounted for the largest numbers of workers on the staff. Rivera had the task of organizing a union, which included "making sure every member had a shop steward, helping negotiate the contract, recruit[ing] shop stewards," and educating the workers about the contract, says Rivera. In addition to working with African Americans at 1199, he became what he calls one of the many Latino "Jackson groupie[s]" who attended Jesse Jackson events when he came to New York in the early 1980s. These two experiences—union organizing and attending speeches by Jackson—explain why and how Rivera became an important figure in forging black and Latino political coalitions in New York within the labor movement.[97]

In response to Ed Koch's budget-cutting policies in the late 1970s and hostilities toward blacks and Latinos, many Puerto Rican activists began focusing on electoral politics. For instance, in 1981 political strategist David Santiago formed the Southside Political Action Committee (SSPC), which aimed to build the political power of Latino residents in Williamsburg. Located at the corner of Bedford Avenue and South First Street, the SSPC conducted major voter-registration drives, supported candidates in local school-board campaigns, and mobilized to win Latino representation on city commissions and task forces. Santiago and the SSPC worked closely with a number of African American activists in the 1980s, people like Sonny Carson, a CORE leader and Black Nationalist who was an organizing force in the Brooklyn neighborhoods of Bed-Stuy and Bushwick. Carson tried to unite with SSPC and other radical Latino groups in Brooklyn to form coalitions and take even more militant steps toward advancing Latino interests in Brooklyn just as he had been doing for blacks in Brooklyn since the 1960s.[98] Like Al Vann, Luis Garden Acosta, and Santiago, Carson is an example of a few black and Latinos leaders who in the late 1970s and early 1980s had become engaged in electoral politics and black and Latino coalition building in Brooklyn.

Santiago also formed a coalition called United Parents to Save Our Children with Acosta and David Lopez, a tenants' rights activist, with José Candelario serving as the lead coordinator. The organization set out to mobilize local parents in Williamsburg to push for decentralization of the school district. Williamsburg's school board was controlled by the Hasidic Jewish community, which began to settle in the area in the 1950s. As they gained control of the school board in the 1970s, they advanced their own interests to the detriment of black and Latino students.[99] This move worked to galvanize black and Latino activists to work together to elect representatives to the local school board.

While the city's Dominican community remained primarily concerned with politics in the Dominican Republic, in 1976 they organized a New York City Dominican Day Parade Committee. The parade participants came from fifty or sixty community-based groups, each with different political ideologies and agendas. One community activist, Giovanni Puello, says that getting Dominicans elected to the organizing committee became a way of demonstrating Dominican unity and potential political power. Puello, along with Zenaida Mendez, would become an important player in Latinos for Dinkins in 1989.[100] Dominicans remained concerned with affordable housing, jobs, and education. They became more involved in local politics as the political situation in the Dominican Republic grew worse and any chance of returning home became unlikely. Their concerns remained more focused on immigration policy unlike the Puerto Ricans, who were already U.S. citizens. Thus Dominicans had more in common with Ecuadorians, Colombians, and Mexicans, many of whom lived among and around them.

The Afro-Dominican Zenaida Mendez grew up in a family that closely followed the U.S. civil rights and Black Power movements. Her father belonged to the Partido Revolucionario Dominicano, which opposed the Dominican dictator Rafael Trujillo. She recalls her father leading family discussions about Dominican and American politics, focusing on the work of Martin Luther King Jr. and the civil rights activist Angela Davis. In 1969, the family migrated to Corona, Queens, becoming part of the large Dominican diaspora that had started settling there in the late 1940s and early 1950s. When Mendez moved to the Hell's Kitchen neighborhood in Midtown Manhattan in the 1970s, she became deeply involved in the fight for affordable housing and day care. "That's how I got started," Mendez remembers, organizing all the mothers in her apartment complex to lobby for better child-care options.[101] She also volunteered at a tenants' rights organization for college credit. At the end of the semester, the group hired her to organize small-business owners in the neighborhood. She testified in front of the City Council and served on the Hell's Kitchen community board. Mendez's work in community activism led to a job offer from David Dinkins when he became the Manhattan borough president in 1985. Mendez had spent so much time picketing outside City Hall that she had reservations about putting her placard down and walking inside.

But she took the job because she respected Diane Morales, an activist from the Upper West Side whom Dinkins hired. Mendez joined the Manhattan borough president office's Community Assistance Unit in 1985 and held the title of Community Board 4 Liaison. In that role she worked as Dinkins's proxy in the Latino communities of East Harlem and Washington Heights. She worked with Latino leaders and activists; she spent almost four years solving individual and community problems and delivering services that gave Dinkins name recognition and political capital. In addition, she persuaded Dinkins to appear before community boards and demonstrate that he supported her work, which further increased his credibility and political capital among Latinos. By the time Dinkins ran for mayor in 1989, the majority of Latino leaders and activists that Mendez worked with while in the borough president's office "knew who David Dinkins was in the Latino community, in particular in the Dominican community," and they supported him, she says.[102]

THE REAGAN ADMINISTRATION: UNITING AGAINST A COMMON ENEMY

In the early 1980s, two issues came to the fore that united black and Latino activists in a way they had not been since the early days of the student movements in the 1960s. Throughout the 1970s, black and Latino Progressive groups had been working on parallel tracks but rarely had they worked in tandem. With the election of Ronald Reagan as president in 1980, Progressive blacks and Latinos found themselves once again facing a common enemy. The Reagan administration's adoption of supply-side economics and its aggressive, militaristic foreign policy galvanized black and Latino activists in New York City and laid the groundwork for the development of future intra-Latino and black–Latino coalitions. Specifically, Latino Progressives opposed the U.S. Navy's bombing of the Puerto Rican island of Vieques. Meanwhile blacks and Latinos, particularly in the labor movement, opposed the Reagan administration's foreign policies in South Africa and South America.[103]

Vieques is a small island-municipality eight miles off the coast of Puerto Rico. The United States took control of much of the island during World War II. After the end of the war, the U.S. Navy continued to conduct military exercises on Vieques, using portions of the land as testing grounds for bombs, missiles, and other explosives. In 1978, several important Puerto Rican activists on the mainland formed the New York Committee in Support of Vieques (NYCSV), which aimed to force the U.S. government to halt all military activity on the island. Among the founders were Sandy Trujillo and Zoilo Torres. They were joined by the Puerto Rican socialist and community organizer Gilberto Gerena Valentín, one of the cofounders of the Puerto Rican Day Parade in New York and an activist whom Frank Espada called "by far the most radical" leader of the Wednesday Night Club. In the 1960s, Gerena Valentín had led protests in response to the hanging of Puerto Rican youth in NYPD station houses, a problem in Brooklyn in the 1960s. He supported the campus takeover at CCNY and served as a founding member of the National Association for Puerto Rican Civil Rights.[104] (He later defeated the Bronx-based political boss Ramon Velez in the 1977 election for New York City Council, a seat he held for brief period before retiring in Puerto Rico.)[105] Dennis Rivera, who became the head of Local 1199 in 1988, also joined the movement to protect Vieques. As Rivera's stature and influence grew within the union, he continued to advocate for Vieques and popularized the cause among 1199's black and Latino rank-and-file members.[106]

The NYCSV first met at El Canario, a now-defunct social club on 116th Street near Lexington Avenue in the heart of the Puerto Rican enclave of East Harlem. For three years, the NYCSV held meetings once a week in this small, second-story walk-up. Trujillo was put in charge of coordinating the activists because she had developed "a good reputation as . . . a coalition builder."[107] Trujillo managed to bring in members of El Comité, PSP, and the YLO. Every week, delegates from the NYCSV's member organizations would meet in a circle of fifty to eighty people to organize and plan demonstrations. As part of its outreach activities, NYCSV's leaders would attend cultural and church events in Latino communities across the city. "For those three years, we did a lot of outreach and awareness around Vieques," says Trujillo. "We also forged a lot of good relations with people." This was the first time Trujillo could recall when members of all the major Puerto Rican groups on the Left worked together in a constructive way. It is no

coincidence, perhaps, that the NYCSV's attempts at broad coalition building found success just as three of the largest Puerto Rican groups in the city
had begun to implode. El Comité, PSP, and the YLO were all going through
significant breakups and reconfigurations, which meant that those activists
were looking for a new political home.

The momentum around NYCSV gave rise to the National Congress for
Puerto Rican Rights (NCPRR) in 1981.[108] This organization was a network
of Progressive Puerto Rican activists from the Northeast and Chicago who
unified around an agenda to tackle the biggest issues facing Puerto Ricans:
housing discrimination, gang violence, unequal education, insufficient
health care, and injustice in the courts. Torres and Valentín became founding members, and Torres served as one of the group's earliest presidents.[109]
Zenaida Mendez joined the NCPRR while serving as the housing conversation coordinator for a tenants' rights organization in Hell's Kitchen.[110]

Torres and other leaders in the NCPRR believed that Puerto Ricans in
the United States had to start building their own political institutions, run
voter-education and -registration campaigns, place candidates on ballots, and
mobilize the Latino vote on election day. Torres argued that organizing Latino
communities around a set of substantive issues would form the basis of Latino
political empowerment on the mainland. José Candelario, Torres's longtime
friend and fellow PSP activist, says the advent of the NCPRR and its political
empowerment strategy was "a clearly defining movement in our struggle" for
justice, freedom, and dignity, and redefined Latino politics in New York.[111]

Members of the NYCSV and the NCPRR created the infrastructure that
would later transform New York's Democratic Party. The core coalition
formed around Vieques was the same one that eventually propelled David
Dinkins, José Serrano, and other politicians into advocating for changes
that party bosses had traditionally opposed: more investment in public
housing, schools, hospitals, and after-school programs, as well as redistricting to increase the number of minority-held seats in city government.[112]
Trujillo says that the experience of working together on democratic rights
and Vieques prepared disparate members of the Puerto Rican community
to work together on Latinos for Dinkins in 1989. "After doing [NYCSC and
NCPRR], we moved out of being just the radical fringe." As activists, Trujillo says, they realized that "we have to register voters and become active in
the political arena."[113]

Before 1984, African Americans and Latino Progressives remained largely engaged in their own struggles. The Vieques movement not only helped unite groups of Puerto Rican Progressives but also reached out to a few Progressive Chicanos, Cubans, and Dominicans. Bill Lynch and Dennis Rivera, along with Torres and other members of the NYCSV and NCPRR, saw the importance of unification among blacks and Latinos. As a result, blacks and Latinos were able to form coalitions that would underwrite the Jackson for President campaign in 1984 and 1988 as well as the Dinkins mayoral campaign in 1989. In the 1990s, Dennis Rivera, Jesse Jackson, Al Sharpton, Charles Schumer, and other leaders formed a second wave of activism around Vieques under the umbrella organization Todo Nueva York con Vieques (All New York with Vieques), a coalition that called for the complete withdrawal of the U.S. military from Vieques.[114]

While the first campaigns around Vieques were taking place, a powerful coalition of black and Latino members of the New York City municipal employees' union, DC 37, also launched a vigorous and public campaign against the Reagan administration's domestic and foreign policies. In the early 1980s, DC 37 included fifty-six local unions and 120,000 workers.[115] Of its members, 60 percent were black or Latino, including large numbers of Puerto Ricans, Dominicans, and blacks from the English-speaking Caribbean and the southern United States, reported Stanley Hill, the former executive director of DC 37.[116]

The union opposed Reagan's plan to cut spending to programs for the urban poor in order to increase spending on weapons systems and military interventions abroad. "It is safe to say that the advent of the Reagan presidency served to infuse many black [and Latino] communities with a sense of political embattlement," writes political scientist Charles Hamilton in his essay "Needed, More Foxes: The Black Experience." Specifically, DC 37 objected to the Reagan administration's tacit support for the apartheid regime in South Africa and explicit support for authoritarian dictatorships in Central America.[117]

But how did DC 37's African American workers become interested in the struggles of Central Americans? And how did Latino workers become interested in the struggles of black South Africans? Hill said that the union's African American leaders had become engaged in Central American liberation because DC 37 had "a very good political and progressive group of people who brought the issue before the governing assembly."[118] The African American members of the union's governing board led organizations that were increasingly filled with black and Latino members. Progressive Latino members who knew about the issues in Central America educated their African American colleagues and union presidents. Black leaders recognized they needed to be responsive to the interests of this growing constituency if they wanted to stay in office.[119]

DC 37's political action committee (PAC) was also involved in putting international causes at the center of DC 37's agenda.[120] Santos Crespo, a second-generation Puerto Rican, was one of the PAC's co-chairs. He grew up in East Harlem and the Bronx, and after a stint in the U.S. Navy, he joined DC 37 and rose up the ranks, becoming its executive vice president in 1999. Crespo says that as early as the 1980s, black and Latino leaders in DC 37 were taking purposeful steps to show their respective constituencies how much they actually had in common. He remembers that the Latino leadership "tried very hard to constantly make the connection" when organizing Latin Heritage celebrations. Organizers of Black History Month events in February included Latinos in their programs and invited Latinos to serve on the planning committee. By 1983, Progressive blacks and Latinos were working together to plan complementary black history and Latino heritage month events in October. By making these connections between African and Latino roots, cultural event organizers made it that much easier to raise the political consciousness of members regarding the plight of people in South Africa and Central America.[121]

The leadership of DC 37 started using the union's newspaper, the *Public Employee Press*, to draw attention to the struggles for justice and freedom in Central America and South Africa. The newspaper was one of the most effective ways for union leaders to reach rank-and-file members. The union published the newspaper on a monthly basis and distributed a copy to every member. According to an internal survey the union conducted in the 1980s, 80 percent of members either "always" or "almost always" read the newspaper.[122]

As early as March 1980, articles appeared regularly in the *Public Employee Press* about South Africa and Central America. In 1985, Hill, then associate director of DC 37, wrote in the newspaper, "Fighting for the rights of workers is inseparable from the fight for all human rights. . . . Civil rights and human rights are trade union values, and this is as true around the world as it is here at home. That's why it should come as no surprise that we at DC 37 are in the forefront of the battle for human rights in South Africa, the only country in the world where racism is a professional national policy."[123]

The articles compared the historic struggles in South Africa with those in Central America. In both regions, a largely white, upper-class oligarchy held the balance of power over a dark, working-class majority. In both regions, right-wing governments granted civil and political rights to a few privileged citizens and disenfranchised the rest. In South Africa, the government violently suppressed black workers' efforts to organize or collectively bargain. In El Salvador, right-wing guerrillas conducted wide-scale assassinations of government critics with impunity.[124]

District Council 37 also used the newspaper as a venue to expose America's complicity with these oppressive governments. In March 1980, DC 37's Allan Howard criticized the U.S. government in the union's paper for not taking steps to halt U.S. corporate investment in South Africa, including the sale of military hardware to the country. "In taking this stance, the U.S. government is aligning itself with the apartheid regime against brave African brothers and sisters who every day risk their lives for rights that Americans take for granted."[125]

It was during this period that DC 37 and other U.S.-based labor unions began to do more than simply report on the conditions in Central America and South Africa. Describing the struggle of poor people in both regions as an extension of America's civil rights and labor movements, DC 37 began to organize meetings and build grassroots activity. In 1981, the union's parent organization, the American Federation of State, County, and Municipal Employees (AFSCME), passed a resolution urging the U.S. government to work with other countries to seek a political settlement to the conflict in El Salvador instead of providing military support for the government.[126] Specialists in the South African and Central American labor movements met with DC 37's committee leaders in small meetings, raised political awareness, and built consensus among the body politic that action must be taken. These leaders then disseminated information at local events organized by shop stewards.[127] The strategy worked. Support for anti-apartheid and anti-dictatorship resolutions increased as did participation in delegations and public demonstrations.

In 1983 black and Latino members of Local 371, a union of social service employees, started a campaign to stop the city from purchasing products made in South Africa. Several black kitchen workers at the Park Avenue Armory homeless shelter learned that the canned pineapple the city bought came from South Africa. The kitchen staff refused to serve it and went to their local shop stewards. "It's cheap [for the city] because black workers under apartheid get paid next to nothing," said one of the shop stewards, Peter Freeman, in the *Public Employee Press*. "We don't think the city should save money on the backs of South African workers."[128] Journalists from Local 371's paper, the *Unionist*, did some additional investigative reporting and found canned fruit was not the only product the city purchased from South Africa.

Local 371 then helped craft a proposal to the New York City Council to prohibit all city agencies from purchasing agricultural or industrial products from South Africa and to investigate all city contracts with businesses that invested in or had operations in South Africa. The plan was approved unanimously by DC 37's executive board in October 1984. Union officials formed an alliance with several key council members who also introduced a bill that called for a ban on any deposit or investment of public funds, including public-employee pension money, in financial institutions or corporations who did business with South Africa.[129] At the time, New York City's employees' retirement fund had an $8 billion portfolio. In addition, the city purchased several billion dollars' worth of goods and services each year and held roughly $4 billion in bank deposits.[130]

The mayor's office and other political leaders stalled, so the union launched public demonstrations to broaden awareness of the anti-apartheid legislation and the city's economic support of the racist white minority rule in South Africa.[131] The size and scope of the protests were reminiscent of the civil rights and antiwar protests of the 1960s, and brought together both black and Latino activists who would later march and protest in New York City and Washington. This coalition was made possible by the union movement, where blacks, Latinos, and a small number of whites came together around a common issue, explained Stanley Hill. At locals such as 420, the hospital local, brown and black minority-majority members influenced its African American president, Jim Butler, to become involved in issues in the Caribbean and Central America. "Jim would go down to the Caribbean and played a major role in Central America too," Hill remembered.[132] President Charles Hughes of Local 372, the union that represents Board of Education support staff, "had about twenty-six thousand members" and a high percentage of them were African Americans, blacks from the Caribbean, and Latinos, stated Hill. "I don't know the exact [number] but it was a nice percentage," and the Hispanics in that union knew the issues in Central America and influenced Hughes to travel to the region, he recalled. "We all went down there." Hughes could best be described as perhaps one of the most radical leaders in DC 37. Activists outside the labor movement influenced his decision to become engaged in left-of-center politics in Nicaragua and other parts of the Central America. Hill recalled, "Charlie would not only deal with Central America . . . but also Russia. He almost gave me a heart attack!" Black and Latino trade unionists in DC 37 worked together on the divestiture fight and on weakening oppressive regimes in Central America. Union leaders such as the black Jamaican Cleve Robinson of Local 65 used his political capital to mobilize black trade unionists behind the freedom struggles in Central America and South Africa. Hill described Robinson as "a major force" who helped mobilize black union members and leaders to get involved in the demonstrations. Bill Lucy, who served as treasurer of AFSCME and president of the Coalition of Black Trade Unionists at the time, similarly provided money and resources and mobilized black workers to support the protest. In the final analysis, "the two issues converged," said Hill. Mobilized black and Latino members of DC 37 got involved.[133]

Finally, on February 26, 1985, the New York City Council unanimously passed the union-backed, anti-apartheid legislation. Both Manufacturers Hanover Trust Company and Citibank agreed to abide by the bill immediately, and other banks quickly followed suit.[134] In the *Public Employee Press*, Hill called the bill "a model piece of anti-apartheid legislation and an example for other cities to follow." New York's was the largest pension fund in the country to divest from South African companies.[135]

This turned into a battle that laid the groundwork for disparate groups to come together toward another common goal: political power.

5

THE CHICAGO PLAN

COALITION POLITICS, 1982–1984

PRIOR TO 1984, black and Latino activists in New York City had made some advances in forming coalitions in the labor movement, student organizations, tenant organizations, and the movement for community control and empowerment. There were also notable black and Latino coalitions protesting U.S. foreign policy in Central America and South Africa. But coalition building around electoral politics continued to present significant challenges. Black politicians could be ethnocentric and paternalistic toward Latino leaders and voters; black politicos assumed they knew what Latinos wanted and did not invite them to join coalitions. Meanwhile, Latino political operatives tended to view black leaders and voters with fear and suspicion. Rather than focus on their common struggles, politicians competed for a small handful of traditionally minority-controlled elected offices at the local, state, and federal levels and the associated political patronage.

In the early 1980s, however, a handful of black and Latino activists inside and outside of New York began building coalitions, organizing voter-registration drives, and recruiting candidates for electoral campaigns. The coalition that helped elect Harold Washington as the first African American mayor of Chicago in 1983 was a pivotal event that had a profound impact on electoral politics in New York City.

The true power of Washington's story isn't just his ascendance to power but how it happened. "It was never going to be possible for Harold [Washington] to be elected just with black votes," says Richard W. (Dick) Simpson, a University of Chicago professor of political science and a former

Chicago alderman. Washington needed coalition partners to get elected and he found them among Latinos and poor whites. Without the support of the Latino community, Washington could not have been elected mayor of Chicago. Jesse Jackson participated in the coalition that worked to get Washington elected and later employed the same coalition strategy when he ran for the Democratic nomination for president in 1984 and 1988. Without Washington's election in Chicago, Jackson would not have had the support of grassroots Progressive Latinos that helped him created the Rainbow Coalition and made him a formidable candidate for the Democratic presidential nomination in 1984 and 1988. And because David Dinkins benefitted greatly from the infrastructure created by Jackson's campaigns and his 1988 primary victory in New York City, his election as Manhattan borough president in 1985 and mayor of New York in 1989 can also be credited to Washington's ascendance.[1]

Washington was able to put together a coalition of black, Latino, and poor white voters with the help of African American leaders and organizations such as Jackson's Rainbow Coalition and Operation PUSH (People United to Serve Humanity). Washington's charisma and political skills also played a major role, but Progressive coalitions that developed with Chicago's changing demographics between 1950 and 1980 were also critical.

Between 1950 and 1980, Chicago's African American population grew from 13 percent of the total population of the city to just under 40 percent while the Latino population grew to more than 14 percent. This meant that together, blacks and Latinos represented more than half of the city's population (54 percent). The shift was even more pronounced in the Chicago Public Schools (CPS). In 1950, CPS enrollment stood at 62 percent white and 36 percent black. By 1983, more than 60 percent of all CPS students were black, with Latino enrollment at greater than 20 percent and white enrollment comprising less than 17 percent. Chicago was now no longer a city of European immigrants. But while the city was becoming majority-minority in its ethnic population, the voter rolls took longer to catch up. The work of Latino and African American independent political organizations (IPOs) to register voters was crucial to creating the foundation of support for Washington's candidacy. In 1983, the work of IPOs swelled the number of registered Democrats to 1,625,000, with 857,000 white Americans, 673,000 African Americans, and 95,000 Latinos. By winning the majority of the African American and Latino vote as well as a share of the white vote, Washington ascended to the top job in Chicago city government. Washington also built on the efforts of coalitions of poor whites, blacks, and Latinos from the 1970s who were united in opposition to the controversial way the longtime mayor Richard J. Daley made city government appointments, hired and promoted civil servants, ran departments, and delivered services to neighborhoods. A sustained opposition movement was forged around issues such as repairing potholes, clearing snow, maintaining neighborhood parks, removing trash, granting equal access to government jobs and contracts, ending police brutality, and extending control over public education, housing, and neighborhood policing.

Although he never held elected office, the community organizer Rudy Lozano was a pivotal force in black–Latino coalition building, and he literally paved the way for Washington's election as mayor. Between 1972 and his possibly politically motivated murder in 1983, Lozano became one of the most important political forces and advocate of black and Latino coalitions in Chicago. He arrived at the position slowly and methodically, first as a student organizer. Growing up in the working-class, Mexican American community in the Pilsen historic district of Chicago, Lozano's activism began when he organized a student walkout to demand that the city public schools increase the number of Latino teachers and include Latino history in the curriculum.

His career as an activist continued at University of Illinois at Chicago (UIC), where he helped organize the school's Latin American Recruitment and Educational Services Program (LARES). Lozano dropped out of UIC to become the director of the Center for Autonomous Action (CASA) where he worked closely with the Mexican American Legal Defense and Education Fund (MALDEF) as part of his efforts to aid and organize undocumented workers, particularly tortilla factory workers. While still in his twenties, Lozano became an organizer for the International Ladies' Garment Workers Union (ILGWU), advancing to the position of chief Midwest field organizer. Lozano began to move beyond labor and community organizing to electoral politics in 1972, the same year that witnessed the first political coalition between blacks and Latinos in Chicago.[2] There was a great deal of political momentum among minority groups during this period as African American IPOs had helped elect members to the U.S. Congress and become important leaders in Chicago's Progressive movement. Meanwhile, Lozano and other CASA activists had begun to form alliances with African American activists and other Latino groups.

In 1972, CASA tried to get attorney Juan Soliz elected to the state legislature. When the Democratic machine maneuvered to keep Soliz's name off the primary ballot, activists organized a third-party candidacy, which laid the groundwork for the precinct organization that supported Washington's opposition movement to unseat Mayor Jane Byrne in 1983.[3]

After the death of Mayor Daley in 1976, the state's consumer affairs chief, Jane Byrne, ran against interim mayor Michael Anthony Bilandic on the promise of reforming Chicago politics. Byrne's electoral victory occurred, in part, because groups like the Alliance of African American and Latino Independence voted for her. Once elected, though, Byrne failed to reform city government and appointed Democratic regulars to important boards. She infuriated the IPOs that served as a critical volunteer base in her defeat of the machine's candidate Bilandic. Byrne also advanced Ronald Reagan–style policies in Chicago, which neglected and alienated her base and, in the process, united coalitions of poor whites, blacks, and Latinos against her administration.[4]

A series of political missteps and slights led to worsening relations with Chicago's minority communities. An incident in 1982 illustrates the tension between the Byrne administration and the city's Latino and black activists. The controversy began after Byrne locked out several activists from a meeting on the Chicago Housing Authority. Marion Stamps, head of the Chicago Housing Tenant Organization, and other activists complained that Byrne appointed a new director of the housing authority without community input. They viewed this as another example of how the mayor ignored and disrespected poor, black, brown, and white public-housing residents across the city. During the July 24, 1982, broadcast of Derek Hill's popular weekly radio show *Sunday Morning Live* on WBMX (102.7 FM), a woman called in and asked, "If Mayor Jane Byrne can lock us out of City Hall, why can't we boycott her upcoming ChicagoFest?"[5] The event was described by her critics as a bread-and-circuses reelection strategy that entertained citizens but provided no long-term jobs for the unemployed. The caller's suggested boycott appealed to activists because the event had wide media coverage, corporate sponsors, and notable artists coming to the city from around the country.

Jesse Jackson, who appeared on the radio talk show the same day, heard the question and shortly thereafter began consulting with other activists around the city. "By that Wednesday, about fifty-odd groups came together" and agreed to support the boycott, recalled Renault Robinson of Chicago's Afro-American Patrolmen's League.[6] The boycott committee not only received the support of Stevie Wonder and other noted artists scheduled to perform at the event but also drew daily coverage in the *Chicago Tribune* and local newspapers, creating opportunities to educate and inform the general public about its opposition to Mayor Byrne. Publicizing the boycott committee's voter-registration drive was, however, the greatest benefit from all the media coverage. "We used the white media that traditionally worked against us to help us," says activist Robinson.[7] Volunteers' efforts to increase the number of blacks and Latinos on the voter registration proved crucial to defeating Byrne in 1983. "At the time, we didn't know who the candidate was going to be," recalls activist Joseph Gardner. "But we knew we had a movement and that in order for that movement to have credibility and strength and power that we had to register people to vote."[8]

Stamps joined four other groups of grassroots leaders, including the radical community activist Slim Coleman, to form People Organized for Welfare and Employment Rights (POWER). The coalition included approximately twenty-three community-based organizations. Before the start of the ChicagoFest boycott, POWER had participated in some 350 protests a year against Byrne at City Hall, often right in front of her office.[9] In addition, POWER started a voter-registration drive to unseat Byrne, Illinois Republican governor James R. Thompson, and President Ronald Reagan. South Side activist Bob Lucas says POWER "did the first leg" of voter registration in Chicago from August to October 1981 "when we registered something like forty thousand people." By 1982, POWER had a fifteen-year history of groups of black, Puerto Rican, Mexican, and lower-income whites united in several struggles: a fight to stop the governor's attempt to push welfare cuts through the Illinois General Assembly, and a fight against Mayor Byrne and city government's plan to make large profits gentrifying neglected and impoverished neighborhoods.[10]

Stamps also became a leader of the voter-registration drive, which she viewed as part of the "struggle around the question of self-determination" and community control for local residents.[11] She helped organize a massive grassroots voter-registration drive involving some sixty community groups working in thirty-three independent wards. They established sign-up locations in traditional spaces and, in the early 1980s, nonconventional spaces such as public aid and unemployment offices.[12] In addition to the coalition partners, organized labor participated, too. The AFL-CIO donated $4,500 to the voter-registration drive.

At the end of August 1982, the movement had netted so many new voters in working-class white, black, and Latino areas that the chairman of the Chicago Board of Elections, Michael Lavelle, said it looked like "the biggest voter registration drive" he had seen in his tenure.[13] It is estimated that between the voter-registration drive months before the ChicagoFest boycott and thereafter, the opposition movement registered about 97,000 new voters.[14]

Movement leaders organized the All-Chicago Community Summer Congress, held at the international amphitheater at the end of August, in order to develop and approve a platform that any candidate for mayor who wanted their support had to endorse. Two hundred representatives attended and developed a platform that supported putting up candidates to run for the Chicago school board, closing elite middle-class magnet schools, a speculation tax on real-estate owners who resell buildings less than five years after purchase, strict enforcement of building code violations to protect tenants, and a citizen review board to investigate reports of police brutality. Movement members then started the vetting process that led to the selection of Harold Washington as their candidate for mayor. They were joined by different coalitions across the city, which also eventually decided on Washington as its candidate.[15]

This mass support and consensus between diverse groups occurred thanks to voter education and empowerment. Following the All-Chicago Community Summer Congress, Lou and Georgia Palmer along with other black nationalists conducted a survey to come up with short list of black candidates to run against Mayor Byrne. In 1981, Georgia Palmer organized a series of Saturday political education classes in southwest Chicago for grassroots people who knew nothing about politics. She continued to teach these classes up until the mayoral election of 1983. "We put out thirty-five thousand survey sheets and seventeen thousand were returned," recalls Georgia. "Out of that, we got ninety-two names." From those, they identified six possible candidates to take on Mayor Byrne. Washington came out as the top choice.

Next, Lou Palmer organized a plebiscite held at Bethel African Methodist Episcopal Church on the South Side of Chicago. Again, Washington emerged as the favorite of black leaders. They strategized how to get Washington to run for mayor, but no evidence exists that Latino IPO representatives like Art Vázquez and Lozano participated in the plebiscite that selected Washington.[16]

WHY WASHINGTON?

Harold Washington was born in 1922 and grew up in modestly comfortable surroundings on the South Side of Chicago. He dropped out of high school during the Great Depression to join the Civilian Conservation Corps, a New Deal public-works program established to create jobs. After several months, Washington returned to Chicago and worked at odd jobs, including a brief stint in Chicago's stockyards. During World War II, Washington was drafted into the Army Air Corps and assigned to an engineering battalion in the Pacific theater. He rose in the ranks and completed his high school diploma during the war. He returned to Chicago after his discharge in 1946 and majored in political science at Roosevelt University. At that time, African Americans made up only 5 percent of the student population, yet Washington became student government president in his senior year. After graduating from Roosevelt in 1949, he received his law degree from Northwestern University Law School in 1952.[17]

Washington's interest in politics started early. As young as age seven, he worked with his father, a Democratic precinct captain steeped in electoral politics. "I know something about big-time politics," Washington told a *Tribune* reporter. "I was a precinct captain in the Regular Democratic Organization of Cook County when I was fifteen years old."[18] Those who knew Washington described him as a gifted politician, political junky, and policy wonk. He began his political career just two years after finishing law school, worked as a lawyer in Chicago's Corporation Counsel, and became a precinct captain in the Third Ward for the African American congressman and political boss Ralph Metcalfe. In 1959, Metcalfe made Washington his alderman secretary and supervisor of Third Ward precinct captains; he also worked ten of the precincts and taught political science and government operation classes to both young and old in the Third. He understood Chicago politics and knew the ins and outs of the Daley machine, which controlled the accounting and casting of ballots, ruled and validated all nominating petitions, certified the results of elections, decided one's legal voting status, and ruled on all suspected cases of election fraud and/or irregularities.[19]

In 1964, with the support of the Daley machine, Washington won election to the Illinois House of Representatives. As a legislator, he straddled a difficult line between acting as a loyal Democratic regular and a political independent on the majority of issues that came before him. Ultimately, he was able to work within the system while also supporting Progressive, anti-machine legislation on immigrant rights, bilingual education, organized labor, the peace movement, self-determination, and community control movements in Chicago.[20]

Pierre Clavel argues that the orchestrated assassination of Black Panthers Fred Hampton and Mark Clark in 1969 by COINTELPRO with the assistance of the Daley-controlled police department put Washington and other black elected officials in conflict with the Democratic Party machine.[21] That year, Washington collaborated with Renault Robinson of the Afro-American Patrolmen's League, which had filed a federal discrimination suit against the mayor. On behalf of the league, Washington sponsored a bill in the state legislature to institute an independent police civilian review board. That action enraged Daley, who moved quickly to end Washington's political career. A senior Progressive Democrat in the state House intervened and kept Washington's political career alive.[22]

Around the same time, several black and Latino organizations came together, along with some whites, over the issue of police brutality. Former alderman Dick Simpson recalls that blacks and Latinos built coalitions "over different time periods, around either elections or around issues" like police brutality or both groups' struggle for jobs with the Chicago Transportation Authority.[23] Washington remained a quasi-independent Democratic insider until 1974, when he finally broke with Daley and unsuccessfully ran against him in the Democratic mayoral primary. After Daley died in 1976, just two years into his sixth term as mayor of Chicago, machine operatives selected Daley protégé Michael Bilandic, a corporate attorney, to serve as interim mayor for six months until a special election could be held for a mayor to serve out Daley's term. Byrne ran as an Independent Democrat and defeated Bilandic in the Democratic primary. She pledged to reform city government and garnered the vote and volunteer power of the IPOs that later swelled the ranks of the ChicagoFest boycott coalition. The coalition provided the margin of difference in a primary in which Byrne and Bilandic split the vote of the white Democratic regulars. After the election, Byrne made peace with Democratic regulars by appointing them to the school board and housing authority, infuriating the IPOs. Byrne also adopted many of Reagan's economic policies, igniting an opposition movement, a very successful voter-registration drive, and the recruitment of candidates like U.S. Representative Harold Washington and Rudy Lozano to run against Democratic regulars in citywide and ward elections in 1983.[24]

Georgia Palmer's African American plebiscite selected Washington, and Latino leaders agreed with the selection. The reasons range from the personal to the political. "Harold had been in the machine but he had become an Independent Democrat . . . who knew forces on both sides" and "had a sense of the machine's 'internal mechanism,'" says Jackson. In addition, Progressives viewed Washington as wise and tough enough to reform city politics. In Jackson's words, Washington "didn't have the money but he had the skill and the will to work" against the entrenched Democratic machine in Chicago and was able to open the government to those who had been systematically shut out for years. Washington's independence gave him credibility to build coalitions between a number of constituencies, including organized labor, liberals, and Progressives, and among black and Latino activists.[25] Several people noted that Washington's charisma and Malcolm X–like speaking style, which mixed substance and candor with humor, mobilized cross-sections of the African American community.[26] Washington "had the ability to analyze a situation and break it down so all could understand no matter where" they lived in the city says Washington's special counsel Timothy W. Wright, and do it "with a sense of humor," says activist Alice Palmer, who served on Mayor Washington's civilian review board.[27] Washington's political experience and name recognition as a sitting U.S. congressman also made him an ideal candidate.[28]

Washington's on-the-job performance won him support of the Latino vote. The Pilsen neighborhood activist Jesús "Chuy" Garcia viewed Washington as "perhaps the most eloquent anti-Reagan critic in the U.S. Congress." Washington had been an advocate for immigrant and labor rights and a supporter of bilingual education. Garcia admired Washington's "understanding of the nature of working-class people and their reality."[29]

Despite support from coalition leaders, Washington remained dogmatically opposed to running for mayor. He preferred his position in the U.S. Congress and so set stringent requirements for his candidacy: registering 50,000 new voters, raising a $200,000 campaign war chest, garnering united support from African Americans, and getting support from a broad coalition, including groups such as POWER and organized labor. The coalition exceeded Washington's request. They registered nearly 400,000 voters and raised almost $500,000. "Harold could not say no," says Jackson, and thus the coalition and the movement it built provided the infrastructure and the political leverage to force Washington to run.[30]

In fall of 1983, registering to vote had become as popular as sit-ins had been in the 1960s. The *Tribune's* Vernon Jarred insisted that the city's blacks, Hispanics, and poor whites had "voter fever." Activists had "registered more than forty thousand new voters in September [of 1983] at the city's welfare and unemployment offices."[31]

After agreeing to run for mayor, Washington then went to work developing a winning campaign strategy and raising campaign funds. A three-part reform program became his standard stump speech. First, he called for transparency and integrity in government, which appealed to whites who had struggled with city government policies since the 1970s. Second, he called for city government to provide equal access to job opportunities and city contracts. Third, linking to the community control movement of the 1970s, Washington insisted that neighborhood organizations, and not City Hall, should make local public-policy decisions about housing, education, and city services.[32] He took his stump speech to Los Angeles, where the African American mayor Tom Bradley and the Speaker of the California State Assembly, Willie Brown, organized a successful fund-raiser for him. An unknown group organized similar events in New York City. The out-of-town fund-raising trips helped Washington circumvent the Chicago

Democratic machine, which had had a long history of hand-picking candidates, financing their campaigns, and punishing those who opposed them.[33]

Next, Washington began making contact with Progressive Latino leaders and discussing his vision and campaign strategy. As an African American congressman from a black congressional district, he had only limited contact with Latinos. But dating back to the 1970s, Latino leaders had been participating in coalitions with Progressive African Americans. By the time Washington had decided to run, black and Latino Progressives had participated in POWER or witnessed the gains it made working collectively. Dick Simpson, a Progressive white political scientist and church leader, introduced Washington to the Puerto Rican preacher Jorge Morales and the Mexican American attorney Juan Soliz. In 1976, Morales had started the San Lucas United Church of Christ in West Town/Humboldt Park with the expressed purpose of engaging in community action and mobilization for low-income community residents. He became an important player in a number of IPO coalitions, including the Black-Latino Alliance for Progressive Politics (BLAPP), which, in 1982, brought together Puerto Ricans from West Town/Humboldt Park and Mexican Americans from the Pilsen area.[34] Garcia, one of Lozano's fellow Mexican American activists, described the difference between BLAPP's principal Latino communities in cultural terms: "You can tell where you are from the sounds and the smell of the cooking. In Mexican areas, people are doing the taco thing with beans and rice; in Puerto Rican areas, it's roast pork and fried rice. If you walk around Pilsen (a Mexican enclave) you'll hear mariachi music; in (Puerto Rican) Humboldt Park, you'll hear salsa and conga drums."[35] BLAPP also included African Americans, the majority of whom resided on the West Side of Chicago and were led principally by activists such as Danny Davis and Richard Barnett.[36]

Soliz worked for the Legal Assistance Foundation of Chicago specializing in immigrant naturalization issues. In 1982, a coalition of organizations such as the Pilsen Neighbors, Mujeres Latinas in Acción, Por un Barrio Mejor, and El Centro de la Causa recruited the thirty-two-year-old Soliz to run for a seat in the state House as its anti-machine candidate against the Italian American incumbent Marco Domico. Domico had worked for twenty years as a low-level Chicago Department of Public Works employee and was backed by Vito Marzullo, the powerful committeeman of the Twenty-fifth

Ward. If elected, Soliz would have become the first Latino representative in the state House and an Independent one as well. Soliz's Progressive stance on immigrant rights stood in stark contrast to Latino machine hacks who rubber-stamped the work of machine aldermen and legislators.

To cripple this fledgling Latino political movement, the Democratic machine successfully challenged the credentials of Independent candidates and, with the support of circuit court appeal judges, removed Soliz and others from the ballots. Nonetheless, the candidates and their supporters were undeterred. Getting back on the ballot as an Independent required 3,000 signatures on a petition and raising campaign funds in an environment in which business owners feared losing city contracts if they fell out of step with the party machine. Activists organized a third-party candidacy under the umbrella of the IPO of the Near West Side with Soliz as president, Lozano its vice president, and members of BLAPP as one of its most important sources for political activists and campaign volunteers.[37]

In 1983, Rudy Lozano ran for alderman in the Twenty-second Ward with Ronelle Mustin, an African American, as his campaign chairman. In a tight three-way primary, Lozano lost to Frank Stemberk and was just seventeen votes shy of what was needed for a runoff. In the Twenty-fifth Ward—which included Little Italy, Pilsen, and the University of Illinois complex—the former Brown Beret and labor organizer Juan Velazquez received 42 percent of the vote as an IPO candidate in the primary against Marzullo.

Neither Lozano nor Velazquez won their seats, but their 1983 primary campaigns created a crucial political base of support for Washington. During the general election, support for Washington among African Americans and whites remained the same. The critical change came from Latinos whose support increased from 13 percent to 75 percent and provided Washington with 50,000 new votes and the margin of victory in the general election. Latino support for Washington became important when his primary victory triggered a racist and bigoted Democratic Party political realignment. Many white Democrats, even the chairman of the local Democratic Party, actively campaigned for Bernard Epton, an obscure liberal Jewish candidate from Hyde Park who won the Republican nomination. After Washington's unexpected win in the Democratic primary, Epton, despite being the Republican nominee, became the de facto "great white hope" of the Democratic machine. The campaign slogan, "Bernard Epton before it's too late," had the not-too-subtle message that a vote for Epton was a vote to keep whites in power. The fear of a black mayor unleashed a high level of racist iconography in campaign posters and other printed materials. One ad claimed that if voters elected Washington mayor, he would make fried chicken and watermelon the official city foods. In response, Washington said, "I'm . . . very pro-black, but that doesn't mean I'm anti anything else. I'm pro-black but I'm also pro-Latino, I'm pro-Polish, but I'm pro-black as well so don't expect anything else from me."[38] His response surprised many because African American candidates had traditionally suppressed Black Power and Black Pride rhetoric to ensure not offending the white-controlled Democratic machine. And indeed, Latinos responded favorably to Washington's handling of racist attacks. Latino neighborhood organizations played a vital role in mobilizing voters for Latino candidates for City Council and for Washington in the general election. The same organizations would also go on to play an important role in supporting Washington after he became mayor.[39]

BLAPP and the other coalitions that supported Washington's three reform issues brought together black and Latino leaders as well as white liberals from the Lake Front section of Chicago. In the general election, 75 percent of all Latino votes went to Washington. Most of his Latino support came from Puerto Rican voters who, compared with Mexicans, shared more cultural similarities with Washington. Mexicans also voted for Washington, but his support was strongest from newer immigrants in Pilsen and Little Village who were attracted to his call for greater equity in the distribution of city services and jobs. Washington defeated his Republican opponent, Epton, in what was a historically close race for an overwhelmingly Democratic city: 656,727 votes for Washington to Epton's 617,159. In his victory speech, Washington said, "The whole nation is watching, and Chicago has sent a powerful message. Out of the crucible of the city's most trying election, blacks and whites, Hispanics, Jews, and Gentiles, Protestants, and Catholics of all stripes have joined to form a new Democratic coalition." The story was reported by Percy Sutton's Harlem-based New York Amsterdam News on April 16, 1983. Washington's victory was accompanied by another milestone: a record voter turnout of 1.3 million citizens.

The Latino votes in both the primary and the general election attracted Washington's attention. He responded by creating an independent advisory commission on Latino affairs to critique the mayor's performance and recommend policy. He signed an executive order prohibiting city police officials from collaborating with the Immigration and Naturalization Services (INS) on raids, roundups, and deportations. Washington also appointed Vázquez, Soliz, and Lozano to his transition team.[40]

Unfortunately, Lozano didn't live to see the impact of Washington's mayoralty. On April 12, 1983, a gang member shot and killed Lozano in the kitchen of his Pilsen home. Richard M. Daley, the former mayor's son, was serving as the state attorney general, but his office never established a motive for the murder. Thousands of supporters marched in the streets of Pilsen and Little Village in response to what they called the politically motivated assassination of Lozano. Garcia suggests that the assassination was ordered by unnamed political operatives exacting revenge on Lozano for his role in "helping to bring together the Latino component of the coalition that was indispensable for Harold [Washington] to win the primary and . . . general election."[41] Daley's superficial investigation into the shooting reads eerily like that following the deaths of Black Panther Fred Hampton and Mark Clayton in 1969.

Washington's election was a milestone not just for black–Latino relations but also for breaking Chicago's political status quo. It strengthened and validated the work of IPOs across the city and contributed to a new governing coalition, which included both the new immigrant Latino and African American communities. Washington had a very different governing style than the old machine; he incorporated neighborhood-based agendas and governing structures, relied on community advisory boards to hold city bureaucrats accountable, and gave the Latino community an advisory committee within his cabinet, which answered not to the mayor but to a board of commissioners. The mayor's Advisory Commission on Latino Affairs included a broad-based group of Latinos from throughout the city, including various nationalities and interest groups.

Mayor Washington also ushered in a new era in Chicago elections. During the campaign, he articulated a city government reform platform that championed honesty, affirmative action, and community control, which appealed to a broad coalition of voters. "We had been fighting the same issues in the City Council since the '60s, but we hadn't been able to win," recalled Simpson.[42] During the campaign, Washington convinced voters through debates, interviews with the media, and while stumping that he had the capacity to win that battle if elected mayor. In 1984, using the same campaign issues that proved successful for Washington, Garcia won the race for Twenty-second Ward alderman, the council seat that Lozano came so close to capturing just a year earlier. The same year, Juan Soliz ran again for state representative and won.[43]

The Progressive coalition that elected Washington inspired similar coalitions in New York City and other parts of the country as well. Zoilo Torres, the New York City Puerto Rican activist, attended a December 1983 conference in Chicago that dealt with such issues as mayoral politics and Afro-Americans. The event included coalition partners in Chicago such as POWER.[44] Torres argued that the Chicago coalition and Washington's victory served as a "very important" catalyst for changing the views of the Left on electoral politics and confronting the Ed Koch–controlled Democratic machine in New York City. Torres learned how the Chicago coalition's "massive voter-registration" drive among blacks, Latinos, poor whites, and white liberals provided the political base necessary for its opposition candidate to win the Democratic primary. As Torres recalls, "We saw what occurred in Chicago and said, 'we could do that here,' in New York City."[45]

AN INSPIRED NEW YORK

Using research from the Chicago election, Richard A. Cloward, a Columbia University professor of social work, and Frances Fox Piven, a CCNY professor of political science, proposed a strategy for registering low-income voters in New York City. Just weeks after Washington's victory, the *Amsterdam News* reported stumping and eating registration drives during which organizations would advertise food giveaways; once the crowds gathered, they made a pitch to register people to vote. In the South Bronx, hundreds of poor blacks and Latinos lined up to receive a five-pound brick of American cheese from organizers from the Westboro Community Development Corporation. While they waited for their cheese, organizers asked if participants wanted to register to vote. In another instance, volunteers from the New York Voter Registration Campaign used a cheese line to register 1,872 voters in front of the Antioch Baptist Church in Harlem. A cheese line at Bronx Lebanon Hospital registered 510 voters.[46]

These nongovernmental organizations (NGOs) belonged to a coalition of about twenty civil rights, labor, and religious groups. The New York Voter Registration Campaign represented a growing movement around the country of groups focused on registering lower-income citizens. Learning from events in Chicago, the New York coalition also set up voter-registration tables in medical clinics, unemployment offices, cheese lines, and waiting rooms as part of a pilot project set to launch in June 1983.[47] A little over a week after Washington's election, an editorial published on April 30 in the *Amsterdam News* presented a vision for defeating incumbent mayor Ed Koch in the 1985 Democratic primary for mayor of New York. As in Chicago, defeating the Koch-controlled Democratic machine in New York City required a massive voter-registration drive and an energized coalition that could get low-income black and Latino voters to turn out on election day. Moreover, African Americans and Latinos had to come together in issue-based coalitions as they had in Chicago in order to develop platforms and select candidates to run. When it came to selecting and supporting candidates for appointments or to run in the primaries for mayor, borough presidents, and district attorneys, New York City independent political organizations had a long and divisive history.[48] So the question was this: Would they be able to get past their divisions to replicate Chicago's success?

Since the 1970s, black elected officials typically controlled the minority candidate selection process in coalitions they formed without input from Latino elected officials. In response, Latino elected officials refused to endorse black candidates and instead cut deals for patronage and appointments with Democratic regulars running against African American–supported candidates in primary elections. "For black elected officials to believe that they can pick a winning black candidate to be the candidate for minorities, without Hispanics being a part of the selection process, is for black elected officials to continue to deal in illusory politics that lacks sober thought. Blacks and Hispanics are not united," said an op-ed piece in a May 7, 1983, edition of the *Amsterdam News*. "In the Manhattan borough president's race, the Hispanic community voted for Andrew Stein over David Dinkins. Also, in the Democratic primary for governor, racist anti-black Koch received a substantial amount of the Hispanic vote." The article went on to explain historical reasons why New York City had not had a Chicago-like Progressive coalition backing one candidate for citywide office like Washington: "From the day when Percy Sutton endorsed Abe Beame over Herman Badillo, there has been a split between the black and Hispanic communities; and, until that gap is eliminated, blacks will not be supported by Hispanics. Unfortunately, black elected officials have not yet moved to heal the wounds; and their present action can only widen the gap."

RUN, JESSE, RUN!

In the early 1980s, Republican Ronald Reagan's and Democratic Ed Koch's harsh budget cuts and seeming indifference to the pain they caused poor communities fueled a strong opposition movement in New York City. Blacks and Latinos who had been working in the political realm for some time began to mobilize their political base and support candidates running for office. They were joined by an influx of former radicals who saw what had happened in Chicago and decided that upcoming elections could unseat both Reagan and Koch. Nationally, the Democratic Party was preparing itself to challenge Reagan for the presidency. Former vice president Walter Mondale and Senator Gary Hart (D-Colo.) were the two front-runners for the Democratic nomination. Both were white men from largely white states, so certain segments of the party had concerns that the hardships and inequities faced by racial minorities, the working class, and other vulnerable groups would not be given sufficient attention by either Hart or Mondale.[49]

Jesse Jackson, as the director of Operation PUSH in Chicago, had been intricately involved in the coalition that helped elect Mayor Harold Washington. During the lead-up to the Democratic primary for mayor of Chicago in 1983, Jackson became incensed when Senator Ted Kennedy (D-Mass.) came to Chicago to support the incumbent Jane Byrne and Mondale supported Daley. Jackson called leading Progressive and liberal Democrats around the country to help persuade Kennedy and Mondale not to validate the Chicago Democratic machine and undermine the Chicago coalition. Nonetheless, Kennedy and Mondale kept their commitments to Byrne and Daley. The decision left Jackson feeling that Mondale and Kennedy, two prominent Progressive liberals within the Democratic Party, had disrespected and abandoned the Chicago coalition and movement. A minority candidate running against them in the Democratic presidential primaries seemed the best way to gain their attention and respect. As he had done with Washington, Jackson tried unsuccessfully to convince some black politicians to run, including Atlanta mayor Andrew Young and the former mayor Maynard Jackson. Meanwhile, a movement was growing for Jackson himself to run. Some unknown person started the chant "Run, Jesse, Run." Jackson recalls, "I wanted to pull back but I couldn't because it would have appeared as if I had been playing" but "I was not playing" or considering running. But after fighting against liberal contempt for Washington's coalition, Jackson decided to run for president.[50] The phrase "Run, Jesse, Run" caught fire in New York in 1983 and gradually led to the formation of a large coalition of black and Latino Jackson supporters in the city.[51]

Despite the energy and optimism that propelled Jackson onto the national political stage, he faced significant early challenges. First of all, he didn't officially enter the race until November 1983, nine months after his competitors. He got a late start on building an organization, locking down endorsements, and fund-raising. He moved quickly to catch up, opening official campaign headquarters in thirty-two states by the end of January.[52]

In many ways, Jackson patterned his national campaign after Washington's in Chicago, calling for massive voter-registration drives and drawing on the support and grassroots activism of coalitions of minority activists, organized labor, and white liberals and Progressives to make up for what he lacked in major media exposure and sophisticated marketing. In July 1983, even before he announced his candidacy, Jackson's Operation PUSH signed an agreement with the 109,000-member League of United Latin American Citizens (LULAC), the nation's largest Latino organization, to collaborate on voter-registration drives and economic issues. Then in November, LULAC entered an agreement with the leaders of the Urban League and the NAACP. With this type of coordination, these organizations hoped to register 1 million new Latino voters by the 1984 election. LULAC's president, Mario Obledo, endorsed Jackson's candidacy because "it mean[t] a lot of important issues [were] going to be discussed." Like Washington's platform in 1983, Jackson called for rolling back Reagan cutbacks, reducing unemployment, and increasing support for education and affirmative action policies. In addition, Jackson denounced U.S. support for repressive governments, particularly in South Africa and Central America. One subject that had a lot of emotional resonance for many black and Latino voters was the Reagan administration's cuts to school lunch programs and food stamps. These cuts most severely affected African American and Latino communities and, most important, took a disproportionately heavy toll on children. While the other Democratic candidates addressed these issues, none attacked Reagan as directly or as consistently as Jackson. He called for a 20 percent reduction in defense spending and a reallocation of those funds toward poverty assistance programs like food stamps, school lunches, job training, and education.[53]

In terms of policy, Jackson had a lot to offer Latinos. He quickly distinguished himself from the other Democratic candidates on immigration and U.S. foreign policy in Central America. Senator Alan K. Simpson (R-Wyo.) and Senator Romano L. Mazzoli (D-Ky.) introduced the first version of their immigration reform bill in March 1982. The bill offered no guest-worker plan like the one the president supported but instead it promised to streamline the existing program for workers from Mexico and other countries and contained provisions for expanding the program. The bill called for a $1,000 fine for employers hiring undocumented workers and required employers to vouch for their employees' immigration status, making it illegal for an employer to knowingly hire or recruit undocumented immigrants.[54] Most Latino organizations opposed the bill, arguing that it would stigmatize all workers who looked Latino, spoke Spanish, or had immigrated to the United States.[55] Jackson was the only one of the three major Democratic candidates for president who opposed the bill. He also pointedly refused to use the term "illegal alien," choosing to use the phrase "undocumented worker" instead.[56]

Rather than a criminal justice problem, Jackson regarded illegal immigration to the United States from Latin America as an economic problem, driven by international debt policies and U.S. foreign policy in Central America. He said that it was racist for the United States to set one standard for white immigrants from Europe and another standard for black and brown "political and economic refugees" from Central America. Jackson argued that the Simpson-Mazzoli bill would "usher in an era of passbooks akin to South Africa" and permit gross injustices against the 20 million Latinos who were living in the United States at the time.[57]

While Jackson opposed the bill, the NAACP, the most powerful predominantly black civil rights organization in the country, endorsed Simpson-Mazzoli. The NAACP supported the initiative as a member of the coalition that included the AFL-CIO and the ILGWU. The coalition argued that undocumented workers competed with U.S. citizens for jobs and worked for less, thus repressing wages.[58]

Jackson clashed with members of his African American base over other Latino issues, including bilingual education, providing sanctuary for Central American refugees, and extending the language of the Voting Rights Act to include Latinos. These positions were controversial in the black community because many held the view that support for bilingual education took resources away from African American students. They also believed that Latin American refugees would compete with African Americans for job opportunities and lower wages and that including Latinos in the Voting Rights Act would put Latinos in direct competition with African Americans in the political arena. Thus, in each of these issues, Jackson had to walk a fine line between trying to win over Latino voters and not alienating African Americans.

Jackson's support for Central America won him friends in the Latino community. In contrast to Mondale and Hart, Jackson decried U.S. support for repressive, authoritarian governments in Central America, and he called the U.S. government's decision to install explosive mines in Nicaraguan ports unlawful and depraved. "Jackson became the favored candidate of the peace movement and of Hispanics," wrote Armando Gutierrez. "Indeed, there were some who felt that Jackson alone stood against a possible United States invasion of Nicaragua."[59]

LATINOS FOR JACKSON IN NEW YORK

As news of Jesse Jackson's positions on immigration and economics spread, Progressive minority activists around the country joined his campaign. "Latinos for Jackson" chapters began springing up across the country with particularly strong support among Puerto Rican communities in New York, New Jersey, and Pennsylvania, and Chicano communities in Texas, California, Arizona, Colorado, and New Mexico. Similar to BLAPP in Chicago, the

Latinos for Jackson committee in New York included Progressive activists seeking political empowerment in the city and Latinos who viewed African Americans as natural partners in that goal.

Nellie Marrero, a Puerto Rican East Harlem resident, served as the Latinos for Jackson cofounder and city coordinator for the committee. The group's activities included a letter-writing campaign to friends and family endorsing Jackson for president and inviting them to a January campaign kickoff event where Jackson addressed an enthusiastic group of 175 people in East Harlem. Marrero insisted, "Jackson speaks of the needs of minorities, in terms of the poor and the problems of the average working person. He emphasizes the building of a mass movement in this country—a Rainbow Coalition."[60] The pioneer hip-hop artist Melvin Glover (also known as Grandmaster Melle Mel) of Grandmaster Flash and the Furious Five, best known for the 1982 hit song "The Message," was born in Barbados and grew up in the Bronx. "The Message" describes the challenges of life in the Bronx under the Koch and Reagan administrations. Melle Mel later tweaked a rap song he had written to create one for Jackson's 1984 presidential campaign titled "Jesse." Melle Mel's lyrics criticized incumbent politicians and envisioned what a Jackson presidency would mean for the country and thereby decrease white fears of a black president.[61]

Latinos for Jackson operated as part of a New Yorkers for Jackson Committee headed by Brooklyn assemblyman Al Vann and had groups in the Bronx, Brooklyn, and Manhattan. By January 1984, its members had already become engaged in voter-registration brigades, leafleting, door-to-door campaigning, fund-raising, and the Jackson delegate selection process. The Latinos for Jackson committee also had the task of selecting twelve Latinos to run for delegates or alternate seats to the Democratic convention.[62]

Harlem congressman Charlie Rangel served as a vice chair of Walter Mondale's national campaign. In doing so, he parted ways with old political ally and close friend David Dinkins, then the city clerk of New York. During the 1984 Democratic presidential primary, Dinkins served as the coordinator for the Manhattan Committee of New York for Jesse Jackson. In early March 1984, he hosted a steering committee meeting and briefing at Sylvia's, the iconic Harlem soul food restaurant. During the meeting, Dinkins announced several "Jackson for President" campaign events in East Harlem geared toward Latino supporters.[63] Latinos for Jackson also had representatives on the steering committee of New Yorkers for Jackson, ran candidates for delegates, and conducted walk-throughs with Jackson in the South Bronx, Williamsburg, and East Harlem.[64]

Like the majority of the New York media, the Spanish-language media in New York City ignored Latino support for Jackson. Likewise, most Puerto Rican and Latino elected officials overwhelmingly supported Mondale, who outspent Jackson at least ten to one in Latino communities. For Jackson, then, it wasn't easy to win the support of grassroots organizations that relied on Latino elected officials and political bosses for funds for their programming. However, some key community activists gave their support, lending credibility to the Latinos for Jackson movement. For example, Ramon Jimenez remembers a visit with Evelina López Antonetty, who had founded United Bronx Parents in 1965. The organization historically worked with Puerto Ricans but had African Americans on staff and worked with black and white parents as well.[65] Jimenez, knowing that Antonetty's program depended on state and federal funds from mainstream Democratic officials who were all backing Mondale, stated, "I just sat down, she looked at my face and she said, 'Ramon, you're here because you want me to support Jesse Jackson.' I said, 'Yes.' Then she said, 'Ramon, I'm with you one hundred percent.' And she supported us totally in that campaign against all the elected officials that helped her get funding."[66]

At a Latinos for Jackson fund-raiser held at El Museo in East Harlem, Antonetty spoke about the sense of political empowerment that Jackson's Rainbow Coalition was creating: "We don't want our children to suffer the way we have suffered discrimination. We don't want our children to inherit our hardships—and I believe, now, that they won't."[67] Nellie Marrero added that "Jesse Jackson provided the opportunity for all of us stuck at the bottom, as he says, to rise up and change the course of this country." Jimenez noted that Latinos for Jackson had united blacks and Latinos for the first time in a long while, increasing solidarity between the city's often fragmented Latino diaspora made up of Puerto Ricans, Cubans, Dominicans, and others.

In the South Bronx, members of Latinos for Jackson canvassed neighborhoods, knocked on doors, handed out bilingual literature, and conducted walk-throughs with Jackson in the Eleventh, Sixteenth, and Eighteenth Congressional Districts and in predominately Latino State Assembly districts, such as the Seventy-third, Seventy-fourth, and Seventy-eighth where

Jackson received 40 percent of the Latino vote.[68] "We beat [Robert] Garcia and all [of the rest of the elected] Puerto Rican politicians who supported Mondale [and] they had all the money," recalled Jimenez.[69]

In Brooklyn, Luis Garden Acosta, the founder and director of El Puente, a community and youth development organization, served as that borough's Latinos for Jackson coordinator. The talented political strategist David Santiago of the SSPC and the National Congress for Puerto Rican Rights also worked with the Brooklyn campaign. In support of Jackson, Santiago brought the members of the SSPC "in line with Sonny Carson [whose] base was Bed-Stuy, Bushwick, [and] central Brooklyn." As in the South Bronx, Latinos for Jackson mobilized large numbers of Puerto Rican voters for Jackson in Williamsburg.[70]

The campaign organized a rally and parade of Jackson supporters in East Harlem on March 31, three days before the April 3 primary. Officials estimated that 10,000 people marched and lined the sidewalks of the parade route through East Harlem to the New York State Office of General Services Building at 125th Street and Adam Clayton Powell Jr. Boulevard in Harlem. The *Washington Post* reported that "the parade stretched seven blocks and included two bands, delegations of Asians, Hispanics, gays, union members, and blacks [carrying signs] supporting Jackson." When Jackson addressed the crowd, he said, "The waking up of the sleeping giant has been a long time coming. But we're here now, our time has come. It's time for black leadership. . . . If not us, who? If not now, when?"[71]

In an impressive showing, Jackson bested Mondale three to one in five city congressional districts in Queens, Manhattan, and the Bronx. Jackson also received 80 percent of Brooklyn votes. Among Latino voters, 24 percent went to Jackson, 51 percent to Mondale, and 21 percent to Hart. Considering that Mondale far outspent Jackson, Mondale's 51 percent did not look like a convincing margin of victory over Jackson. Likewise, Jackson almost won the city itself while Mondale won the state. Jackson's results in New York were even more impressive considering they happened without one television commercial or advertisement. Instead, the campaign depended on a strong ground game, rallies, and a parade.[72] Jackson's primary victory in the Eighteenth Congressional District in the Bronx inspired the African American Wendell Foster to organize a follow-up Rainbow Coalition meeting at Christ Church in the Bronx on April 10 and "continue the momentum for change" that the Jackson campaign had created. The Jackson result, Foster said, "increases my chances of success for the [Bronx] borough president's race in 1985 and Basil Paterson's race for mayor."[73]

Jackson's victories in the heavily Latino Eleventh, Sixteenth, and Eighteenth Congressional Districts sent the Koch machine and the Latino Democratic regulars who depended on it for their survival into a panic. Shortly thereafter, rumors of a "black conspiracy" began to spread. One such disinformation campaign suggested that Paterson and Dinkins used the Rainbow Coalition and Latinos for Jackson to mobilize Latino voters to unseat Latino elected officials, elect a black mayor, and put African Americans in control of city government.[74] After the primary vote, eighty-four Latino Democratic regulars running for office and reelection employed anti-black and black conspiracy stump speeches, and mobilized Latinos in their districts to "defend their political gains," wrote Ramon Jimenez in the pages of the *Amsterdam News*:

> This is indeed strange because when confronted with a genuine attack by Koch and Reagan, during the past few years, the mode of combat [Latino politicians] selected was silence and compliance. Hospitals and school closings, threatened wars in Latin America, and deep cuts in Human services . . . never resulted in these politicians planning weekly meetings and initiating a massive voter registration drive. Instead, Jesse Jackson's campaign advocating full employment, the full implementation of the Voting Rights Act, minority empowerment, human rights policy in Latin America, and other significant positions has caused them to mobilize and organize. Indeed, racism is certainly still alive and well, not so much among the Puerto Rican masses—but among many of the Puerto Rican elected officials.[75]

Politicians such as City Council members Rafael Castaneria Colon and Fernando Ferrer, Assemblyman Hector Diaz, and those friendly to South Bronx political boss Ramon Velez were viewed by Jimenez as obstacles to progressive change in the county. But others like Representative Robert Garcia and Assemblyman José Serrano had "one last moment to decide whether they wish to continue to play the role of mercenaries" for the Koch machine while fanning the flames of disunity between blacks and Latinos.

"If they continue to ignore the new political reality of New York City and the consciousness of their communities—they will indeed face challenges . . . Puerto Rican challenges in 1984 and 1985." Jimenez went on to say, "Conspiracy is indeed being planned . . . a conspiracy to the control of real estate interest over New York City politicians . . . a conspiracy to bring new programs and policies to deprived communities . . . a conspiracy to end the reign of Koch, Simon, and their cohorts . . . a conspiracy to bring JUSTICE to New York City. Are you finally ready to join this 'conspiracy'?"[76]

Jackson's candidacy for president reintroduced the debate over the merits and possibility of a black and Latino political coalition in Democratic Party politics in New York City; it also revealed the rifts between Latino political leaders, who supported Mondale, and Latino activists, who supported Jackson.[77]

CHALLENGES AND MISTAKES

Despite the many successes of his campaign, Jesse Jackson made some major strategic errors in 1984 that cost him votes. During the campaign, New York media outlets increasingly asked questions about how Jackson financed what they described as a lavish lifestyle, including a large home in Chicago, and the sources of PUSH's funds and his campaign funds. Jackson provided angry and inadequate answers, and accused the media of unbalanced treatment compared with the other candidates in the race. His off-the-record "Hymie Town" comment to a group of African American journalists serves as perhaps his most remembered gaffe. Jackson argued that Jewish sectors in New York (which he labeled "Hymie Town") had been responsible for media criticism of his finances. Jackson failed to quickly apologize for the comment, which further distanced him from Jewish leaders who had an ongoing disagreement with African American leaders like Jackson over affirmative action and U.S. support for Israel.

Following the "Hymie Town" incident, Jackson selected Al Vann to chair the campaign in New York State. After the election of Mario Cuomo, Vann had become one of the most powerful politicians in Albany and had demonstrated an ability to help candidates win elections outside his home district in Bedford-Stuyvesant, including José Rivera and Representative Major

Owens. The selection of Vann as the state's campaign manager was a colossal misstep, since it meant basing the office in Brooklyn, where the New York City press corps rarely ventured for press conferences and other media events. Moreover, Jackson preferred spending time in Manhattan because his network of closest supporters lived and worked there. With the leadership of the statewide operation somewhat isolated in Brooklyn, the campaign was not run as professionally or effectively as it had to be to take New York State away from Walter Mondale.[78]

The bigger problem was that the African Americans who led Jackson's national campaign did not let Latino strategists into their inner circle, nor did they develop a comprehensive strategy to win over Latino voters. Armando Gutierrez, who headed the campaign's national Hispanic desk, says he never felt like the campaign leaders listened to his recommendations or empowered him.[79] Likewise, Ramon Jimenez remembers being "the only Puerto Rican on the New York State Committee for Jesse Jackson."[80]

There were three main reasons for this shortcoming. First, with the possible exception of Washington's Chicago mayoral campaign, black and Latino leaders at both the national and local levels had had very little regular contact since the civil rights and Black Power movements of the 1960s and 1970s. As a result, African American campaign staff had few close contacts within the Latino community. When the campaign did try to recruit Latino staff, they did not have any trusted confidantes to vet the candidates. Sheila Collins, a campaign staffer, admits that Jackson's black campaign staff made the mistake of hiring Latinos with leadership titles but no history of grassroots organizing. In New York, they ended up with staffers who had good-looking resumes but no real pull on the street.[81]

Second, Jackson's campaign managers were slow to appreciate the national importance of Latino voters and put too little money behind the effort. In San Antonio, the campaign failed to support Laura Sanchez, a local activist who was working to get Jackson a spot at the podium during that city's Cinco de Mayo festival. As a result, Jackson missed the opportunity to speak to a crowd of 30,000 Mexican Americans. During the 1984 presidential race, Sanchez had to "fight the city's black campaign leadership for the resources to reach her people as well as for a place on Jackson's itinerary," recalls Collins.[82] Sanchez believes that the black Democratic machine in San Antonio viewed her efforts to mobilize Latino voters as threatening to their agenda and a drain on resources that should have been spent reaching black voters.[83]

Third, the Jackson campaign had a generally fraught relationship with elected Latino officials. The majority of elected Latinos would not endorse Jackson because they had close ties to the Democratic Party apparatus, and the establishment wing of the party endorsed Mondale. They feared reprisals in the form of lost support for their own agendas and campaigns if they backed Jackson. In New York especially, Latino officials would not support Jackson. These officials assumed, at first, that Jackson would make no inroads among their constituents because they did not think Latinos would support a black candidate for president. They were taken by surprise when support for Jackson grew among Latinos in some areas of New York City. They responded with racist anti-Jackson rhetoric, warning Latino voters about a black conspiracy.[84]

While Jackson came in third in the New York primary, he drew 25 percent of the vote in the state, a much better showing than predicted. He missed bumping Gary Hart out of second place by just 25,000 votes. Apparently, Jackson was able to compensate for not having a national Latino strategy or a network of supporters among the Latino elites by having a compelling policy agenda and a team of excellent grassroots organizers like Nellie Marrero and Jimenez.[85] According to Collins, Jackson's favorable showing in New York "placed the campaign on the map for the first time as having the potential of building a Rainbow Coalition."[86]

The importance of Latino votes for Jackson both in New York and nationally during the 1984 primary is more significant for local elections thereafter than for Jackson's bid for the Democratic nomination. From the beginning, Jackson had the goal of making Democratic regulars respect and respond to a united organized independent coalition of blacks, Latinos, and poor whites within the Democratic Party and their issues. Latino activists proved that with far less money they could deliver more voters to the polls in primary elections than Democratic regulars. The example of how to defeat local Democratic machines with fewer financial resources in minority-majority congressional districts was the most important legacy of Jackson's bid in 1984. Looking back, Gutierrez says that despite Jackson's pro-Latino policies, Latino voters viewed Jackson with "some degree of skepticism." While overcoming this skepticism was too monumental an undertaking, Gutierrez still feels that important progress was made during the campaign.[87] And Saul Nieves, who attended the 1984 convention, says it was the first time in his life that he saw "African Americans and some white Progressives and Latinos" all attending the same meetings and getting along.[88]

After the convention, the Rainbow Coalition faced a debt of $1.4 million and a Federal Election Commission requirement that all campaign offices be closed. At the national level, coalition organizers held a meeting in August to discuss the future of the group. Ambitious plans were suggested to build a voter-education and -registration apparatus and to form a public-policy research institute; a political action committee to select, nurture, and fund Progressive candidates; a leadership training program; and a public-relations office that could better shape the coalition's overall message and response to fast-breaking news.[89] They also discussed how to better position minority candidates for upcoming races. Gutierrez argued that candidates should visit the twenty U.S. cities with the largest black and Latino communities to develop relationships with Progressive individuals and organizations. Candidates, he said, should lay the groundwork for electoral coalitions well in advance of a campaign and have a strong network already in place. By reaching out to grassroots organizers and activists, not necessarily elected minority officials, potential candidates would be better positioned to mobilize voters in critical districts.[90]

As a national organization, the Rainbow Coalition had plans that started, stopped, and ran into many roadblocks, including a lack of funding. As a result, on the national level there was a lull in activity immediately after the convention. "Without an immediate political focus for cooperative activity, the hope and energy of the campaign dissolved as activists returned to their organizations and communities," wrote Collins.[91] But examples at the local level in New York provide evidence that the coalition and its partners continued to organize against local Democratic machines in primary elections. There are also examples that Jackson's campaign did build a voter-registration movement and a ground game that remained intact after the 1984 Democratic convention had ended.

The African American Bennie O. Batts declared his candidacy for Congress in Westchester County's Twentieth Congressional District in the September 1984 Democratic primary, becoming the first non-white candidate to run for Congress in the history of the county. The county's Rainbow

Coalition volunteers helped collect the 1,250 signatures required for him to get on the ballot for the Democratic primary for the U.S. House of Representatives. Moreover, Jackson's support of Batts's candidacy resulted in local endorsements from ministers representing fifteen of the largest black congregations in Westchester. In explaining why they endorsed Batts, the ministers said that they sought to broaden and strengthen the Rainbow Coalition in that county and thus transform the politics. The ministers argued that after the Democratic convention, the Rainbow Coalition remained "alive and well" in Westchester County.[92]

In southern Queens, Jackson also endorsed the former family court judge Simeon Golar's candidacy to represent the Sixth Congressional District. This was a seat created in 1982 by order of the federal courts and the U.S. Department of Justice to increase minority representation in Congress. Golar ran as an Independent Democrat and Rainbow Coalition candidate against the incumbent, Joseph Addabbo, backed by the Queens County Democratic political machine. In the largely Latino section of Bushwick, Brooklyn, the Rainbow Coalition supported the Puerto Rican Nydia Velázquez's run in the Democratic primary in the Twenty-seventh District seat on the New York City Council.

At the end of September 1984, a coalition of black and Latino elected officials and organizers who supported Jackson as well as Mondale during the Democratic primaries started a united, national registration drive to add 165,000 new voters to the polls by the registration deadline of October 6, 1984. Former Jackson campaign delegate and Manhattan coordinator David Dinkins and former Mondale delegate Hazel Dukes announced at a joint press conference at the campaign headquarters of Walter Mondale and Geraldine Ferraro in New York that the goal of defeating President Ronald Reagan in the general election on November 6, 1984, united the coalition.

Starting with the Progressive anti-machine coalitions in Chicago in the 1970s, voter-registration drives led to the movement to unseat Mayor Jane Byrne and elect Harold Washington as mayor in 1983. Jessie Jackson ran for president in 1984 as a protest candidate who had condemned those Progressive Democrats who came to Chicago during the Democratic primary for mayor and endorsed Washington's opponent. Jackson's presidential campaign employed the same political strategy used to defeat the Chicago Democratic machine: a long and sustained voter-registration drive, which created a multiethnic Rainbow Coalition and establishing a Progressive stump speech that addressed issues facing working-class Americans and immigrants from Latin America. In the process, blacks and Latino activists who supported Jackson in New York and other parts of the country developed Progressive political organizations like the Rainbow Coalition, which registered and mobilized voters. During and after the 1984 presidential campaign, they increased their ranks through the voter-registration drive, particularly in Brooklyn and in suburban New York, thus changing New York's political landscape.[93] Coalition partners continued to run opposition candidates in Democratic primaries against machine-backed politicians. They lost more than they won, but in the process they learned how to recruit candidates, fund-raise, establish and run campaign headquarters, and develop a ground strategy that got voters to the polls on election day.

6

WHERE THE STREET GOES, THE SUITS FOLLOW

COALITION POLITICS, 1985–1988

DEMOCRATIC REGULARS (THE SUITS) understand the ins and outs of deal making in order to pass legislation and gain access to patronage and appointments. As their careers advance, they often lose touch with their base and forget how to mobilize them. Grassroots organizers (the streets) know how to mobilize people. But activists are poor at the compromising and deal making involved in unions meeting the needs of their base. Both party regulars and activists fail to recognize that they need each other in order to advance common goals.

Al Vann took two things from his experience as Jesse Jackson's New York State campaign chairman. First, with the proper support, a minority candidate could make a real showing at the polls. Second, registering new voters from historically underserved black and Latino communities would be the key to toppling the Ed Koch–controlled Democratic machine in New York City. Unfortunately, lessons learned did not translate to accomplishments achieved. Vann had the opportunity to build a coalition that would unseat Koch but lost it after infighting, conspiracy theories, and divided loyalties caused the fragile black–Latino coalition to crumble.

Vann was an ambitious man, for both himself and his cause. His personal goal was to become Brooklyn's first black borough president and then unseat incumbent mayor Koch. After the 1984 Democratic National Convention, Vann held a number of leadership positions, including chairman of the Black and Puerto Rican Legislative Caucus in the New York State Assembly and founder and chairman of the Brooklyn-based Coalition for a Just New York.[1] Vann started the coalition in 1983 during a struggle to get Mayor

Koch to appoint Dr. Thomas Minter, a black educator, as schools chancellor. From the start, the coalition was an all-black, Brooklyn-based political organization of notable and generally Progressive political, religious, and community leaders from across the city. They met twice a month in the summer of 1983 at Vann's Fulton Street clubhouse in Brooklyn.[2] By 1985, the coalition was working to advance its agenda for evaluating and endorsing candidates for mayor, borough presidents, City Council president, comptroller, and other elected offices.

A BROAD-BASED COALITION

The coalition met with a delegation of labor leaders in the city and later with Latino leaders to broaden the group's base of support for the candidate it would endorse. By the end of January 1985, the coalition started interviewing candidates to decide who it would endorse to run against Ed Koch in the 1985 Democratic mayoral primary.[3]

By this time, many informal conversations about who would run against Koch started taking place throughout the city. A good number of those conversations took place at Jack Newfield's house at in Manhattan's Greenwich Village. An investigative journalist and editor for the liberal weekly newspaper the *Village Voice*, Newfield had worked behind the scenes for years to bring African Americans and Latinos together. And he was a close friend of Al Vann and Herman Badillo. The activist and Harvard Law School–trained attorney Ramon Jimenez remembers attending a number of gatherings at Newfield's house. "You had a who's who in terms of Progressives in New York," he says. The main topic of discussion, Jimenez says, was simple: Could a black and Latino coalition beat Mayor Koch?[4]

Instead of ushering in a period of unity and shared purpose, though, the candidate-selection process created bitter rifts between black and Latino activists as well as between black leaders in Brooklyn and Harlem because black political elites often practiced the politics of exclusion, ethnocentrism, and presumption in speaking and acting for others. As a result, the ability of a black or Latino candidate to win citywide office in 1985 was compromised. Latino politicians had a history of mistrust of black politicians. Having spent so much time fighting against them for coveted seats, they viewed African Americans as a threat. They seldom shared staff resources, political connections, or funds, even when it might have put the movement for minority rights a step ahead. When they did work together, swapping campaign assistance or endorsements across districts, it was often out of political expediency and not out of principle. It rarely led to sustained partnerships.[5] Therefore, while black and Latino activists had been united and energized by Jackson's showing in New York City, elites went into the candidate selection process divided and uncommunicative.

When black and Latino elected officials did cooperate, it was often along the lines of backroom deal making and the quid pro quos of classic machine politics. None of the officials were able to capitalize on the upsurge in grassroots mobilization—even as it had the potential to augment their own power and status. They, particularly state officeholders, had grown so dependent on realtors and corporations for reelection funds that over time they not only became detached from the communities who elected them but had become so attached to power that they could no longer enact real change.[6] Once in office they failed to remember the reason why people voted for them in the first place.

DEMOCRATIC PRIMARY FOR MAYOR, 1985

Amid the continuing tensions between black and Latino politicians, a few prominent minority candidates emerged as early favorites to challenge Ed Koch in the Democratic primary: former deputy mayor Herman Badillo, former Manhattan borough president Percy Sutton, and former New York secretary of state Basil Paterson. By spring 1984, Paterson had emerged as the consensus candidate among black and Latino Progressives.

At the age of fifty-eight, Paterson had a long track record in New York politics. He had served as state senator, vice chairman of the Democratic National Committee, deputy mayor for labor relations, and head of the Harlem Clubhouse. He also ran unsuccessfully for lieutenant governor of New York in 1970 on a ticket with Supreme Court Justice Arthur Goldberg, a pairing that earned him credibility among Jewish voters. His work as a labor lawyer for Local 1199 gave him insider status with labor leaders.[7]

In June 1984, a Friends of Basil Paterson political action committee was formed. The group included a several Progressive politicians of that era: Badillo, Brooklyn Borough President Howard Golden, DC 37 president Victor Gotbaum, state Democratic chairman William C. Hennessy, City Council president Carol Bellamy, and State Assembly Speaker Stanley Fink. The committee paid tribute to Paterson's twenty years of public service by hosting a stumping-and-eating fund-raiser in the ballroom of the Sheraton Centre Hotel. The $200-a-plate dinner raised more than $100,000 for a potential campaign. When Paterson stood to address the crowd, he warned that New York City would not prosper unless blacks, Hispanics, and other minorities took their "rightful place in the civic, economic, cultural, and political life of this city." Badillo agreed that Paterson's credentials gave him the right of "first crack" at being the anti-Koch coalition's mayoral candidate. But if Paterson declined, he and few others were ready to take a chance on the mayoralty. Badillo was confident that if blacks and Latinos remained united, Koch would be defeated.[8]

The coalition did remain united until Paterson surprised his supporters in September 1984 with the news that he would not run for mayor for unnamed "personal reasons." "I had triple bypass several months later," Paterson recalls. "I did not disclose details about why I declined to run then because I made my living as an attorney and who's going to hire a lawyer with a bad heart? A lot of people gave me a hard time about that, but I couldn't tell people the real reasons for years or it would have jeopardized my career."[9]

Bellamy and Badillo then emerged as the two most likely alternative candidates. Bellamy had several strikes against her, though. For one thing, she was white. Expectations had been raised about the possibility of a black mayor in New York City following the election of African American mayors in Los Angeles, Chicago, Detroit, and Philadelphia.[10] She was also seen as being too close to the Koch administration. Bellamy had endorsed Andrew Stein over David Dinkins in the Democratic primary for Manhattan borough president in 1981 (a race that Stein won) and had supported Koch over Mario Cuomo in the 1982 governor's race, despite Cuomo's strong support in the black community.[11] Moreover, she regularly voted for Koch's austerity budgets that included plans to shut down city-run hospitals in black and Latino communities. According to Wilbert Tatum, the editor in chief of the

New York Amsterdam News, Bellamy's pro-Koch record "spat in the face" of African Americans.[12] As a result of her history of pro-Koch endorsements, the Coalition for a Just New York refused to support her.

Badillo, on the contrary, seemed to have the coalition's support going into the group's final deliberations and preparations. Badillo had tremendous credibility as a political leader. He embodied the Horatio Alger story as a poor non-English-speaking orphan who had achieved the American dream. After high school, he graduated magna cum laude from CCNY and was first in his class at Brooklyn Law School. By age twenty-five, he became a lawyer and a certified public accountant; later he became the first Puerto Rican to be elected Bronx borough president, a U.S. congressman, and the first Hispanic to run as a candidate for mayor of New York City. Badillo's legal defense of members of the coalition who were arrested during the takeover of Hostos Community College gave him some street credibility among Latino Progressives. Badillo's credibility among Progressives increased when he openly supported the informal "Dump Koch" coalition that had developed over time. The *Amsterdam News* called Badillo the "leader best positioned to bring out the critical Hispanic vote" in the 1985 Democratic primary in New York City.[13] "If we don't work together, Ed Koch will win again," Badillo said, and he committed his support to any "coalition that will bring about change."[14] Badillo had the ability to turn out a large number of Latino voters on election day for himself as well as the candidates the coalition endorsed, including Vann for Brooklyn borough president.

Like Dinkins in Manhattan and José Serrano in the Bronx, Vann needed a black and Latino coalition in Brooklyn to win the Democratic primary for borough president. An endorsement from Badillo would give him the needed credibility and support among Latino voters in Kings County. Vann openly supported Badillo's candidacy for mayor. Bill Lynch, who worked as a political strategist for Local 1707, also supported Badillo. If Badillo won at the top of the ticket, Lynch and Vann believed that with Serrano running for Bronx borough president, Dinkins running for Manhattan borough president, and Vann running for Brooklyn borough president, blacks and Latinos would control the New York City Board of Estimate. That immensely powerful board, composed of the mayor, City Council president, comptroller, and borough presidents, controlled the city's $20 billion budget that funded local programs and services in the boroughs.

After Paterson declined to run, the Coalition for a Just New York agreed that it would support Badillo. The coalition held meetings, the members agreed, and Vann told Badillo he would get the endorsement. However, the support was brief. During one coalition meeting, Badillo left the room and a secret discussion ensued; Badillo was summarily dumped as the coalition's candidate of choice. On February 8, 1985, the coalition threw its support to Herman "Denny" Farrell, the African American assemblyman representing Harlem and Washington Heights (figure 6.1).

Dumping Badillo, the Latino candidate, in favor of Farrell, an African American, destroyed the black and Latino coalition that had formed around the upcoming mayoral race. Without the coalition's united political power, Koch was reelected.[15]

Rumors surrounding the reason for Farrell's nomination were more damaging to the coalition than the actual motivations that spurred it. A rumor

FIGURE 6.1 David Dinkins (*second from right*) and Assemblyman Denny Farrell (*front*). (Courtesy NYC Municipal Archives)

of a "black conspiracy" to keep a Latino from attaining the most powerful political seat in the city surfaced. The rumor went that after Badillo left
the room that fateful night, Sutton, Dinkins, Paterson, and Representative
Charles Rangel—the so-called Gang of Four—conspired to back a black
candidate and ignore their commitments to the Latino community. It was
a compellingly sinister story that tapped into historic Latin American views
of black leaders as narcissistic, nationalistic, and disinterested in coalitions
with Latinos. This view became a powerful political allegory that is still alive
today.[16] The only problem was this: it wasn't true.

Many Progressives—blacks and Latinos alike—questioned the wisdom
of a Badillo candidacy. Many Latino activists never forgave Badillo for serving as Mayor Robert Wagner's henchman during the forced relocation of
Latinos from the Upper West Side twenty years earlier. "We remember what
Badillo did," says Sandy Trujillo, "and we did not want him to be a candidate." Polling showed that Badillo lacked support in Latino communities,
and, if given the choice, Latinos would back Koch over Badillo.[17] As the
first Puerto Rican elected to the U.S. House of Representatives, Badillo had
the bad habit of presuming to speak for all Puerto Ricans and Latinos. He
did this even though he lacked popular support in Latino communities.[18]
Even some who might have supported him on the grounds that electing
any Latino was important questioned Badillo's ability to win. He had tried
and failed to the win the nomination numerous times since 1969, which
dampened the buzz.[19] Even Bronx elected officials such as Representative
Robert Garcia and Serrano showed little excitement about his candidacy.
Furthermore, there was still anger against Badillo in the African American
community in Harlem for his muted support of Jesse Jackson in the 1984
Democratic presidential primary, even though Badillo did nothing to assist
with Jackson's campaign and denounced the candidate as divisive and polarizing after Jackson's "Hymietown" comment.[20]

But the Harlem crew was not simply dissatisfied with Badillo but also
frustrated with the leadership of the Brooklyn-based coalition. Opposing
Badillo's candidacy appeared to be a good way to take power back across
the East River. Vann's importance had increased tremendously as a result
of Mario Cuomo's election in 1982 as governor of New York, the founding
of the Coalition for a Just New York in 1983, and his chairmanship of Jackson's state campaign in 1984. "There was quite a rivalry at one point between

Brooklyn and Harlem," Dinkins says. Percy Sutton "understood that better than anybody, long before I understood what the hell was going on." Sutton, for example, had the sense to alternate meeting sites between Harlem and Brooklyn when the legislature was in session.[21] But during the candidate selection process, Ramon Jimenez says, the "historic division" between Harlem and Brooklyn was as wide as ever.[22]

In a meeting just three days before the coalition was due to announce its endorsement of Badillo, Jimenez says he sat outside the door of the meeting in which leaders of the Harlem Clubhouse decided "that Brooklyn shouldn't be making deals for the entire black community." It was at that point that the Harlem-based group decided to put forward its own candidate.[23] The passing over of Badillo shocked Vann and aimed to undermine Vann's leadership. The real issue was geographic power, not a conspiracy to undermine or slight Latinos.[24]

The Harlem Clubhouse found a willing challenger in Farrell. Not a particularly confrontational person by nature, Farrell now says that he agreed to run because he did not think Badillo had demonstrated sufficient passion and engagement to be mayor of New York City: "When I saw him, I said, 'This guy is no candidate.'"[25] Farrell felt that if they could not find a candidate more committed to becoming mayor and making significant citywide change than Badillo, then the black and Latino coalition had already failed.

The Gang of Four did not conspire to undermine support for Badillo. The coalition had a process whereby candidates for public office would seek the group's endorsement by coming in for interviews, recalls Dinkins. Once the interviews were complete, the coalition members met to discuss the merits of each candidate. Dinkins recalls that during the Badillo discussion, neither he, Sutton, Rangel, nor Paterson said a word. "I mean literally zero," Dinkins insists. "We said nothing."[26] Paterson agrees: "Not one of us spoke for or against [Badillo] deliberately. We went in the meeting saying, 'We are not getting into that.'"[27] At the first balloting meeting, Lynch recalls that Badillo had the necessary support to win the coalition's endorsement and that there were no other candidates for mayor under consideration. The coalition tabled the vote and agreed to meet again shortly to issue its endorsement.[28]

But when they reconvened, Farrell requested that his name be added to the ballot for mayor alongside Badillo's.[29] After secret ballot voting, Farrell was pronounced the winner. The coalition contained some forty-odd voting members. The two largest groups came from Brooklyn, which had a delegation of thirteen members, and Harlem, which had twelve representatives. With secret ballot voting, no records exist, nor do we know if coalition members voted in blocks based on their borough affiliation. Interviews and the *Amsterdam News* reveal that Lynch, the Harlem-based civil rights attorney C. Vernon Mason, and the Reverend Calvin Butts of Harlem's Abyssinian Baptist Church supported Badillo. But exactly how coalition members voted and what alliances were struck is known only to those in the room.[30]

The fallout from the decision was swift and severe. Some argue that *Village Voice* reporters Wayne Barrett and Jack Newfield—who had tried to orchestrate a black, Latino, liberal, and Progressive white coalition in support of a Badillo candidacy—spread the story throughout the "New York press corps that the Harlem Gang of Four, Rangel, Dinkins, Paterson, and Farrell, colluded to block the candidacy of Herman Badillo," according to an editorial in the *Amsterdam News*.[31] Those who failed to deliver the coalition's endorsement to Badillo and thus resurrect his political career sought to spread black conspiracy rumors and thereby destroy any chance of a black-Latino coalition behind Farrell's candidacy.

Barrett and Newfield joined forces with Badillo's campaign strategist Hank Sheinkopf to destroy Farrell's candidacy. They argued in the pages of the *Village Voice* that Farrell had conspired with Bellamy and that Farrell had agreed to stay in the Democratic primary just long enough to erode African American support, thus forcing him out of the race. They said that once Badillo was out, Farrell would drop out as well, clearing the way for Bellamy to gain the support of the coalition. In exchange, Farrell expected Bellamy to endorse Dinkins for Manhattan borough president. By calling the group of Harlem-based black politicians a "gang" who beat up on Badillo and his Brooklyn sponsors, Barrett and Newfield poured gas on the fire.[32] An editorial in the *Amsterdam News* said, "it will take years to repair the damage" among black political leaders in Brooklyn and Harlem and blacks and Latinos.[33] Vann became convinced of the conspiracy and abandoned Farrell's campaign. Lynch, who had supported Badillo, did not like

Farrell's last-minute inclusion on the ballot and refused to work on Farrell's campaign team.[34]

The "Gang of Four" appellation incensed Latino political elites and activists who had been backing a Badillo bid. The Dominican activist Apolinar Trinidad published a Latinos United for Political Action (LUPA) pamphlet that referred to Farrell as a "Judas who sold out the black and Latino community and did not even obtain thirty pieces of silver." The pamphlet was distributed to 8,000 blacks and Latinos attending a conference at the Nelson Rockefeller Empire State Plaza Convention Hall.[35] Shortly after, Farrell was greeted at one of his first stump speeches by a group of Latino activists picketing and shouting "Judas."[36]

State senator Olga Mendez of East Harlem called the coalition's refusal to endorse Badillo, "a clear message to Puerto Ricans and Hispanics that the blacks don't want to share power with us." She considered challenging Dinkins in the Democratic primary for Manhattan borough president even though she knew that she couldn't win. She did not enter. But if she had, it would have made a much steeper climb for Dinkins.[37] Ultimately, the lie about the Gang of Four undermined solidarity among blacks and between blacks and Latinos and weakened the city's anti-Koch coalition.

As unpleasant as the mayoral race became, Farrell did not drop out. He says that staying in through the primary, again winning his own assembly district, and getting more black votes than any other mayoral candidate was a matter of political survival. "If I dropped out, I would have been out of government," says Farrell, who still represents the Seventy-first District in the New York State Assembly. But Farrell also acknowledges that he had no idea just how difficult the campaign would be when he agreed to run. "In retrospect, it was a silly thing to do. . . . I thought if I gave the community a black candidate, I would get support."[38]

With his political clout intact, Jesse Jackson remained silent during most of the fallout from the fight over Badillo versus Farrell. He returned to the city three times during the Democratic primary campaign season in 1985. In June, he came to New York to endorse Vann for Brooklyn borough president and in the process gave Vann's candidacy a "psychological, financial, operational boost," according to the *Amsterdam News*.[39] Jackson's endorsement increased Vann's support among whites, blacks, and the Latinos who had supported Jackson in 1984.

In late June 1985, Badillo, along with younger Latino leaders such as Nydia Velázquez, the first Latina on the City Council, attended a jam-packed event held at the Ferry Bank Restaurant on Front Street in Brooklyn. A renovated Brooklyn bank located under the Brooklyn Bridge, the Ferry Bank Restaurant had become a space for Brooklyn activists and elected officials to meet and cut deals, hold press conferences, and raise money. In an effort to unite African Americans in Brooklyn behind Vann, Jackson said at a press conference held at the restaurant that "nothing separates us but ship stops" at a few ports between West and Central Africa and the Americas on the Atlantic slave trade. Jackson insisted that with the potential to deliver 21 million votes to a candidate, the world cannot "move without taking you into account."[40] Jackson ended his stump speech with a call for campaign donations and volunteers for Vann's campaign. In August 1985, Jackson returned to the city to participate in a voter-registration drive in the Bronx, Brooklyn, and Harlem that the coalition of black trade union-ists, the Grand Council of Guardians, and Percy Sutton's AM and FM radio stations WLIB/WBLS cosponsored. Jackson conducted a similar rally in the Bedford-Stuyvesant Restoration Plaza in Brooklyn. Farrell, along with Vann, attended the event. Jackson's voter-registration blitz targeted areas with major black and Latino voting potential for his 1988 presidential bid. It was a success: the three rallies added some 5,000 new people to the city's voter-registration rolls and kept him out of the sticky Farrell versus Badillo controversy for most of the campaign.[41] Just days before the September 10 primary, Jackson returned to the city "in support of Farrell," according to an article in the *Amsterdam News*.[42]

However, the damage to the Dump Koch coalition had sufficiently strengthened Koch's chance of winning the primary and thus reelection in a city where registered Democrats outnumbered registered Republicans five to one. The same proved true for the Democratic regulars running for office who supported Koch. Black and Latino elected officials and organizations in the city endorsed Koch, who controlled the city's budget appropriations for their areas. As a result, groups like the Brooklyn-based Caribbeans for Koch supported the mayor and his candidate Howard Golden, the incumbent for Brooklyn borough president. Koch promised patronage to the organization in the form of a new resource center and a commitment to increase Carib-bean culture broadcasting on WNYC, the city-owned public-radio station.

The promise of Koch support and patronage kept Vann from gaining needed endorsements from Representative Edolphus Towns and the three African American and one Latino City Council members from Brooklyn. These black and Latino elected officials refused to risk angering the white-controlled Democratic machine in Brooklyn just to endorse a weak candidate.[43] Vann had a poor showing in the 1985 primary. Golden received 47 percent of the vote; state senator Marty Markowitz, 24 percent; Vann, 21 percent; and former teacher, five-term assemblyman, and Reform Club candidate Joseph Ferris, 7 percent.

Vann did not rebound from the very public blow of Farrell's candidacy. Before that, Vann had been well positioned to become the first non-white Brooklyn borough president. But afterward, some black and more Latino voters left his camp. Thanks to Caribbeans for Koch volunteers who lent their support to Golden's campaign, Kings County's large Caribbean community voted for Golden. Instead of Vann's two white opponents, Golden and Markowitz, splitting the white vote in Brooklyn, they split his black base and, as result, he came in third in the voting.[44]

Progressive Latinos in Brooklyn, upset over the Committee for a Just New York's refusal to endorse Badillo, took their anger out on Vann, the coalition's chairman. Latinos stayed home on election day or voted for Markowitz or Golden. Other more conservative Latino Democrats no doubt followed the lead of the Brooklyn Democratic machines and Latinos for Koch activists and voted for Golden. Vann's poor third-place finish in the primary heralded the decline of his political career (he would never hold citywide or even boroughwide office) and the weakening of Brooklyn as a black power center. The "dominance of the entrenched old-line Harlem leadership" returned, wrote journalist Ron Howell in *City Limits*, and Brooklyn's "black leaders became increasingly parochial in their concerns."[45] Even as the number of black elected officials grew in subsequent years, those same leaders in Brooklyn did not regain their earlier ability to unite voters behind an opposition movement against Democratic regulars in Brooklyn and in citywide elections. Vann's failure to get sufficient coalition support to mobilize voters in the Brooklyn Democratic machine contributed to Koch's defeating the fragmented and weakened coalition that aimed to unseat him.[46]

Koch won the Democratic Party primary for mayor in a landslide, with 64 percent of the vote, including support in most of the black and Latino districts. The incumbent mayor also received more votes than he had in either his first- or second-term primaries. Bellamy came in second, with 18 percent, and Farrell third, with 13 percent. Farrell actually won his own black and Latino districts in Washington Heights, as well as a district in Harlem and in southeastern Queens. Bellamy won the Sixty-ninth District around Columbia University. Dinkins became the new Manhattan borough president by a two-to-one margin. In the Bronx, Serrano lost to Stanley Simon by 3,475 votes. C. Vernon Mason gave Robert M. Morgenthau, the Manhattan district attorney, the closest challenge of his long tenure. But in the end, the incumbent won with 68 percent of the vote. Perhaps most interesting are the turnout numbers. Only 30 percent, or 650,000 out of a possible 2.1 million, of eligible Democrats voted. However, black and Latino turnout proved relatively higher than white turnout but lower than during Jackson's 1984 presidential bid. Overall, Koch received 79 percent of the vote in Staten Island, 71 percent in Queens, 65 percent in Brooklyn, 62 percent in the Bronx, and 54 percent in Manhattan. The predominantly white contingent of the Dump Koch coalition, along with labor leaders, supported Bellamy. The majority of blacks and Latinos supported Koch and a smaller percentage supported Farrell.[47]

Farrell's candidacy suffered for a number of reasons, including his late entry into the 1985 Democratic primary for mayor. Latino voters opposed him because they believed his candidacy was a plot by blacks to keep a Latino from being elected mayor. Second, some journalists, particularly Barrett and Newfield, remained critical of Farrell's candidacy, insisting that it was a plot to help Bellamy win the Democratic primary.[48] "I was killed off within three days of my announcing my running," says Farrell. His opponents outspent him and had larger campaign staff. He went on to say that campaigning in a big city like New York "is very strenuous especially when doing it with like five people helping you," Farrell says. In addition, Farrell received no support from the Brooklyn contingent of the coalition, which had never had solidarity among its delegates. Some key political bosses among them, most importantly Al Vann, did not support Farrell's campaign in Brooklyn.[49]

Dinkins's victory represented the political potential of a united coalition made up of black and Latino elected officials and organized labor. Bill Lynch intentionally reached out to Latino Progressives when staffing the office of the Manhattan borough president under Dinkins. These hires gave Dinkins credibility within their activist networks and Latino communities in Manhattan. The Latino staff in Dinkins's office would go on to work for Dinkins's mayoral campaign in 1989 as part of the Latinos for Dinkins group.

Conversely, Serrano's loss to the Democratic machine in the Bronx worked to strengthen his ties to independent black and Latino elected officials across the city who opposed Koch. After 1985, Serrano's political future depended on supporting Progressives and organized labor, and their black and Latino registration drives to unseat Koch.

After the 1985 election, relationships among black and Latino state representatives in Albany hit a new low. In 1986, just two years after the Badillo–Farrell debacle, five of the eight Puerto Rican legislators resigned from the Black and Puerto Rican Legislative Caucus. Led by Olga Mendez, the secessionist group in 1987 formed the New York State Assembly and Senate Puerto Rican/Hispanic Task Force.[50]

The 1985 election also transformed Badillo's career. While he had never been a true leftist or particularly committed to street-level constituent work, his years of serving in high-level political appointments and elected offices had greatly increased the distance between himself and his supporters. Shirley Gray, a labor leader with DC 37, observed Badillo's political transformation up close. She argues that by the early 1980s, he seemed to know a great deal more about the best French restaurants in Manhattan than the lives of the underemployed Puerto Ricans in the South Bronx who had elected him. Gray was able to see the reaction of Latinos she worked with in the union. The higher Badillo climbed in the Democratic Party, the more he seemed to lose touch with his people. "He sort of switched over to another level of politics," Gray says. "Grassroots politics is important to a person like me, who's in a labor union, because we don't represent the managers and the big money people. So, Herman sort of got out of that dimension."[51] Some even argue that Badillo used his rejection by the Coalition for a Just New York as an excuse to pursue his own political and economic interests. "At one time, he could have been influenced greatly by Progressive folks," says Ramon Jimenez. If they had elected him mayor, they might have had his ear. Instead, Badillo listened to white Democratic powerbrokers and fund-raisers.[52]

Badillo later ran as the Democratic candidate for New York State comptroller. He lost in the general election, his first statewide race, to

Republican Edward Regan. In 1993, Badillo withdrew his support for Din-kins, then the mayor, on the basis that the incumbent had done a poor job managing the city during his first term. He endorsed Dinkins's rival, Rudolph Giuliani, and ultimately ran in the general election for city comp-troller against Alan Hevesi as the candidate on the fusion Republican–Liberal Party ticket, which featured Giuliani as the party's candidate for mayor. That decision to run on the Republican–Liberal ticket gave Badillo the political backing of Republicans, the Liberal Party faithful, and anti-Dinkins Latinos like Ruben Diaz of the Bronx, thus increasing the size of his political base. Running on the coattails of Giuliani also expanded his donor and political base among white voters. Like Giuliani, Badillo campaigned for comptroller on a platform that called for a smaller city government, tougher law enforcement, and higher educational standards. These, however, had little to do with the responsibilities of the city comp-troller. He eventually lost the general election to Alan Hevesi, the Demo-cratic candidate.

After his victory over Dinkins in 1993, mayor-elect Giuliani made Badillo one of his chief advisers on education and appointed him chair of the Board of Trustees of CUNY. In that position, Badillo ended the open-enrollment policy that black and Latino students had fought for in 1968. In the late 1990s, Badillo became a registered member of the Republican Party and ran unsuccessfully in the 2001 Republican primary against former Democrat and businessmen Michael Bloomberg.

When Badillo endorsed Giuliani over Dinkins, many came to view him as a serial candidate who seemed focused on getting elected at any cost, including undermining the emergence of the united black and Latino politi-cal coalition in the city. Like Giuliani and Bloomberg, pragmatism along with political expedience and ambition persuaded Badillo to become a registered Republican.[53] Dinkins still holds that a look at these men's core political views and philosophies provides evidence that they are not "real" Republicans. Rather, he says, Giuliani and Bloomberg are conservative New York Democratic regulars who could not get the support of left-of-center and liberal voters to win a Democratic primary. In 2011, Badillo announced that he was switching back to the Democratic Party. His rationale for doing so is unknown.[54]

JOSÉ SERRANO'S CAMPAIGN IN THE BRONX, 1985

The collapse of the black and Latino coalition around the mayoral race in 1985 often obscures the fact that blacks and Latinos did indeed work together in other city races that year. While unsuccessful, José Serrano's campaign for Bronx borough president against Stanley Simon, the white incumbent, exemplified both the challenges and the opportunities that came from black and Latino political collaborations at this time.

Like most Latino elected officials in the Bronx, Serrano had long been a champion of Ed Koch and supported Democrat Walter Mondale over Jesse Jackson in 1984, despite having a large black constituency in his assembly district. He had dutifully deferred to Koch's lieutenant in the Bronx, the Democratic leader Stanley Friedman, and refrained from publicly criticizing Simon. Indeed, Serrano did not seek the Democratic nomination for Bronx borough president in 1981 because Friedman had asked him to wait. Bronx insiders expected Simon to run for the New York Supreme Court in 1985, so Friedman promised that he and Koch would back Serrano for the Bronx borough presidency. But Simon decided instead to run again for borough president with the endorsement of Koch and Friedman.

This broken promise infuriated Serrano and pushed him to become politically independent. To do so, he needed the support of anti-Koch organizations such as Latinos for Jackson, the Alliance Party, the Coalition for a Just New York, and LUPA. But gaining the support of Latinos for Jackson and the Coalition for a Just New York would be difficult, since Serrano had openly criticized Al Vann as a troublemaker on the New York political scene and had not endorsed Jackson the year before. In addition, Serrano had consistently supported the Democratic machine in the Bronx; the same machine blocked minority-majority political empowerment.[55]

In a 1984 editorial in the *Amsterdam News*, Ramon Jimenez wrote that "political insiders" had told him that Koch and Friedman had tried to get Serrano to run for City Council president on a Koch ticket, which would have given the mayor a Latino running mate and split any coalition of black and Latino voters supporting Koch's opponents. Friedman had long stayed in power as the Democratic Party chair in the increasingly black and Latino Bronx County by dividing black and Latino coalitions. He would convince Latino candidates to run in races where they would face an African

American candidate rather than aim for seats held by whites and Jews. Friedman counted on a bench of Latino regulars to endorse machine candidates
or to run against Latino independents.[56] Once Serrano declined to join the
City Council race, Friedman convinced the East Harlem Democrat Angelo
Del Toro, who was running for City Council president with the backing of
the Coalition for a Just New York, to endorse Simon instead of Serrano—but
in exchange for what? Del Toro and Serrano had a fierce political rivalry,
with each man wanting to be the leading Latino official in the city. Also
joining the Democratic primary in the Bronx was the anti-Koch candidate
Ishmael Betancourt, who attacked Serrano for having been a machine politician and said that he could not be trusted to make real changes.[57]

Julio Pabon, the Bronx Puerto Rican activist, had known Serrano for
fifteen years and served as an unofficial adviser when Serrano was in the
New York State Assembly. When Serrano decided to run for Bronx borough
president, no elected official in the Bronx would support him, including the
South Bronx political boss Ramon Velez, for fear of alienating Friedman
and Simon. So Serrano immediately enlisted the support of Pabon and his
Progressive colleagues in the Bronx. As a campaign volunteer, Pabon helped
register black and Latino voters. He argued that it was time for "a brother"
to be Bronx borough president. He would describe how the white-run
machine had told Serrano to wait in line and then skipped his turn, despite
the fact that a majority of residents in Bronx County were black and Latino.
"When the residents heard that, they got angry and registered to vote in
order to support Serrano in his election against Simon," says Pabon.[58]

From day one, Pabon insisted that black folks would vote for Serrano
if the campaign devised the right strategy. But Serrano's campaign leaders were adamantly against it, telling Pabon to "lay off the black vote and
just concentrate on the Latino vote."[59] They insisted that black folks were
jealous of Latinos and would never vote for Serrano. Pabon responded
that the classic divisions might hold true for middle-class blacks but
argued that the county's poor blacks saw things differently. "If you go to
the projects and get those people who are not registered to vote, and you
get those people who can vote," Pabon said, "they are with us all the time.
Poor black and poor Latinos share the same horrible living conditions and
the same bad schools. They suffer with us in the welfare lines, they suffer just like us." Pabon said that if the campaign reached out and spoke a

common language, they could bring a critical number of blacks on board. But Serrano's campaign advisers disagreed.

After months of internal disagreement, Pabon rebelled against Serrano's campaign chairman and began trying to work the black vote on his own. Pabon employed a strategy he learned as an activist, gangbuster, and recruiter for the unions. It relied on identifying and showing respect to leaders in the neighborhood (not necessarily those holding official offices) in order to win their approval. In practical terms, this meant going to the corner, playground, or parking lot; meeting with local leaders face to face; and explaining what he wanted to do. Pabon would ask to work the turf and would explain how the campaign could benefit the people in the community. Once the leader approved, Pabon could then work in the community without fear. "I didn't learn this in school," he says. "I learned it on the streets here in the Bronx. If you go into a park and want to organize or campaign there, you have to let [the local dealer] know who you are and get their blessing." He had used this strategy as a Puerto Rican union recruiter in predominately black neighborhoods in Harlem and he did the same with the Serrano campaign.

Soon, without the knowledge of the campaign manager, Pabon was taking Serrano with him into the black neighborhoods to walk precincts. "I said, José trust me, we have your back," recalls Pabon. When they first knocked on black folks' doors in the projects, they would get curt responses, such as "What do you want?" But once residents started recognizing Serrano from his television ads, they were both surprised and delighted to meet him. On one occasion, Pabon commandeered a Serrano caravan heading for Latino communities and redirected it into the majority-black Morrisania section of the Bronx. "You should have seen it. People were coming out . . . touching the car [and] wanting to touch him, saying, 'Yo, Serrano, how are you doing,'" Pabon remembers. Serrano himself seemed very flattered and "caught off guard" by the "celebrity treatment" he received in Morrisania.

The effort to mobilize black voters was too little and too late. With only two weeks until the primary, there was not enough time to register sufficient numbers of new African American Serrano supporters. Pabon still maintains that a better strategy for building a coalition between blacks and Latinos could have gotten Serrano elected Bronx borough president. But by the time his campaign advisers correctly understood the class differences among African American voters in the Bronx, the opportunity had passed.[60]

Simon won the election by 3,013 votes out of 113,000 votes cast—a margin of less than 3 percent. Immediately, the Serrano campaign protested, calling for local, state, and federal investigations into voting irregularities and possible discrimination against Latino voters whom poll officials had prevented from voting. The Serrano campaign charged that an unusually large number of voting machines had broken down in Latino districts, and as a result election officials required large number of Latino voters to use paper ballots. Thereafter, election inspectors made mistakes, unintended or otherwise, that invalidated hundreds of those paper ballots. In other instances, English-only poll workers improperly turned away large numbers of Spanish-speaking voters because the workers couldn't communicate in Spanish to obtain the voter's name and address. And finally, recent arrivals from Puerto Rico, where voting laws require voter-registration cards at the polls, did not know that in New York City there was no such requirement. When they tried to clarify voting laws, election inspectors failed to elucidate the voting requirements. Some requested the cards so they could read the person's name and address off of it and turned away those who did not have the card; some poll workers directed Latino voters to incorrect voting locations where poll workers would not let them vote because they were not on their voting rolls.

As a result of these voting irregularities, Serrano insisted that large numbers of Latinos were unfairly prevented from casting votes in the Democratic primary. While Serrano's campaign and supporters suspected foul play, they failed to produce evidence that the Bronx Democratic machine had stolen the election. However, Serrano's complaint forced the U.S. Department of Justice to send 107 observers to New York City to monitor the treatment of Spanish-speaking voters in the November 5, 1985, general election, which Simon easily won.[61]

The loss forced Serrano to break entirely from the party regulars, including Koch, Friedman, and Simon, who controlled Bronx politics. Before the election, Serrano was a Velez-inspired ethnocentric machine politician. After the campaign, the same Democratic regulars who had supported Serrano in the New York State Assembly came out slinging dirt, throwing low punches, and perhaps tampering with votes, leading Serrano to seek independence from all associations with the Bronx machine and Velez. The election proved decisive in driving him farther away from the party. Independence meant he was also marginalized by Puerto Rican political elites throughout the city who still depended on the party machine to endorse and bankroll their reelection campaigns.

To establish a new center of gravity, Serrano began solidifying his relationships with black leaders and in the black community. "Serrano ha[d] always been close with the black leadership," says Paterson.[62] And he'd been "cool" with black folks on the street, according to the former African American district leader Leroy Archibald. "He was one of the first guys that really started hiring blacks [as staffers] when he got elected," remembers Archibald. "He had a couple of them that were chief of staff . . . and Sherrill Olive is still there, and she has been with him since day one."[63] And now, suddenly, Serrano found himself in the unique position of being a Latino official who relied on black leaders to support his political career.

After the 1985 election, Serrano established the South Bronx Independent Club on Melrose Avenue near 150th Street in order to create some distance between himself and Ramon Velez. He also needed a political base from which to lobby decision makers for jobs, funds, and other community services. If Serrano had learned anything from watching Velez for so many years it was that political power comes from an official's ability to serve his constituents and, in turn, his ability to rely on them to mobilize voters at election time. Serrano built his independent club into a vibrant organization and one that would play an important role in Dinkins's campaign for mayor.[64] The 1985 election gave Serrano credibility among Latino Progressives. In addition, over the years he endorsed and curried favor with local black Democratic Party leaders in the Bronx and elected officials, like Dinkins and Vann, who supported his campaign for the U.S. Congress. His maverick political identity and close ties to the black community helped Serrano win a congressional seat in 1990.[65]

DAVID DINKINS TAKES MANHATTAN

In 1985, Manhattan Borough President Andrew Stein decided to run for New York City Council president, thus creating an opening in the race for his seat. When David Dinkins decided to run for Manhattan borough president in the Democratic primary in 1985, he had had a lot of experience to draw from, having already made two unsuccessful attempts in 1977 and 1981. In the 1977 Democratic primary, Stein defeated a less-funded Dinkins, who came in third to Stein and Robert Wagner Jr. In 1981, Dinkins came in second, with 47 percent of the vote, to the incumbent Stein, who outspent Dinkins and had an impressive list of endorsements.[66] Arnaldo "Arnie" Segarra, a friend of Dinkins, remembers when people used to ask him, "What do you do?" Dinkins would joke, "I run for borough president." Now with Stein gone, the fifty-eight-year-old Dinkins ran as an experienced campaigner with a broader base of support than in his previous attempts and a lot more funds. With a larger war chest and strings of endorsements, he ran as a quasi-incumbent against Jerrold Nadler, a thirty-eight-year-old attorney, leader of the Upper West Side Community Free Democratic Club, and maverick independent Democrat who had represented the Sixty-seventh Assembly District in Albany since 1976. Nadler ran a poorly funded campaign that few thought would win; some even questioned if the young, ambitious insurgent had entered the race to gain notoriety for a future election.[67]

How did Dinkins do in Manhattan what Vann and Serrano had failed to do in their campaigns for borough president in Brooklyn and the Bronx, which was to build a multiethnic and united Progressive coalition? And how did he do it when there was so much bad blood from the Denny Farrell versus Herman Badillo ordeal? During the primary, Bill Lynch became the campaign's proxy manager and strategist from his post at DC 1707 after Dinkins's campaign manager, Bill Green, had personal issues that limited his effectiveness. Lynch had supported Badillo and thus he was in good standing with many of the city's Latino leaders. He leveraged those relationships to increase Latino support for Dinkins.

With the exception of Badillo, Latino leaders, particularly in the labor movement, turned out in support of Dinkins's campaign for Manhattan borough president.[68] Dinkins had a reputation as a class act, nice guy, and Progressive who championed what he called the "colorful mosaic that is New York." His city clerk and campaign staff included men and women, Jews and Gentiles, and across-the-board representation from the city's Asian, Caribbean, African American, and Latino communities.[69] The

Puerto Rican activist and political strategist Zoilo Torres recalls that Dinkins "treated others with respect." He "was always walking around with a
multiracial, multiethnic entourage" and "you never saw Dinkins get angry"
in public. Dinkins's cool reputation as an inclusive Progressive kept Latinos
in his electoral coalition.[70]

Similarly, Latinos could relate to Dinkins's stump speech that called for
an end of taxation without representation and the end of minority-majority
representation on the New York City Board of Estimate. Dinkins insisted
that a vote for him would return minority representation to a board, which
for some twenty-four years had had African American Manhattan representation until Percy Sutton left the office of Manhattan borough president in
1977.[71] The Asian American and Latino leaders resonated with this message.

Dinkins's campaign was also aided by the fact that state senator Olga
Mendez chose not to run. She would have likely won many Latino votes
and been a formidable opponent. In fact, Mendez originally stated that she
would run for the open seat in retaliation for the coalition's snubbing of
Badillo, but in the end she agreed instead to co-chair Dinkins's campaign
committee for Manhattan borough president with Basil Paterson.

Dinkins also enlisted the help of Segarra, his old friend from East Harlem. Segarra was well known to elected officials, activists, and political
operatives in both the African American and Latino communities. He had
been a nightclub manager, community organizer, and Harlem-based liaison
to Mayor John Lindsay after the 1968 riot in El Barrio. "Also, I was a pretty
decent basketball player and that put me close to African Americans," says
Segarra. "We shared the gym together, we shared the locker room together,
[and] we shared the housing projects together." So when Dinkins called and
told Segarra that he needed his help to win the borough presidency, Segarra
agreed to help. He chaired the campaign's Hispanic Task Force and became
a critical force in driving Latino votes to Dinkins from El Barrio.[72]

The Latino surrogates Mendez and Segarra helped Dinkins receive
endorsements from the Grand Council of the Hispanic Societies (which
included sixteen public-service organizations) and Yolanda Sanchez of the
Hispanic Women's Political Caucus. In the Bronx, Representative Robert
Garcia and Serrano endorsed Dinkins. Felipe Luciano, the former leader of
the YLO (which included Latinos of various ethnic and national origins)
and a television personality, reporter, and news anchor—did the same.

Jack Aguerros, executive director of El Museo del Barrio in East Harlem, endorsed Dinkins along with Dr. Victor Alicea, president of Boricua College, and Olga Cassis, a member of the New York State Democratic Committee and Woodrow Wilson Democratic Club of Manhattan, which also endorsed Dinkins.[73]

Dinkins also received strong support from Jewish and Asian American community leaders. A number of Progressives endorsed Dinkins, such as the left-of-center Democratic Socialists and the organization's co-chair Michael Harrington, author of the award-winning book *The Other America: Poverty in the United States* (1962). With the help of Bill Lynch, Dinkins had unprecedented support from labor leaders, including Harry Van Arsdale, Victor Gotbaum, Jim Bell, and the Teamsters' Barry Feinstein. The *Amsterdam News* observed, "Dinkins's labor support blanket[ed] the city."[74] Dinkins also won the backing of a range of prominent white politicians, including Carol Bellamy, former mayor Abraham Beame, and Governor Mario Cuomo. Dinkins's campaign benefitted from endorsements from the *Daily News*, the *New York Post*, the *Amsterdam News,* and the *New York Times.*[75]

Dinkins won the primary in a landslide, with 64.9 percent of the votes compared with Nadler's 34.1 percent. With the exception of the Jewish vote, which he split with Nadler, Dinkins overwhelmingly won the city's major ethnic and racial groups, including capturing 95 percent of the black vote.[76] The victory gave minorities in the city representation on the Board of Estimate for the first time in eight years. Moreover, Dinkins's win stood in stark contrast to Vann's and Serrano's defeats, illustrating the different political landscapes that minority candidates had to negotiate in Democratic primaries.

Manhattan had more black and Latino political operatives controlling the county machine and in positions such as district leaders, precinct captains, and political club heads. These operatives helped get voters to the polls on election day. Farrell controlled the county's Democratic Party, and black and Latino political operatives like Charles Rangel, Paterson, Dinkins, Sutton, and state senators Leon Bogues and Mendez had power in the county (figure 6.2). In addition, Dinkins ran for an open seat and did not have to compete against an incumbent; neither Vann nor Serrano had these advantages in Brooklyn or the Bronx. In short, the political landscape of all

FIGURE 6.2 Percy Sutton (Manhattan borough president, 1966–1977); David Dinkins (candidate for Manhattan borough president) and his wife, Joyce; Basil Paterson (Local 1199 attorney, state senator, 1966–1970); and Leon Bogues (state senator, 1980–1985). (Courtesy NYC Municipal Archives)

three boroughs made Dinkins's election far more probable. Organized labor focused its efforts on the Dinkins campaign and identified Manhattan as a more winnable place to elect a Progressive borough president.[77]

On the recommendation of Paterson and Councilwoman Ruth Messinger, Dinkins hired Lynch as a consultant for the transition. Lynch took the borough president–elect to a retreat center on Long Island where they spent three days putting together a transition. Lynch brought together experts and advisers from a broad range of communities, fields, and backgrounds to help set priorities for the new administration. Dinkins's goals incorporated using the power of the borough president's office to improve essential services and provide better education, housing, health care, and job development for those most in need and underrepresented. Dinkins pledged to represent all the people, "Black, Hispanic, Asian, white, women, lesbians, gay men, all religions, young, the old, and the disabled" in every neighborhood in Manhattan. He championed a "government that is concerned about human needs as well as the physical needs of our borough." It was during the transition retreat that Lynch agreed to serve as his executive assistant and chief of staff with the title of deputy borough president. Over the next eight years, the two would become an inseparable team.

One of Lynch's duties was to help staff the president's office as well as recruit people to fill key leadership posts throughout the borough. He had by then internalized the lesson of the Farrell debacle: as a black politician, Dinkins had to have highly skilled and dedicated Latinos in his inner circle, and he had to fully commit to serving their constituency.

Some of Lynch's hirings included thirty-seven-year-old Puerto Rican attorney Sally B. Hernandez-Pinero as one of several deputy borough presidents. Hernandez-Pinero represented the borough president on the New York City Board of Estimate, advocating for "minority employment and community development in the Board's contract decision." She also served as the borough president's representative on the Board of Trustees of the New York City Employees' Retirement System, where she helped implement the first phase of the South African divestiture program.[78] A year later, Lynch hired an openly gay Mexican American attorney, Dennis DeLeon, as deputy borough president with a focus on civil rights and equal opportunity. Both DeLeon and Hernandez-Pinero would go on to play important roles in the Dinkins mayoral campaign, and Hernandez-Pinero served as Dinkins's deputy mayor for finance and economic development from 1990 to 1992.

Lynch also hired Diane Morales, a Puerto Rican community activist and the former New York City Department of Social Services project manager, as the office's director of community services. The staff she hired probably had the greatest impact on the Latinos for Dinkins movement, which mobilized support for Dinkins's 1989 mayoral campaign.

Morales supervised the borough president's office's liaisons to every community board in Manhattan and served as the face of the president's office at the most local level. She hired a dozen other activists and organizers, many of them Latinos, who worked as community liaisons to the president's office. Morales was connected enough to the Latino community to be able to recruit people who had little formal political experience but who had been effectively organizing on the streets for years. Morales remained deeply involved in advancing Latino community empowerment and brought on experts from specific neighborhoods, people who knew their area of the city extremely well and could help connect residents to city services. Mendez later worked as a liaison with Community Boards Eleven and Twelve, which covered El Barrio and the largely Dominican community in Washington Heights. "What I liked about Diane Morales the most was she would listen to us," says the Afro-Dominican activist Zenaida Mendez. "When she hired me, she knew that I knew my community. So when I said, this is what is going on, she would trust me and that gave me a lot of confidence. I knew that she valued my [opinion and] contribution."[79] Morales hired Sandy Trujillo, Victor Quintana, Carmen Martel, and Angel Herman, activists who had spent years organizing residents around tenants' rights issues in Manhattan. "Morales brought on those of us she knew from El Comité that were still activists and committed to a social justice perspective," says Trujillo. "Most of us had never been involved in government, so this was our first entrée." Trujillo, who served as a liaison to the Upper West Side community boards, credits Lynch for taking the risk to hire Morales and then empowering her to fill the liaison posts with activists instead of Democratic Party regulars. In contrast to previous administrations, recalls Trujillo, Dinkins had a set of "real Progressive, left-leaning activists" operating within the president's office at a time when the city's borough presidents had much more autonomy and power than they do today. "We had real authority around issues like land use," Trujillo says. "It was a really good platform for Dinkins, not only in terms of addressing Manhattan issues, but taking on larger citywide issues."[80] Mendez adds, "The communities all knew David Dinkins, and they all knew us. It was still a time when . . . if somebody had a problem, we could call a city agency and take care of that problem." If someone suddenly became homeless, Mendez continues, "we would call the city and definitely find housing for that person or family." Mendez insists that hiring community activists helped Dinkins give "a greater voice to those voiceless in the city" and keep his campaign promises: "We were working on behalf of David Dinkins. And whenever it was important for him to come to the community board, or Bill Lynch, or Diane Morales, I would come with them to the board and say, 'This is my superior who backs what I say,' and people respected that."[81]

"We were conscious that the work that we did had long term implications," says Trujillo. Even before Dinkins announced his candidacy for mayor, the Latinos in the office started mobilizing and organizing meetings in East Harlem that brought politically inexperienced people from the neighborhoods together with Democratic Party regulars. When they did a youth outreach program, Trujillo remembers inviting "young people from all over the city. [We] identified a lot of youth groups that were more progressive, and we wanted young people to get exposed to political activity." When a census count started, "we organized a lot of Latinos around promoting the census" and, in the process of doing so, built a base for Dinkins conducting its work with an "eye toward an eventual campaign" for mayor in 1989.[82]

Meanwhile, a major shakeup was occurring at the headquarters of the hospital and health-care employees' union, Local 1199, where Dennis Rivera was, in his words, an organizer who "didn't have much power or influence in the union" but wanted to reform it.[83] The outcome of the power struggle within 1199 would arguably have as great an impact on Dinkins's mayoral chances in 1989 as would his administration's efforts to build a better relationship with the Latino community.

In 1985, Local 1199 was headed by Doris Turner, who three years earlier had become one of two African American women in the country to lead a major labor union. During her tenure, views of her changed from that of a dynamic, strong, empathetic, and tough but good-humored leader to a corrupt, opulent, and autocratic obstructionist.[84] Lynch went to visit her once to offer his support and guidance regarding an ongoing strike, and he remembers that she kept him waiting outside her office door for three hours. Turner often kept people waiting until she was ready. Lynch recalls getting up and leaving the office, thinking, "I am too grown for this."[85]

A 1993 profile on Rivera in the *New Yorker* argued that from the beginning, Turner had him high on her enemies list while he worked as an organizer under her control. In 1982, he urged old trade union associates in Puerto Rico to join a rival union that Turner wanted to weaken by persuading them to join 1199. When she learned that Rivera had undermined her objectives, she was enraged. Rivera began receiving anonymous death threats. Turner assigned Rivera to organize hospital workers who showed no interest in joining a union, thus isolating him from rank-and-file workers. From December 1983 to May 1984, she even stopped Rivera's salary in order to get him to support her attempt to organize the workers in Puerto Rico, but he remained defiant.[86] In 1983, he began participating in the formation of a multiethnic coalition opposed to Turner's authoritarian leadership and reelection. At the time, 1199 had about 70,000 members. Three-quarters were black and Latino and of those, 80 percent were women. The African American Georgiana Johnson emerged as the opposition slate's candidate for president, and Rivera was one of several candidates for executive vice president. A paper called *Unity & Progress News*, which Rivera produced in collaboration with others, served as the coalition's principal tool for communicating its message.[87] The paper articulated the coalition's platform, which called for "increasing democracy within the union and reducing the power of the president," reported the *New York Times*. Members of 1199 who openly read, distributed, or discussed the contents of *Unity & Progress* paid a heavy price. Turner's supporters threatened and harassed them to the point that some quit the union.[88]

The *Amsterdam News* reported that during the April 1984 union election, Turner secretly called for and supervised the alteration of some 3,000 paper ballots, giving her a 22,187 to 9 win, the largest margin of victory in the history of the union.[89] Dave White, the African American executive vice president of the union, witnessed the election fraud and subsequently filed a sworn affidavit with the U.S. Department of Labor about Turner's wrongdoings. White's affidavit also charged that in July 1984, Turner mismanaged contract negotiations with the directors of the League of Voluntary Hospitals, called a strike against the league without the authority of the union's executive committee as stated in the union's by laws, and wasted $5,000 in union funds on "riotous living" in a hotel with union officials who supported her—all this while rank-and-file members picketed for forty-seven days without receiving strike benefits.[90] Turner ended the strike on August 27, 1984, without negotiating a contract or a 5 percent pay increase, thus deceiving members that she had gained both.

Conditions grew even more tense in February 1985 when some 15,000 Latino members of 1199, most of whom could not read English proficiently, opposed a Turner-led proposal to amend the organization's bylaws to centralize power in the hands of the highest-ranking union officials. Union bylaws and long-standing practices called for printing and distributing copies of important documents in both English and Spanish. This time, however, Turner failed to do so, and Latino union members sued Turner and 1199, charging them with intentionally and willfully discriminating against them, depriving them of their right to participate on an equal basis in union business.[91] Members of the Save Our Union coalition provided voter education on their platform and reported on the history of Turner's indiscretions in *Unity & Progress*. Open and sometimes hostile partisanship among the union's membership plagued the organization from late 1983 to the special elections in April 1986. [92]

Several months before the special elections, Lynch met with Rivera to talk about Save Our Union's strategy. Lynch provided the insurgents with a strategy. In order to win an elected office, the union's bylaws stated that a candidate had to win a majority in every division in the union. "The weakest division [for] Doris was the pharmacy division," recalls Lynch. "So I said, 'You are not going to beat her outright. You just have to stop her from winning all the divisions. So go and put all your energy in the pharmacy division.'"[93]

Rivera and the Save Our Union coalition adopted the strategy. It worked, giving them a 4,800 to 2,100 win over Turner. After several months, federal officials validated the election results and announced that the slate of Progressive labor leaders from the Save Our Union movement had won. Georgiana Johnson was elected president, and Dennis Rivera was elected executive vice president. The other eleven senior posts were divided among three Latinos, five African Americans, and three whites.[94] Rivera urged the forging of coalitions in labor and in politics, and vowed to end the inertia and bitterness that had dogged the union during Turner's tenure as president. By April 1988, Rivera had consolidated the necessary support to win the presidency himself by a margin of nine to one and went on to lead Local 1199 from 1988 to 2007. When he took office, 1199 had 85,000 members, the majority of whom were black and Latino women. By the time he left, it had more than 250,000 members and had become the largest service employees' union in the country. In 1998, he oversaw the merger of 1199 with the Service Employees International Union (SEIU), which greatly increased the size and political strength of the union. Rivera became known as one of the labor movement's best political strategists.[95]

JESSE JACKSON'S PRESIDENTIAL RUN, 1988

In the four years since Jesse Jackson had lost the Democratic presidential nomination to Walter Mondale in 1984, he had been involved in a number of activities, not the least of which was preparing for another run in 1988. He traveled across the country to endorse and campaign as a surrogate for Progressives who had belonged to his Rainbow Coalition in 1984. He also supported unions during labor disputes and promoted minority business opportunities. In preparation for the next presidential primary, Jackson started doing one-minute media spots on important issues of the day on radio stations countrywide and published an autobiography. In terms of his activism, he returned to strategies used during his days as director of PUSH and in 1987 threatened to organize a boycott of Major League Baseball, the National Football League, and the National Basketball Association if league officials did not take steps to hire African Americans in their front offices. He did not limit his activism to domestic issues. He held face-to-face meetings with foreign leaders in Europe, Asia, and Africa and remained active in the anti-nuclear and anti-apartheid movements. All these events were part of a strategy to improve Jackson's foreign policy acumen and his mettle as a Democratic Party presidential candidate in 1988. As a *New York Times* reporter put it, Jackson had become as "omnipresent internationally" as he had been domestically.[96] Jackson vowed to run a more sophisticated, flexible, media-savvy, and well-funded campaign than he had in 1984. Jackson's national campaign chairman, the highly skilled fund-raiser and California Assembly Speaker Willie Brown, organized separate fund-raising events with Bill Cosby, Roberta Flack, Melba Moore, and Aretha Franklin.

Jackson schmoozed with Democrats in elegant spaces that contrasted sharply with his pass-the-hat civil rights fund-raising tactics of 1984, speaking at a $500-a-person luncheons and a $1,000-a-person San Francisco dinner. In just one day, Jackson raised $100,000 as compared with his 1984 campaign, which had raised $300,000 in total. Jackson also sought to strengthen and broaden his coalition, and in March 1988, the Queens-based Asian American Union for Political Action (AAUPA) held a "Jazz for Jackson" fund-raiser at the Dong Restaurant in Sunnyside, Queens. The AAUPA's John Yong, a candidate for a Jackson delegate slot to the Democratic National Convention in Atlanta, insisted that Jackson represented "the only candidate whose platform reflects the concerns of the Asian and all oppressed minorities."[97] A group calling itself the Asian-American Clergy for Jesse Jackson offered its endorsement, stating that Jackson "speaks to the

FIGURE 6.3 Jessie Jackson campaigning in New York City in 1988 and sporting a Local 1199 baseball cap. (Local 1199 Archives; courtesy of Kheel Center for Labor-Management Documentation and Archives, Cornell University, Ithaca, N.Y.)

disenfranchised, the outcast, the most oppressed segments of our society. He's the only presidential candidate who so eloquently articulates our call for human rights here and throughout the world." As he did in 1984, Bill Lynch managed the campaign in New York City. Lynch worked closely with Dennis Rivera, now Local 1199's executive director, and DC 37's executive director Stanley Hill, realizing that Jackson needed the support of organized labor and Latinos to win the New York Democratic primary against the Governor Michael Dukakis of Massachusetts, at this point the frontrunner, and Senator Al Gore of Tennessee.[98]

Thanks in part to the close involvement of Rivera and Hill, labor played a much larger role in Jackson's 1988 campaign than it had in 1984, when it supported Walter Mondale. In 1988, the Jackson campaign used 1199's Midtown offices as its New York City campaign headquarters and had access to 1199's mailing lists, direct-mail production center, and call banks (figure 6.3). That infrastructure made it easy for activists who had little hands-on electoral experience to volunteer for the Jackson campaign, and it provided Jackson with a huge amount of ready-made muscle. New York unions held a fundraising event at the Jacob K. Javits Convention Center in Manhattan and some 4,000 members came to hear Jackson speak. Thirty different unions organized and worked for months to turn out a Jackson vote in New York. As many as 6,000 volunteers from a variety of unions donated thousands of hours to the Jackson campaign, producing mailings, calling voters, canvassing precincts, and handing out campaign materials.[99]

In addition to shoring up union support, Rivera was also a key part of the Jackson campaign's attempt to become more inclusive of Latinos. He was joined in these efforts by Olga Mendez, the state senator who served as the campaign's national adviser for Puerto Rican and Hispanic affairs. Speaking at a press conference held in late January 1988 at Jackson's campaign headquarters, José Serrano said, "We are happy to be here with our candidate for president. He speaks on issues we represent and he is bringing the country together," and he rejects calls for the U.S. military to invade other countries. Robert Garcia stated that Jackson was "the one candidate in our party who has been clearest on the problems facing the poor."[100] Other prominent Latino elected officials joined Garcia and Serrano in supporting Jackson, who was also able to capture the March 21 Puerto Rico primary with 32 percent of the vote to Dukakis's second-place finish with 26 percent of the vote. (However, based on the Democratic Party rules, voting had no bearing on who the island's fifty-six delegates would support at the national Democratic Party convention in Atlanta.)[101]

Jackson also had a very strong showing on Super Tuesday, winning several states, particularly those in the South, and capturing 95 percent of the African American vote.[102] In the wake of Super Tuesday, New York's primary became increasingly important. While other Latino elected officials in New York City endorsed Jackson, Bronx Borough President Fernando Ferrer had held back until the final days of the Democratic primary in New York on April 19. He had planned with Fordham University to have all the Democratic candidates' debate urban policy before he made his formal endorsement. But Jackson's main opponent and the favorite to win the Democratic nomination for president, Michael Dukakis, decided not to participate in the Fordham debate in order to attend a Washington, D.C., fund-raiser for

his campaign. Upon hearing that Dukakis would not show, Ferrer immediately endorsed Jackson. "More than any other candidate, and certainly
more consistent than any other candidate, [Jackson] has brought concerns
of urban America to the very forefront of national presidential debate," said
Ferrer.[103] With Ferrer's endorsement, Jackson secured the support of almost
all Latino elected officials in New York City.

Three days before the primary election, the Jackson campaign received an
endorsement from the Spanish-language newspaper *El Diario–La Prensa*.
The endorsement represented one of the campaign's most significant break-
throughs. The paper called Jackson "the only choice" for Latinos because he
"carries the message . . . about removing the obstacles holding back Latinos
and other disenfranchised people." The paper went on to state that Jackson
represented the best and "brightest hope" for "positive change" for Latinos,
and that only Jackson had "a real agenda" for the empowerment of "Latinos,
blacks, and all minorities. . . . As Latinos, we must seize this moment in history [and] . . . vote for Jesse Jackson."[104]

At the local level, Latino activists in Brooklyn, Harlem, and the Bronx
became the face of the Jackson campaign. Rivera served as their point person and link to the campaign's leadership at 1199 headquarters. If they had
a question, about either the campaign strategy or Jackson's position on an
issue, Rivera was the one who could get an answer.[105] Lynch, who did not
have Rivera's help in 1984, ran a very organized campaign in Latino neighborhoods. Fifty sound trucks were commissioned to roll through, blasting
Jackson's campaign message to an Afro-Cuban beat. They had Jackson himself on the streets, talking about low-income housing, job opportunities,
and drug abuse. The campaign widely distributed a bilingual copy of the
campaign's message in Latino communities through door-to-door outreach
and direct mailings.[106]

Dukakis spoke fluent Spanish, but the Puerto Rican political strategist
and pollster Angelo Falcon argued that his stump speech could best be
described as "boring in any language." In contrast, Jackson was a charismatic speaker who connected with his audience and had far greater visibil-
ity at the street level, which gave him increased ability to identify with and
win over New York City voters.

A majority of Jewish voters refused to support Jackson because of the accusations of anti-Semitism that hounded him. Similarly, Ed Koch had alienated

large numbers of black and Latino voters. In the mid-1980s, New York City could best be described as a city full of racial conflict about to explode.

In the end, though, Jackson narrowly beat Dukakis in New York City, 45.2 percent to 44.8 percent, but Dukakis carried the state. And although he did not win the Democratic nomination, Jackson made a very credible showing. Nationally, Jackson came in second, winning nine states and the District of Columbia. Jackson's candidacy in 1988 forever altered the American political landscape, and it had particularly important implications for politics in New York City.

In New York City and elsewhere, every campaign comes down to who can turn out the vote. This was part of Lynch's genius, recalled Zoilo Torres, the leader of the National Congress for Puerto Rican Rights. Lynch recognized that grassroots activists, tenant organizers, and union leaders were the people who could get people to the polls on election day—not the Democratic Party hacks and certainly not elected officials. Lynch put the right people in place to strategically distribute campaign resources and mobilize at the street level. "If anybody knows grassroots organizing," Torres says, "it's Bill Lynch."[107] On election day, Lynch, working closely with Rivera and Hill, mobilized eight hundred people from different unions who took the day off to help get Jackson voters to the polls.[108] The political scientists Asther Arian, Arthur S. Goldberg, John H. Mollenkopf, and Edward T. Rogowksy argue that Jackson's campaign united "black and Latino elected officials [who] had been highly fragmented and competitive with one another" since the 1985 Democratic primary for mayor. They maintain that Jackson's 1988 campaign "brought virtually all [black and Latinos elected officials] together, even bridging over the division between those blacks and Latinos identified with the county party organizations and the insurgents who had been challenging them."[109]

Nonetheless, the Jackson campaign did not heal the rifts between black and Latino officials, nor did it force these officials to put aside petty concerns for the larger good. In pragmatic terms, black and Latino officials needed each other for the purpose of mobilizing voters and defeating their political opponents. Support for Jackson served as the political reality for elected Latino officials up for reelection in districts that overwhelmingly voted for Jackson in 1984. They also needed the help of organized labor, which supported Jackson.[110] But in fact—and in private—black and Latino elected officials continued to distrust each other. Few elected Latino officials with the exception of Mendez, Angelo Del Toro, and Rivera actively campaigned for Jackson.[111]

Even if the Jackson campaign should not get credit for healing all wounds, it certainly does deserve credit for altering the status quo in New York City in a way that set the stage for future coalition building. Jackson's troops registered huge numbers of black and Latino voters, and brought them into the political process. His achievement demonstrated that a minority candidate could have citywide success and potentially defeat Mayor Koch in the upcoming 1989 Democratic primary. But most important, the Jackson campaign built a vibrant political infrastructure, which brought together the resources of diverse Progressive institutions and united black and Latino trade unionists, activists, and community organizers.[112]

It was that political infrastructure that benefited David Dinkins when he ran for mayor in 1989. Dinkins used the same campaign managers and many of the same staff members who had run the Jackson campaign. Lynch, Rivera, and Hill ran the Dinkins campaign in an almost identical fashion, leveraging their ties to the labor movement, local political clubs, and leftist organizations to build commitment and enthusiasm on a grassroots level. "Through a conscious and continued fostering and development of the coalition that had formed during the Jackson campaign the previous year, Dinkins was able to mold relations between blacks, Latinos, Asians, and trade union leaders, and white reform clubs to put forth a strong alliance," writes political scientist Shelly L. Anderson.[113] "A critical part of Dinkins's electoral success, in fact, seemed to lie with his ability to take advantage of the bonds created between blacks and Puerto Ricans during the Jackson campaign." If anyone deserves credit for building the minority coalition that finally led to the defeat of Koch and the election New York City's first black mayor, "that would be Jesse," says Basil Paterson.[114]

7

LATINOS FOR DINKINS

THE COALITION'S COMPLICATED VICTORY, 1989

E D KOCH WAS ELECTED mayor of New York City in 1977. By 1981, despite a
recession that resulted in city government budget shortages and cuts to
city services, Koch had become the most popular New York City mayor
since Fiorello LaGuardia in large part by cajoling and leveraging members
of the New York media corps. By 1981, Koch had become a vulnerable candidate due to corruption and scandal allegations, voter fatigue, and racial
tensions sparked by his divisive statements about blacks and Latinos made
during public appearances.

He held on to power for twelve years in part by convincing the public
that he was a reformer who made decisions and appointments based on
merit instead of political deals, favors, and patronage as his predecessors
had done. He remained popular among conservatives, white ethnics, and
business leaders for openly criticizing labor leaders, members of the Board
of Estimate, the state legislature, and black and Latino leaders. At the same
time, Koch appointed more black and Latinos to high positions in city government than had his predecessors.

New Yorkers expressed a love–hate relationship with his combative,
outspoken personality, but they also admired his love of the city, his work
ethic, and his reputation as a regular New Yorker who didn't put on airs.
Koch lived in Gracie Mansion, the official mayoral residence, during the
week, but he spent the weekends in his rent-controlled Manhattan apartment. He made public his love of Chinese takeout and inexpensive wine.[1]
But dissatisfaction with Koch's rule had been brewing on the left side of
the Democratic Party for years, and Progressives received an enormous

boost in organizational power and morale from the success of the Jesse Jackson presidential campaign in 1988. By 1989, many middle-of-the-road Democrats had grown weary of the drama and bluster that seemed integral to Koch's performance as mayor. This combination of factors gave new hope to left-leaning Democrats whom Koch could potentially fell in the 1989 mayoral election.

Thus Manhattan Borough President David Dinkins's 1988 mayoral campaign grew out of the rich protest tradition in New York City's black, Latino, and labor communities. Over the decades, black and Latino activists, students, and unionists jointly protested discrimination in the trades, federal and city budget cuts, and U.S. foreign policy. These groups constituted a majority of Jackson's Rainbow Coalition in the 1984 and 1988 Democratic presidential primaries in New York City, as well as a majority of Dinkins's supporters in his 1985 run for Manhattan borough president. Jackson's campaigns, especially in 1988, sparked the minority-rights movement in New York City that subsequently elected Dinkins as the city's first black mayor.

Most observers agree that Dinkins was not a charismatic leader or speaker on the order of Dr. Martin Luther King Jr. or Jesse Jackson. Yet he was the one who was finally able to unite the disparate Dump Koch forces and build a successful political movement. Coming out of the primary election, Dinkins had an enormous advantage against any Republican opponent in a city where registered Democrats outnumbered registered Republicans 5 to 1. And yet, the contest between Dinkins and the Republican nominee, Rudolph Giuliani, could not have been closer. During the months'-long race, voter tide shifted from a predicted Dinkins blowout to a photo finish, due in part to Giuliani's success at using what Dinkins had coined, New York's "gorgeous [ethnic] mosaic" of support against him.[2]

Dinkins's coalition was made up of black and Latino supporters who hoped that a black mayor would politically empower minorities citywide. Giuliani cleverly used Dinkins's supporters against him by using their images to stoke the fears of white, wealthy, and Jewish voters who were already anxious about the rise of street crime and the drug trade. Dinkins managed to eke out a victory in 1989, but he was left with what proved to be an insurmountable challenge: that of fulfilling his campaign promises to blacks and Latinos without alienating white voters.

WHY DINKINS?

David Norman Dinkins was born in 1927 in Trenton, New Jersey. The son of a barber and a manicurist, who later divorced, he spent his childhood between Trenton and Harlem. After high school, in 1944 he joined the Marine Corps and two years later attended Howard University on the GI Bill. After graduation, he returned to Harlem, where he married Joyce Burrows, a Howard sociology major, classmate, and Harlem native. Her father had been a noted black politician and businessman with close ties to the Harlem political boss J. Raymond "Fox" Jones, the leader of the George Washington Carver Democratic Club. Dinkins, through his father-in-law, became associated with Jones and his political club. Jones took a liking to the young Dinkins and helped launch his political career, first noticed as a district leader in Harlem for many years. In 1956, he graduated from Brooklyn Law School and practiced law in Harlem before his election to the New York State Assembly in 1965. In 1972, he ran successfully to become president of the New York City Board of Elections, making him the first African American to hold the office. Dinkins remained in the post until 1973 when Jones facilitated an appointment for Dinkins to serve as one of Abraham Beame's deputy mayors (figure 7.1). However, his lapse in paying all his taxes between 1969 and 1972 proved problematic, forcing Dinkins to withdraw his name from consideration for the post.[3] He next ran for New York City Clerk, holding that office from 1975 until his election as Manhattan borough president in 1985.[4]

Dinkins's finances continued to dog him; he received far more scrutiny about his personal finances. Between 1989 and 1993, the media turned back to Dinkins's tax problems as justification for regularly questioning his handling of city finances.[5] But it wasn't only his finances that were held up to the light. With help from the Rudolph Giuliani campaign, the media also raised questions about Dinkins's views of New York's Jewish community, accusing him of anti-Semitism due to his association with Jesse Jackson and the Brooklyn activist Sonny Carson.[6]

By temperament and training, Dinkins was and still is a pleaser. He doesn't take unnecessary risks but seeks common ground and consensus when possible. On a person-to-person level, he is friendly and open. In some sense, his political career was founded on his reputation for being a

FIGURE 7.1 David Dinkins, Abraham Beame (mayor, 1974–1977), and Charles Rangel (*far right*). (Courtesy NYC Municipal Archives)

"nice guy." While many politicians in his cohort were marginalized or dismissed as strident black militants, Dinkins never gained that reputation. No matter the audience, Dinkins's approach was to ingratiate himself and build friendly relations.

The accepted storyline is that as soon as he won the Manhattan borough presidency in 1985, Dinkins became the Dump Koch coalition's presumed Democratic nominee.[7] But the story is more complex. Dinkins was indeed a uniquely popular and well-known elected official among the city's black and Latino voters.[8] He bridged the divide between the black power centers in Harlem and Brooklyn better than most. Al Vann and other Brooklyn-based Dump Koch leaders found him to be an acceptable member of the Harlem political elite. His nice-guy personality and political style set him apart from Koch and other possible challengers.[9] And, according to author Chris McNickle, a former New York City government official, Dinkins's long history as a moderate Democrat meant he had the most crossover appeal to both white and black voters than any other black candidate. Koch would not be able to portray Dinkins as being a "militant" the way he labeled Jackson.[10]

Although these points contributed to Dinkins's ultimate victory, he was not the automatic selection to lead the Dump Koch forces. As they had in 1985, Progressive elites first turned to the former New York secretary of state Basil Paterson. Right after Jackson won the most votes in New York City during the New York Democratic presidential primary in 1988, the leaders of the major non-uniformed municipal unions invited Paterson to dinner. The group included Stanley Hill, executive director of DC 37 of the American Federation of State, County, and Municipal Employees (AFSCME); Victor Gotbaum, president of DC 37; Dennis Rivera, president of Local 1199; Barry Feinstein, president of Local 237 of the International Brotherhood of Teamsters; and several others. Those at the table agreed that Jackson's victory proved that an African American candidate could carry the city and defeat Koch in the upcoming Democratic primary for mayor. Paterson recalls the group around the table, saying, "'Basil, we know you're playing basketball again. We know you are in good enough health to run [for mayor]. We want you to run and we will back you.' My response was, 'The bug is gone.' I no longer had the interest. I also thought . . . the guy you need to induce to run is David Dinkins."[11]

In contrast to Ed Koch or Jesse Jackson, both of whom could be abrasive, Dinkins was affable, pleasant. Zoilo Torres, who would serve as a Dinkins's aide during the campaign, recalls, "You never saw Dinkins get angry." He had a reputation for treating people "with respect, and he always walked around with a multiethnic entourage."[12] According to Jamie Estades, who worked as a Latinos for Dinkins campaign organizer in East Harlem, Dinkins was known in leftist black and Latino circles as a rare politician "who reached out to other groups, regardless of race."[13] With this reputation, Dinkins seemed the perfect antidote for the toxicity that had built up in the city over the course of Koch's twelve years in office. Koch had "picked fights with so many groups" that voters had grown "emotionally exhausted," says Rivera.[14] Paterson agrees, saying, "Ed Koch makes a lot of noise, but Dinkins is who everybody likes."

Interestingly, it was not easy for the Progressive coalition to convince Dinkins to run. He had a relatively safe position as Manhattan borough president and likely could have held the post until he retired from public office. Paterson remembers, "Dinkins was rational. He wondered, 'Why should I run for mayor? The odds are against me winning, and I can remain borough president for as long as I want.' It took a lot of convincing."[15] Rivera and Bill Lynch, who had run Jackson's successful campaign the year before, insisted that a Dinkins candidacy would leverage the support of the It's Our Time movement that Jackson had started.[16] Without Dinkins's knowledge, Lynch hired a pollster from the borough president's office to test the viability of a Dinkins mayoral run. The poll showed that Dinkins had the support necessary to win. Sometime between Jackson's 1988 primary victory in New York City and Paterson's decision not to run, Lynch, Rivera, Gotbaum, Feinstein, and the singer and social activist Harry Belafonte went to Dinkins's house in Washington Heights in Manhattan. They showed Dinkins the poll results and argued that the time was right for a run.[17] According to Dinkins: "It was labor that in many ways caused me to run for mayor. Keep in mind, I had run three times for borough president. Finally, I succeeded. I'm perfectly happy being borough president. It's a significant, important position. If I run for mayor and lose, I have zero. I have nothing. It wasn't like I woke up one morning and said I want to be mayor. It didn't happen that way. I don't want this to sound like I was drafted, but I was persuaded by a lot of people."[18]

"We went back and forth," says Lynch about that meeting at Dinkins's house. According to Lynch, "Dinkins said, 'I don't have any money.' So I said, 'If we raise a million dollars, would you run for mayor?' Dinkins said, 'Yes.'" Lynch and the labor leaders organized a fund-raiser at Tavern on the Green, the famous restaurant in Central Park. With support from the labor movement and wealthy left-leaning whites, they met Dinkins' fundraising goal.[19]

In Lynch's mind, Dinkins was the right candidate at the right time. "I think it would have been hard to do somebody else," Lynch says. "While he was borough president, he had huge crossover appeal." Dinkins had a solid base of support in the black community due to his long record of public service and track record for breaking the color barrier as he climbed the ladder. He also had a degree of white support unparalleled by any other major black official in the city. Dinkins had come to know a lot of potential liberal white donors through his involvement with tennis and the U.S. Open. Dinkins had played tennis for years but became a true fanatic after reading a memoir by Arthur Ashe. Lynch argues that this involvement with tennis gave Dinkins a connection to people with "deep pockets" who helped fund and support the campaign.[20] Dinkins was also able to form strong ties with some Jewish leaders and Progressive Hasidic Jews who had grown tired of Koch. Dinkins had also built a base of support in the Latino community that was unusual among black politicians. Zenaida Mendez worked in the Manhattan borough president's office and recalls watching Dinkins serve on the city's Board of Estimate, which oversaw budgeting and land use, and listen to citizens' concerns and complaints for hours at a time. Dinkins "was someone who could represent us all."[21] Despite historic and deeply ingrained racism within the Dominican community, Mendez and her fellow Dominican Giovanni Puello said that Dinkins's race was an asset, not a liability, within their community.[22] Mendez and Puello viewed African Americans and other Latinos as their "natural allies." While the struggle for control of school districts and community boards in Harlem caused local conflict between Dominicans and African Americans, these groups recognized that supporting Koch on a citywide level would do little for "us working-class people."[23] Dominicans identified with Dinkins as a black man from a working-class background and found his rags-to-riches story inspiring. "I mean, Dinkins was black, he came from a poor community, he made it through college, he became an attorney, he was a success," says Puello. "This guy had so many personal accomplishments. He was black, and he was one of our own."[24]

ORGANIZING LATINOS FOR DINKINS

The first meetings of what would later become Latinos for Dinkins were organized by a group of Latino women who worked in the Manhattan borough president's office. This group of Latinas included Zenaida Mendez, a Dominican, as well as Carmen Martel, Carmen Rivera, and Diana Morales, all Puerto Ricans. They sent out personal invitations to activists in the city's dozen largest Latino communities and to old friends from El Comité, the PSP, the former YLO, the NCPRR, and the NYCSV.[25]

"Women [particularly Sandy Trujillo, Mendez, and Awilda Rodriguez] played a major role" in building the Latino movement, says Dinkins's close friend Arnaldo "Arnie" Segarra. This group of Puerto Rican and Dominican women had been deeply involved in the leftist Latino organizations of the 1970s and had risen over the years to leadership positions. "We were not shy," says Trujillo who had been a member of the NYCSV. "We elbowed in as much as anybody else. The men were strong and outspoken, but I don't think any of us were inhibited."

The earliest unofficial meetings of Latinos for Dinkins took place at Willie Nieves's nightclub, El Canario, in East Harlem, the same place where the NYSSV got its start in the early 1980s. The experience of working within NCPRR and the Vieques movement "better prepared us to" work on the Dinkins campaign in 1989, says Trujillo. She became the activist coordinator for Latinos for Dinkins and helped chair many of the early meetings. Latinos for Dinkins became an official arm of the campaign under Dennis Rivera in April 1989, seven months before the election.[26]

As with the Jesse Jackson campaign, Rivera's support proved critical in the mayoral race (figure 7.2). By 1989, Local 1199 had 125,000 members and was able to provide troops, resources, and campaign personnel. As he had done on the Jackson campaign, Rivera worked as Lynch's right-hand man. Lynch and Rivera ran Latinos for Dinkins out of 1199's offices, and Dinkins's

FIGURE 7.2 David Dinkins, speaking at a gathering of members of Local 1199, with Dennis Rivera and Basil Patterson on the dais to his left. (Local 1199 Archives; courtesy of Kheel Center for Labor-Management Documentation and Archives, Cornell University, Ithaca, N.Y.)

headquarters were based next door in a building owned by 1199 and rented by the campaign.[27] "There was a very close relationship between both of them," remembers Jaime Estades, who ran Latinos for Dinkins in East Harlem. Lynch and Rivera consulted with each other constantly, Estades recalls: "Lynch depended a lot on Dennis because of all the resources that he brought, and Dennis depended on Lynch in order to have access to the candidate that he needed. It was a good marriage." Estades says that 1199's assistance not only made the difference in the election but also "changed the role of unions in campaigns forever. [Local] 1199 was all over the place. The resources, the army, the money—no other union in the history of the city did what 1199 did under Dennis Rivera." In terms of Rivera's political strategy and electoral force, "Everybody is trying to catch up to him on that."[28]

Other unions did play an important part in the Dinkins movement, though. Lynch recalls having to use "subway diplomacy," riding the subway throughout New York City to meet with various labor leaders and keep them informed, engaged, and on board. He would talk with them individually about campaign strategy, polls, and support. "I would never bring them together," Lynch says, because too many egos in one room tended to lead to power struggles.

One of the first activists Lynch hired to work for the campaign full time was Zoila Torres, who both Lynch and Rivera knew through the labor movement and the NYCSV. "I joined the Dinkins campaign because I understood it to be an historic campaign," says Torres. He had been following the electoral scene since Harold Washington's victory in Chicago and saw Dinkins as part of that "same historic process." Immediately after Torres joined the campaign, he began trying to create a compelling narrative for Latino voters to counter the negative and false messages coming out of some quarters, including the largest Spanish-language newspaper, *El Diario*, about Dinkins's role in the Gang of Four and alleged sabotage of Herman Badillo. Torres recalls that during early planning meetings of Latinos for Dinkins, a discussion began about the "need to recognize the strategic importance of a black and Latino alliance in New York City. There were very few districts in New York City that we [as Latinos] could win alone. And the [people] talking against that were the older sector in the Latino community, like the Herman Badillos. They were saying, 'We don't need the blacks for anything. Every time we get into a coalition with them, we lose.'"[29] Segarra says they tried to get Badillo to join Latinos for Dinkins, "but he just refused. He was so upset over being turned down [in 1985] . . . saying that the African American leadership had abandoned him."[30]

To overcome the narrative that Latinos could never trust a black mayor, Torres developed a message of political empowerment. The campaign "was more than just getting Dinkins elected," explains Torres. "It was setting up a political machine in the city that Latinos could use to elect other Latino officials, particularly from their communities and from their districts." Torres came up with the idea of creating political action committees in Latino-heavy districts: "I had been doing [activist work] at the time for almost twenty-five years. It came from the idea that in order to have real empowerment it had to be grassroots and it had to be geographically based. We looked at the assembly districts with the highest rates of Latino votes and that's where we targeted to set up these committees. . . . The political committees would run candidates afterwards and also hold candidates accountable, do voter registration, voter education." Lynch, Rivera, and Dinkins were on board with this strategy, says Segarra. "African Americans had gone through this themselves," so they understood the importance for Latinos of controlling their own destiny.[31] "When they brought us in, they knew that's what we were about," says former PSP member José Candelario. He argues that African Americans had no choice but to accept Latino involvement on these terms because the rest of the traditional Democratic Party had rejected them.

Torres discussed the formation of the political action committees and public messaging with Williamsburg tenant rights' activist David Santiago. From 1981 until 1986 Santiago's organization, the SSPC, had been involved in a number of electoral campaigns in coalition with African American activists. Santiago worked with Latinos for Jackson in 1984 and 1988 and got the SSPC to support Al Sharpton's campaign for the U.S. Senate in 1988. During the Jackson and Sharpton campaigns, the SSPC became closely aligned with Sonny Carson, a black nationalist and the former director of CORE in Brooklyn. He was a powerful figure in Bed-Stuy and Bushwick in central Brooklyn, and ultimately played an important role in turning out black voters for Dinkins.[32] José Rivera and José Serrano rounded out the initial planning group of Latinos for Dinkins. These organizations helped fulfill Lynch's strategy to build on the network of union members and Latinos who had supported Jackson in 1984 and 1988.[33] A key part of that work also focused on incorporating the leftist Latinos who had remained outside electoral politics during Jackson's campaigns, but who were connected to members of Dinkins's staff in Manhattan. Their jobs in the Dinkins administration had been their entry into Democratic Party politics, and these activists became crucial to the success of Latinos for Dinkins. They leveraged their old activist networks to mobilize voters and bring new people into the electoral process.

By 1988, Lynch understood the New York City political landscape better than most political strategists. This knowledge informed every aspect of the campaign organization and strategy he devised. For example, Lynch organized a voter-registration campaign before the official campaign even began. It "united a lot of people and brought a lot of people who never talked about politics, especially in the Latino community, to start talking about politics," Lynch says.[34] He understood that in a Democratic city like New York, the campaign would depend on grassroots African American and Latino activists to win over their communities because the Democratic machine and overwhelming majority of elected Democrats either supported Mayor Koch or believed that Dinkins had no chance of defeating him in the primary. Lynch's concept was to attach the Dinkins campaign symbolically to the "train" that had already sped through Cleveland, Los Angeles, Chicago, and Philadelphia, driving one black candidate after another to City Hall.[35]

As mentioned, in the spring of 1989 Lynch and Rivera officially incorporated Latinos for Dinkins into the campaign organization and created space for it to operate out of 1199's headquarters. Lynch named Sandy Trujillo as the full-time coordinator of Latinos for Dinkins. She partnered with Awilda Rodriguez, who had served as Rivera's communications chief and confidante. After the group moved into 1199, Rivera attended many of the meetings, but he did not get involved in the day-to-day of the organization. Trujillo says, "We were having conversations about what was our platform [and] what did we want to see this administration do for Latinos. That conversation was happening parallel to the [campaign's] strategy planning across the city."

Next, the group talked in detail about how to implement a Latino empowerment initiative across the city. "We found that there were about twelve community districts where the bulk of the Latino votes resided," says Torres. "There were six or seven in the Bronx, three in Manhattan, three districts in Brooklyn, . . . a number of districts in Queens, and very little in Staten Island. We determined how many votes were needed from the Latino community for Dinkins to win the primary." Torres goes on to say, "We determined that he had to get at least 45 percent of the [Latino] vote to be able to get elected, along with 80 percent of the African American vote and at least about 35 percent of the white vote, mainly Jewish white Progressive."[36] They began to search for activists in each of those targeted twelve districts willing to support Latinos for Dinkins. "For a lot of them, it was the first time that they had been involved in citywide politics, much less Democratic Party politics," says Trujillo. "But they were [well known] in their communities for activism they did do on housing and youth services."

Latinos for Dinkins in Brooklyn

Another key Bill Lynch appointment was the political strategist and Brooklyn native Dr. John Flateau as the campaign's Brooklyn field director. José Candelario credits Flateau with doing "more for electing black officials in Brooklyn than anybody else." Flateau's most critical role during the 1989 campaign was to coordinate and mobilize elected officials in Brooklyn. In an effort to build the Latinos for Dinkins operation in Brooklyn, Zoilo Torres and Flateau ultimately selected Candelario, who had run several local political campaigns prior to 1989. In contrast to the Latinos for Dinkins operations in other boroughs, in Brooklyn it had been firmly established on a long history of PSP and SSPC grassroots mobilizing initiatives. The SSPC and independent black democrats in Brooklyn had been engaged in electoral politics earlier and therefore had more experience running campaigns than activist in East Harlem and the Bronx.

Candelario ran the Brooklyn field operations of Latinos for Dinkins out of a theater on the corner of South First Street and Bedford Avenue in Williamsburg. The theater owner, Chris Veneer, was part of the first wave of young artists and intellectuals to move into Williamsburg at the start of the neighborhood's gentrification process in the late 1980s. Veneer's involvements started when he called the Dinkins campaign office to find out how he could help. Santiago and Candelario visited Veneer at the theater. "The minute we saw it, we said, 'You want to help? We need this place for the campaign in the evenings,'" recalls Candelario. "He said, 'Okay,' and gave us his place and his food." The theater became headquarters for Latinos for Dinkins in Brooklyn.[37]

But Latinos for Dinkins in Brooklyn faced serious obstacles from Latinos for Koch supporters such as Vito J. Lopez and Victor L. Robles of Brooklyn, elected officials all. Their organizations, patronage power, and money sought to undermine the campaign activities of the Brooklyn Latinos for Dinkins office. Early in the campaign, Lopez and Robles convinced many Latino voters that Dinkins could not beat the Koch machine.[38] In addition, as a white candidate, Koch was able to stay one step removed from the vicious feuds between African Americans, Latinos, and Hasidic Jews in Williamsburg. But most important, Dinkins was negatively received by some members of the Latino community on purely racial grounds. Spanish-language newspapers published stories about how African American politicians, including Dinkins, had betrayed Herman Badillo in the 1985 mayoral election. Editorials argued that Latinos would be foolish to support Dinkins for mayor. Candelario remembers that when he first hit the streets in Williamsburg, he ran into a Puerto Rican resident who said that if Candelario asked him to support a "nigger," he would spit in Candelario's face. "I could not believe it," remembers Candelario. "I had never heard that kind of racism before . . . in our neighborhood."[39] In some parts of Brooklyn, racial antagonism and political competition led to fist fights between Latino Koch and Dinkins supporters. Campaign workers would even tear down each other's posters and flyers.[40]

Two factors explain this level of opposition to Dinkins's candidacy among Latinos. First, the 1985 incident with Badillo was still a fresh wound to some in the Latino community, who still incorrectly blamed Dinkins. Second, Latin American and Caribbean immigrants arrived in Williamsburg and other parts of New York City with an ethnocentrism formed by Iberian domination of their native countries. Colonialism's paradoxical result was that Latin Americans treated white people with respect and treated non-whites, particularly dark-skinned, non-Spanish-speaking people, with distrust and even disdain. While this ethnocentrism tended to change and soften after living in New York, the regular arrival of new immigrants from

Latin America and the Spanish-speaking Caribbean ensured its survival and retention.[41] Cubans tended not to be bilingual, nor did they feel any kind of racial solidarity with African Americans. Many Cubans operated within the confines of culturally isolated Latino diasporas and, other than their family, interacted primarily with entrepreneurs of their same nationality who operated local bodegas, theaters, and barbershops.[42]

In these tight-knit diasporic communities, Dinkins's campaign workers and volunteers encountered resistance to the idea of voting for an African American candidate. Candelario invested significant time and campaign resources in trying to improve Latino voters' view of Dinkins in Brooklyn. First, he turned to his network of "socially committed progressive Latino activists" who focused on mobilizing Latinos located throughout that borough.[43] Dinkins volunteers would gather up stacks of campaign literature and hit the streets, knocking on doors and handing out materials. Campaign workers also tried to create some cultural bonds by associating Dinkins with important Latino practices such as playing dominoes, listening and dancing to salsa music, and enjoying food from the Spanish-speaking Caribbean.

So the campaign had Dinkins walk the streets to meet people and form connections to the dominoes subculture in Brooklyn. Photo ops turned into campaign posters as Latinos looking at the posters saw someone who, like them, enjoyed dominoes. The campaign used a similar strategy with salsa music. Rivera commissioned Manuel Oquendo y Orchestra Libre, a popular salsa band, to compose a campaign jingle in Spanish. Andy Gonzalez, the band's musical director, wrote the music and remembers the lyrics: "Para alcade de Nuevo York David Dinkins is el major, Para alcade de Nuevo York David Dinkins is el major" (For mayor of New York, David Dinkins is the best). The song talked about corruption in the city and the need for a change in leadership. "There were a lot of homeless in those days [and one of the verses talked about] better housing and working conditions" for the city's Latino residents," says Gonzalez. "I remember that we knocked out that jingle in one day, and just a day later they started running it on sound trucks all over the Latino neighborhoods." It had a salsa rhythm that "was very danceable," says Gonzalez, a "swinging jingle" that contributed to mobilizing Latinos voters for Dinkins in Brooklyn and other parts of the city.[44]

PUERTO RICAN TAMALES (PASTELES)

Latinos for Dinkins in Brooklyn used Puerto Rican food to attract supporters to its events. The smell of the food and the sound of the music drew interest, and when people stopped to investigate, they would see David Dinkins. The campaign wanted to associate Dinkins as much as possible with the music of El Gran Combo and Ismael Rivera, plates of rice and tamales, roasted pig, and cups flowing with wine and beer.*

All food items in these recipes can be found at a Latino bodega or market.

* * *

1 lb ham steak or vegan substitute, diced

1 green pepper, diced

6 garlic cloves, diced

1 large yellow onion, finely chopped

1 small jar green olives

½ small jar capers

1 bunch cilantro, finely chopped

1 small piece salt pork (*tocino*) or vegan substitute, chopped

Sofrito

1 6-oz can tomato paste

10 sweet green peppers (*ajicitos dulces*), diced

6 lbs pork or vegan substitute, chopped

Salt and pepper to taste

4 cups vegetable broth

MASA

3 lbs *yautía blanca* (tuber)

2 lbs *guineos verde* (green bananas)

5 green plantains

1 tbsp salt

Achiote or achiotina

Small piece of pumpkin

* * *

(continued)

25–30 banana leaves, cut into squares

Wax paper and strings to wrap the *pasteles*

Brown the ham and add the green pepper, garlic, onion, olives, capers, and cilantro. In a separate 6–8-quart pot, brown the salt pork, then combine all the ingredients with the sofrito followed by water and the tomato paste. Stir and cook until the liquid cooks off and the mixture thickens.

In a large bowl, peel the *yautía*, the *guineos*, and the green plantains. You can grate them or use a food processor. Stir in the salt and enough achiotina to dampen the dough and give it some color. Set aside.

WRAPPING THE *PASTELES*

Prepare the banana leaves by spreading a bit of achiotina to help avoid the masa sticking to the leaves after cooking the *pasteles*. After refrigerating the masa dough overnight, take a piece of the masa and spread it on top of one banana leaf. In the center of the masa, place the desired amount of filling and close the *pastel*. Wrap the *pastel* starting at the longer side of the banana leaf and continue with the one right across from it. End by folding the shorter edges. Tie with the string.

COOKING THE *PASTELES*

Fill a large pot with water and let it boil. Make sure there is enough water to cover the *pasteles*. Boil the *pasteles* for 1 hour. You can test if they are ready by unwrapping one and testing the masa to see if it is soft. If soft, your *pasteles* are ready.

Makes 26 *pasteles*.

——

*José Candelario, interview with author, 2011.

Latinos for Dinkins in Queens

In the late 1980s, Queens had several predominantly Latino districts with large numbers of Dominicans as well as some Puerto Ricans, Mexicans, and Ecuadorians. In contrast to Brooklyn, the Latinos for Dinkins in Queens did not have a long organizational history of Progressive movements with

Latinos at the helm largely because Queens remained a political strong-hold of conservative Italian, Irish, and Jewish voters. Until 1989, most of the Dominicans in Queens had remained focused on politics in the Dominican Republic. They, like most Mexicans and the Ecuadorians in Queens, had not yet become citizens and eligible to vote.

Bill Lynch coordinated with Brian McLaughlin, the leader of the New York City Central Labor Council, as well as the political boss Archie Spigner from southeast Queens and Dinkins's staffer Zenaida Mendez to mobilize Queens-based members of the Dominican community. Lynch's behind-the-scenes work to coordinate the efforts of McLaughlin, Spigner, and Mendez in Queens illustrates how Lynch leveraged the relationships he had developed during his years as a community activist as well as the contacts Rivera was able to help facilitate in Latino communities.

Events in the Dominican Republic itself accelerated the engagement of Dominicans in the 1989 mayoral campaign in New York City. Caudillo Joaquín Balaguer served as president of the Dominican Republic from 1960 to 1962, 1966 to 1978, and 1986 to 1996. He was infamous for incarcerating, torturing, and assassinating political opponents, and during the 1960s and 1970s his regime forced many of his critics into exile in New York City. When Balaguer returned to power starting in 1986, many Dominican political refugees finally concluded that they and their families would never return to the Dominican Republic. Thus for many Dominicans in Queens, Dinkins's campaign was the first time they became formally engaged in New York City politics. Much of the work of the Dinkins campaign in Queens centered on moving Dominican immigrants toward citizenship and registering them to vote.[45]

Dinkins also built support among Latinos in Queens and throughout the city by seizing on issues important to Latinos in the small-business community. His support for mandatory arbitration for merchants facing rent increases distinguished him from Mayor Koch, who opposed such a policy and helped him win the support of Latino merchants, especially bodega owners in Washington Heights and Queens.[46] An association of Dominican supermarket and bodega owners called the Association of Dominican Merchants and Industrialists played a leading role in mobilizing the Dominican business community to support the Dinkins campaign in 1989. At the time of the election, the association had about five hundred members who owned profitable bodegas and supermarkets in Queens and Washington Heights. Then, as now, bodegas specializing in Dominican and other Latin American food staples and spices served as a stepping-stone for entrepreneurs to enter the food industry. Turning a profit as a bodega owner greatly increased one's chances of qualifying for a bank loan to purchase and operate a much larger supermarket. Mendez, who grew up in Queens, knew many of the families who owned these businesses. She met with them and gained their support in her efforts to organize other Dominican business owners.

Mendez, working with members of the Association of Dominican Merchants and Industrialists, conducted a voter-education and -registration drive. They argued that just as he had as Manhattan borough president, Dinkins would create more opportunities for qualified Latinos to serve in city government. The Latinos for Dinkins infrastructure would translate into Latino political action committees, which could organize newly registered voters, push for new electoral districts, and support candidates dedicated to Progressive unity politics.[47]

Queens's African American population had grown considerably since the 1960s, and there was a huge amount of enthusiasm around Dinkins's candidacy. The campaign depended on Spigner, a powerful black political operative, to get out the black vote in Queens. Once the campaign had Spigner and his influential southeastern Queens political club on board, Lynch knew that minorities among the Democratic Party leadership in the county would come on board as well. Spigner's political club provided the ground troops necessary to collect petition signatures and deliver votes on election day.

Latinos for Dinkins in East Harlem and Lower Manhattan

In 1989, East Harlem was a stronghold for powerful Puerto Rican elected officials, such as the state senator Olga Mendez and the assemblyman Angelo Del Toro. It had once been a hotbed for Progressives and radicals, but they had long since moved on and Democratic regulars controlled the district. The situation in East Harlem was so dire politically that the Dinkins campaign had to assign an outsider to run its Latinos for Dinkins operation.

Jaime Estades had learned how to organize as a member of the PSP and DC 65, but this was his first time working on a political campaign. "And I did it with the criticism of members of the Puerto Rican Socialist Party," Estades says. "I broke with them over that issue." During the course of the campaign, he says, many Latinos he knew from his PSP days and other networks ended up coming to the Dinkins campaign office he set up on the second floor of a building on 116th Street in East Harlem. In order to work for Dinkins, though, he had to separate himself from the leftist Puerto Rican organizations, which maintained a 1960s era anti-electoral stance rooted in a distrust of elected officials and members of the Democratic and Republican Party establishments. The real task was forming good working relationships between blacks and Latinos in East Harlem. Historically, black and Latino political bosses in Harlem had fierce political rivalries, which would often spill out to the rest of the population and reverberate in buses, subways, barbershops, and beauty salons.

During the primaries, a political realignment occurred among Puerto Rican political elites in East Harlem. Del Toro had never supported Koch, but the incumbent mayor's offer of a housing development plan for East Harlem and property to build a Latino cultural center persuaded Del Toro to endorse him. Similarly, Mendez, whose district straddled Manhattan and the Bronx, had supported Dinkins when he ran for Manhattan borough president in 1985 and Jackson's 1988 bid for the White House. But in 1989, she stuck with Koch. Del Toro and Mendez jointly controlled the East Harlem party machinery, including the polling-site inspectors.[48] The Central Labor Council in New York City sent volunteers to assist Estades to help counter Dinkins's lack of support from the local political machinery in East Harlem, which controlled all the neighborhood's polling sites and could potentially manipulate the voting process in Koch's favor. Estades recalls that Del Toro "had everyone against me and my little office" on 116th Street. But the Central Labor Council sent reinforcements. "There was a line of [volunteers] from every union you could mention" outside the 116th Street headquarters, many of them white workers, Estades recalls. While some of those conscripted white workers threw campaign materials in the trash, others campaigned very hard for Dinkins.

Estades said that collaboration took place between Latino and African American activists in Harlem because the African American community (politicians, preachers, and activists) realized that a black candidate could not win a citywide election without support from Latino voters in Harlem.[49] Lynch made sure that his network in Harlem's African American community maintained an open-door policy to Latinos for Dinkins volunteers in East Harlem.[50]

After weeks of Latinos for Dinkins volunteers conducting door-to-door outreach in Manhattan, Dinkins's popularity among Latinos and Asians (whom the Democratic Party machine had also marginalized) began to increase. On August 18, Dinkins did a walk-through in East Harlem from 116th Street and Second Avenue to La Marquetta on Fifth Avenue with Jaime Estades as his advance staff and guide. The massive turnout indicated that a political realignment had occurred. Estades had planned what he expected to be a half-hour leisurely stroll to a number of *cuchifritos* (takeout eateries that sold *morcilla* [blood sausages], *papas rellenas* [deep-fried potato balls stuffed with meat], *chicharrón* [fried pork skin], and tropical fruit juices). But once locals caught sight of Dinkins, people flocked to see him and shake his hand. Estades estimates that roughly 1,000 people surrounded him as Dinkins tried to make his way through East Harlem. "Once he stopped, people were all over him and he had to shake hands, talk to people," Estades says. "It took almost two hours to walk three blocks. It was amazing!"[51] Estades had expected to introduce the candidate to key people but recalls being pushed aside as the crowd tried to get closer to Dinkins.

"People were sick and tired of Koch, wanted him out," reported Estades.[52] Dinkins supported mandatory arbitration for merchants facing rent increases, which Koch opposed, and earned a reputation as helping his constituents and "sid[ing] with the community.[53] On Labor Day weekend, Dinkins did several walk-throughs in Lower Manhattan, where crowds of supporters also thronged him. In Hell's Kitchen, Mendez's neighborhood, a Spanish-speaking advance team led him through the streets with the influential Latin jazz superstar (and Bronx native) Willie Colón and the former professional boxer José Torres at his side. Dinkins did a similar walk-through in Chinatown, greeting enthusiastic supporters with a Mandarin-speaking advance team from the group Asian Americans for Dinkins. For the first time, the Chinese Consolidated Benevolent Association, an association of sixty business families, endorsed a mayoral candidate, putting its full support behind the sixty-two-year-old African American candidate from Harlem.[54]

PUERTO RICAN PAPAS RELLENAS

1 lb ground beef or vegan substitute

5 lbs potatoes

½ cup potato flakes or flour

2 packages anatto powder seasoning (sazón) for coloring

2 tsp salt

Enough cooking oil for deep frying

2 tbsp adobo

2 tbsp sofrito

Season ground beef to taste and cook until brown. Cook potatoes as you would for mashed potatoes. Mash the potatoes, add potato flakes, annato powder, and salt. Mix together. Make sure the potatoes are not too soft or too hard. Heat oil in a frying pan while mixing potatoes. Make half a ball out of the mashed potato and create a well. Spoon some meat into the well. Make another half ball and flatten over the stuffed half, making a full ball out of the potato. If needed, add some potato flakes or flour to make sure the ball stays intact. Deep-fry the potato ball in hot oil and cook until the ball turns bright orange and crispy.

Latinos for Dinkins in Washington Heights

Activists in Washington Heights built their Latinos for Dinkins operation on the established infrastructure of the Dominican parade organizers and the Progressive wing of the Dominican chamber of commerce. By 1982, Washington Heights had replaced Queens as the center of New York's Dominican community and was home to dozens of Dominican restaurants, grocery stores, travel agencies, and social clubs. In addition to her organizing responsibilities in Queens, Zenaida Mendez was in charge of setting up a Latinos for Dinkins office in Washington Heights. She recruited Giovanni Puello, a grocery store owner whose family was active in local politics, to help.[55]

Mendez and Puello organized a kickoff fund-raiser at La Calidad Restaurant at 134th Street and Broadway. The minimum contribution was $250 per plate, and they served a traditional Dominican breakfast, which included fried plantains, eggs, sliced salami, *mangú* (mashed green plantains with fried red onion), and *queso frito* (fried cheese). Mendez and Puello reached out to Progressive Dominicans living in New York as political exiles. Approximately eighty influential community leaders attended, and the campaign netted between $10,000 and $15,000. News of the fund-raiser's success boosted Dinkins's credibility and launched a movement in Washington Heights.[56]

In addition to the now-shuttered La Calidad Restaurant, other Dominican cultural and social institutions played a key role in the campaign. El Club Deportivo Dominicano on 163rd Street and Audubon Avenue, where members of the city's Dominican diaspora socialized on the weekends,

MANGÚ

4 unripe plantains, peeled and cut into 8 pieces

2 tsp salt

2 tbsp oil

1½ large onions, chopped

Salt to taste

1 tbsp vinegar

4 tbsp butter

1 cup cold water

½ large onion, sliced

Boil the plantain pieces, adding 2 tsp salt to the water. When the plantains are very tender, turn off the heat. While the plantains are boiling, heat oil in a shallow pan. Sauté the chopped onion, and add the salt and vinegar. Take the plantains out of the water and mash them with a fork. Add the butter and the cold water, and keep mashing until the plantains are very smooth. Garnish with the onion slices and serve with scrambled eggs or deep-fried slices of salami.

allowed the campaign to set up a voter-registration and citizenship information table in the club on the weekends. "So we would go there almost every weekend to talk and tell people about [our] voter-registration and citizenship drive," says Mendez. "You are talking about reaching hundreds and hundreds of families every week through the social club."[57]

As she did in Queens, Mendez had campaign workers in Washington Heights focus on education, citizenship, and voter registration among naturalized Dominicans, Colombians, Ecuadorians, and Cuban immigrants who had not previously taken part in politics. But when the registration drive started to gain success, some Democratic district leaders complained to Bill Lynch, including the longtime Dominican Democratic Party district leader. Sandy Trujillo recalls that the district leader viewed that territory as their own political fiefdom and worried that they would be displaced by Dinkins's independent base of newly registered voters. Party regulars pressured Denny Farrell, the Manhattan Democratic Party leader, into calling a meeting. The district leader along with Trujillo, Zoilo Torres, and Lynch demanded that Lynch end the voter-registration drives. Lynch and his team pointedly refused. They saw the voter-registration drive as a way to not only get Dinkins elected mayor of New York but also empower marginalized Latino residents in Washington Heights and elsewhere. These new registrants could force candidates for public office to address community issues in order to win votes. Trujillo remembers saying, "This is our movement, and we are not going to stop."[58] As in many areas around the city, Torres says, when activists with Latinos for Dinkins "went up against the Democratic Party regulars in their communities, they were not always embraced."[59]

Latinos for Dinkins in Washington Heights also faced racist ethnocentrism and challenges from small groups of Latinos for Koch. Luis Miranda, who did not support those kinds of racist attacks, was Koch's director of Latino affairs and gained the endorsement of some community organizations in Washington Heights by promising them community development block grants, federal funds that can be used for community services such as housing and job creation.

Latinos for Dinkins faced several challenges. Members in Washington Heights tended to be older, more conservative professionals who were financially stable and owned homes. These members did not participate in grassroots organizing or street activism, and as a result they were less likely

CANDIED ORANGE YAM EMPANADAS

2 medium yams, peeled and cut into 2-inch cubes

1 can yams

1 tbsp vegetable oil

1 cup orange juice

½ jar orange marmalade (with rinds)

1 cup firmly packed dark brown sugar

¼ cup pecans

¼ tsp ground nutmeg

½ tsp ground cinnamon

[Pie crust recipe]

About 4 cups cooking oil for frying

½ tsp salt

Preheat oven to 400 degrees.

Toss the yams lightly with vegetable oil and roast in the oven for about 20 minutes or until the yams become slightly tender. Remove from oven and set aside.

In a large saucepan, combine the orange juice, orange marmalade, and brown sugar and bring to a low simmer, making sure the sugar has completely dissolved. Add the roasted yams to the syrup and simmer over low heat for about 15 minutes.

To prepare the empanadas, spoon about a third of the yams into a bowl along with plenty of syrup. Mash the yams with a fork until almost smooth, adding more syrup if they are too dry. Continue with the rest of the yams. Add the pecans, nutmeg, and cinnamon and stir. Follow a pie crust recipe and roll out the uncooked crust. Cut out a circle from the crust using a medium-size cereal bowl and a butter knife. Place 1 tablespoon of the yam filling into the center of the cut-out pie crust; fold the crust over the filling and use a fork to seal in the filling. Continue with the rest of the crust and the filling. Bake or deep-fry the empanadas until done, then brush with melted butter or coconut oil, sprinkling the salt. Serve with a side of extra syrup, and garnish with orange zest. Makes 12–15 mini empanadas and about 1 cup extra yams and syrup.

Source: http://www.poorgirleatswell.com/2009/11/foodbuzz-24–24–24-after-thanksgiving.html.

to vote for the more Progressive Dinkins.[60] But the vast majority of Latinos in Washington Heights had experienced severe hardships under Koch, including declines in public support for poverty programs and schools, and evictions at the hands of greedy Koch-supported landlords who benefitted from the administration's real-estate policies. These challenges proved insurmountable for Latinos who campaigned for Koch and against Dinkins, even with the grant money available to buy support.[61]

Latinos for Dinkins in the Bronx

The Latinos for Dinkins activists in the Bronx operated in a politically hostile environment controlled by the Bronx County Democratic party. They faced an uphill battle in the Bronx among Puerto Rican elected officials and political operatives who supported Koch, and others who did not support Dinkins because they distrusted blacks. Still others with large numbers of black constituents in districts they represented provided superficial support for Dinkins for their political survival.

For example, Fernando Ferrer, the Bronx borough president, did not endorse Dinkins until late in the campaign. He insisted that he waited so long "in order to hear the candidates . . . express their respective visions for New York."[62] He criticized Dinkins for being too slow in his decision-making process, but he admired the job he had done as Manhattan borough president. "David and I have had disagreements from time to time, but on balance he and I are in synch," Ferrer reported.[63] Ferrer concluded that after a divisive Koch era, Dinkins represented the best hope for uniting the citizens of New York City. On a Sunday afternoon in early September, "enthusiastic crowds of Latinos estimated at 10,000 to 15,000" greeted Dinkins at the Livery Taxi Drivers Festival at 156th Street and Third Avenue in the Bronx.[64] The Washington Heights–based association, in cooperation with Ferrer, José Rivera, José Torres, and Willie Colón, sponsored the event. The festival represented the second-largest crowd to cheer any candidate during the 1989 campaign. (The largest was the million-plus crowd that turned out to see Dinkins as he rode with Harry Belafonte during the West Indian Day Parade earlier in the campaign.) Ferrer gave a hardy introduction to Dinkins in Spanish: "After careful review of the agendas, I'm proud today to endorse the candidacy for mayor of my friend and colleague, David Dinkins, because I believe he is New York's best hope for unifying the spirit and people of our great city. Dinkins will be a friend and advocate of all the residents of all five boroughs."[65] The crowd of mostly Dominicans and Puerto Ricans along with Colombians, Ecuadorians, and some Cubans erupted in cheers of support for Dinkins. After addressing the crowd, Dinkins descended the speaker's platform to greet the crowd and shake hand with onlookers

Ferrer's endorsement of Dinkins seemed pragmatic, considering that his own election as Bronx borough president relied on support from African American voters in the Bronx. After Ferrer, Dinkins gained endorsements from other Bronx elected officials, but their support was often perceived as lukewarm.

Meanwhile, Assemblyman Israel Martinez supported Koch; the former Bronx borough president and congressman Herman Badillo refused to endorse Dinkins, who "never supported me" when he had run for the Democratic nomination for mayor three different times. However, in setting up the Latinos for Dinkins office in the Bronx, "we did not rely on [elected officials] because we were bucking the [Bronx County Democratic] party on a grassroots level," Zoilo Torres says. "They did not like it, but we went into their territory anyway."[66] Trujillo, who ran the Latinos for Dinkins desk in the headquarters of Local 1199, adds, "A lot of the resistance from the Latino elected officials dated back to the rejection of Badillo's candidacy in 1985. What happened in 1985 was definitely to some extent an obstacle to getting some people in the Bronx to join Latinos for Dinkins."[67]

José Serrano had set up his own political club after his loss to Stanley Simon in the election for Bronx borough president in 1985. He did this to free himself from all association with the Bronx machine. Serrano wanted to attract the support of the brightest community leaders, mobilize registered voters, and help bring jobs and services to the neighborhood. He did not care much for Badillo and had become a close political ally of Dinkins in 1985 when they were both running for borough presidencies. Serrano allowed Latinos for Dinkins to set up shop in the storefront he rented for his South Bronx Independent Democratic Club on Melrose Avenue. In addition to the office space, Serrano lent his chief of staff, Michael Benjamin, to the Latinos for Dinkins movement in the Bronx.[68]

Mickey Melendez, a former Young Lord, helped set up the office and recruited Vicente "Panama" Alba, another former Young Lords member, to serve as the Latinos for Dinkins coordinator in the Bronx. Alba served as the only full-time paid staff of the Latino for Dinkins organization in the Bronx and worked to gain the support of tenant association activists, business owners, shopkeepers, and residents of the public-housing projects.

Over time, the Latinos for Dinkins organization in the Bronx developed a campaign strategy and figured out how to mobilize voters in the South Bronx. As part of the campaign strategy, Garcia says they focused on getting people registered to vote. The Latinos for Dinkins operation set up voter-registration drives around the South Bronx, and campaign volunteers regularly came by the office to replenish their supply of voter-registration forms.[69]

As in Brooklyn, the Dinkins campaign confronted racist ethnocentrism in the Bronx's Latino communities.[70] Volunteers for Latinos for Koch equipped caravans with speakers and drove around the Bronx as a man shouted into a microphone, "No vote por este cocolo," the Spanish word for "nigger," Trujillo says, and "Dinkins will rob us and benefit the blacks and not the Latinos."[71] Angel Garcia tells a similar story. He remembers going to an annual community carnival held in the Third Avenue shopping district to hand out campaign materials. When he arrived, he stumbled across a campaign rally for Koch led by Ruben Diaz, a dark-skinned Afro-Puerto Rican, who gave a stump speech in support of Koch, heavily laced with racist ethnocentrism and Puerto Rican nationalism. "Boricua! Viva Puerto Rico! You can't vote for the black guy," Garcia remembers Diaz saying. "If you're really going to vote Puerto Rican, you're going to vote Ed Koch."[72] On another occasion, Carmelo Saez, chairman of the community school board in the Highbridge section of the South Bronx, argued that Latinos might not get their fair share under a Dinkins administration because he would favor African Americans over Latinos. Diaz questioned the wisdom of supporting the Dinkins campaign, noting that Dinkins's staff "gets really dark at the top." These statements surprised Garcia, and he realized that a black candidate could bring out the Latino community's most ethnocentric biases. Most disconcerting was how effectively Latino bosses could manipulate these biases to mobilize undereducated residents.[73]

To combat the racial slurs issued by the Latinos for Koch camp in the Bronx, Latinos for Dinkins did "unconventional and conventional" campaigning. When Dinkins did the walk-through with Colón in the Bronx,

Pabon says, Latino residents in the Bronx "all recognized Colón and got excited about seeing him on the street." Pabon introduced Dinkins and urged people to vote for him. "And they said, 'Sure,'" Pabon says. "We did that and it worked." Pabon also arranged walk-throughs with former Young Lords Felipe Luciano, Pablo "Yoruba" Guzmán, and Juan González, who also had a sizable following. The campaign complemented these celebrity appearances with a traditional ground operation—voter-registration booths, door knocking, phone banking, and leaflets.[74]

THE ATTACK ON YUSEF HAWKINS

On August 23, 1989, just weeks before the September 12 primary election, the young African American Yusef Hawkins was killed by a group of white teenagers in Bensonhurst, Brooklyn. Hawkins, sixteen, and three of his African American friends had come from East New York to see a used car that a resident had listed for sale. Thirty white teenagers carrying baseball bats and at least one gun surrounded Hawkins and his friends in the predominantly white Italian Brooklyn neighborhood. The white teenagers mistakenly thought that Hawkins or one of his companions was the new boyfriend of an eighteen-year-old neighborhood white girl who had recently ended a romantic relationship with one of the attackers. She had planned a birthday party at her house that same evening. Her former boyfriend had warned her not to bring blacks and Latinos into the area.[75] One of the white teenagers fired four shots: two hit Hawkins in the chest, killing him. The attackers did not know that the girl had cancelled the party, fearing the outbreak of violence. The *New York Times* called the killing "perhaps the gravest racial incident in our city" since white teenagers caused the death of the twenty-three-year-old African American Michael Griffith in a racial attack in Howard Beach in nearby Queens in 1986.[76] In that tragedy, a group of white attackers chased Griffith onto a busy highway from the almost all-white neighborhood of Howard Beach, where a van struck and killed him. Black activists added the name Yusef Hawkins to the list of some thirty-three black victims of racial violence in New York City during the Koch years.[77]

The murder outraged African Americans across the city. Racial tensions surged when Koch opposed efforts by the black activists Al Sharpton and

Sonny Carson to hold a demonstration in the same place where Hawkins had died. Koch's base, middle- and working-class Italian, Irish, and Latino conservative Democrats, lined up behind Koch, and the city's African American and leftist Latinos supported Sharpton and Carson.[78]

Carson organized a protest that he called the "Day of Outrage." He mobilized 7,500 demonstrators to protest the Koch administration's handling of the Hawkins case. As Carson led the crowd over the Belt Parkway bridge, straight toward a line of police officers in riot gear, they chanted, "Whose streets? Our streets! What's coming? War!" The confrontation ended after a long brawl in which forty-five NYPD officers and many more demonstrators were injured.[79] The tense ethnic standoff following the Bensonhurst murder alarmed many white and Latino voters loyal to Koch, who feared having a black mayor, even one as moderate as Dinkins, would lead to greater black militancy.[80]

Bill Lynch resolved to get in front of the issue, meeting directly with leaders of the movement. Victor Quintana, Lynch's special assistant, remembers a "cast of characters" coming and going out of Lynch's office day and night.[81]

In addition to co-opting Carson, the campaign also leveraged Dinkins's unique ability to serve as the conciliatory candidate in the midst of racial turmoil. In contrast to his opponents, Dinkins was depicted as the one who could build bridges between the city's ethnic communities. In the span of a week, the theme of the campaign shifted from "who's the toughest guy to run the city?" to "who can best bring us together?" That message resonated with undecided voters who were tired of Koch's polarizing politics and gave Dinkins a helpful boost.[82]

On September 2, 1989, just two weeks away from the primary election, the activist Carol Taylor published an editorial in the pages of the *New York Amsterdam News*. "If we don't start holding politicians who say they're in control accountable, at the ballot box, for the continuous murders of Black brothers and sisters, we are allowing our brains to be lynched along with our people," Taylor wrote. Any African American who doesn't vote against politicians like Koch who do nothing as "racist white thugs" kill our black boys, she continued, "should be sent for a nice midnight stroll through the streets of Howard Beach or Bensonhurst!" She then went on to say that "in the midst of a conservative backlash, and with it, its inherited racism, the Society apparently has no intention of doing the right thing" by our black boys, in reference to the title of Spike Lee's hit movie about police brutality against black youth in Brooklyn, *Do the Right Thing* (1989). The editorial ends with "It's time to clean house! Dump Koch![83] On September 10, two days before the primary election, Dinkins and the filmmaker Spike Lee served as the grand marshals for the twenty-first annual African American parade held in Harlem. Parade organizers dedicated the event to "the unity of African Americans in the fight against racism and killings of African Americans" with the theme, "African Americans: The Right Thing for the 90s." Thousands turned out along the parade route in Harlem on Adam Clayton Powell Jr. Boulevard from 111th Street to 142nd Street.[84]

Koch's apathetic response to the Hawkins case and other incidents of racial violence mobilized large numbers of black and Latino voters to support Dinkins over Koch. Ultimately, Dinkins's ability to fuse a coalition of voters gave him enough votes to win the Democratic primary on September 12, beating Koch, Harrison Goldin, and Richard Ravitch.[85] Dinkins shocked the establishment by winning 51 percent of the vote, more than the other three white candidates combined and enough to win the Democratic nomination without a runoff.[86] Koch won 42 percent of the vote; Ravitch, 4 percent; and Goldin, 3 percent.[87]

It was Dinkins's "gorgeous mosaic" that pushed him over the top: he won almost 100 percent of the black vote, 62 percent of Asians, 55 percent of Hispanics, and 27 percent of Jews. He also won 60 percent of women and 74 percent of all voters under the age of twenty-five (figure 7.3).[88] "I'm rejoicing," said Ekua Wilson, a schoolteacher in the Bronx. The Reverend Herbert Daughtry of Brooklyn called it "the brink of a new day," and Clementine Pugh, a Harlem resident, called Dinkins's victory "the biggest thing since Joe Louis beat Max Schmeling."[89]

Following Hawkins's killing, the campaign became a referendum on which candidate could unite a racially polarized city. The racial violence in Bensonhurst helped guarantee support for Dinkins among the city's minority-majority and young, liberal, white Democrats.[90] Jesse Jackson called the victory, which included lots of grassroots organizing and mobilizing, "squarely in the tradition of the civil rights movement."[91] Just days after Dinkins's primary victory the *Washington Post* wrote, "A generation after the Civil Rights revolution ended . . . race remains the nation's most divisive political factor." At the time of the Democratic primary in New York,

FIGURE 7.3 Assemblyman Richard Gottfried, Jessie Jackson, Dennis Rivera (*standing*), Charles Rangel, and Andrew Stein (City Council president, 1986–1994) at a breakfast fund-raiser, 1989. (Courtesy of Tamiment Library & Robert F. Wagner Labor Archives, New York University, New York, N.Y.)

"race had become again [referring to the civil rights movement] perhaps the single most critical issue facing the country, far more important than drugs and crack dealers dominating the news and public debate," reported the *Washington Post*. "Take away all drugs and the country still would face the problem of increasing racial tension," the *Post* continued. Violence and drug related violence in urban America "are a testament to the failure of attempts by politicians to solve the legacy of racial inequalities in this society. . . . Racial insults are traded publicly and public officials make remarks revealing deplorable racial insensitivity. Demagogues, on both sides, have played to fears and anxieties." The results of the primary in New York "were the most positive sign in months that reason is beginning triumph over prejudice. . . . Dinkins was able to assemble the kind of broad biracial coalition that offers promise for the future. . . . In this election at least" New Yorkers indicated that race would not control their decisions when they voted.[92]

During a time in which class and racial divides had devastated political coalitions in American cities, voters in New York demonstrated their viability with a "convincing victory" over incumbent Koch, reported the *Chicago Tribune*.[93] Dinkins also benefited from an endorsement by the United Federation of Teachers, a largely white union, which had not supported a mayoral candidate since 1973. That kind of support helped Dinkins win Manhattan, the Bronx, Brooklyn, and nearly half the city's sixty Assembly districts. In addition, he doubled the votes received by Jesse Jackson on Staten Island in 1988, once a Koch stronghold. The *New York Times* defined the results as a "monumental" victory.[94] Across the Atlantic, the *Guardian* wrote, "Very few other candidates anywhere have ever put together such a multi-racial coalition," something "which Ken Livingstone" of the British Labour Party had dreamed of as the leader of the Greater London Council, which ran that city until 1986.[95]

CELEBRITY FUND-RAISERS

On the Monday after the primary, a Who's Who of entertainers participated in a Dinkins fund-raiser at the Apollo Theater in Harlem. The jam-packed Harlem venue featured Bill Cosby, Harry Belafonte, Quincy Jones, Spike Lee, and other luminaries. Dinkins's supporters organized similar fund-raising events in Los Angeles, Chicago, Boston, Baltimore, Hartford, Detroit, and Arkansas. Bill Lynch then kicked off the general election campaign with a unity breakfast for state and city Democratic Party officials and those interested in supporting the campaign. Tickets sold for $100 for supporters, $500 for individual sponsors, and $1,000 for corporate sponsors.[96] Governor Mario Cuomo, Attorney General Robert Abrams, Democratic state committee chairman John Mariho, Mayor Koch, every borough president, county and district leaders, and primary election opponents and rivals attended the breakfast. Cuomo and Koch shared remarks that led the effort to mobilize the party behind Dinkins.[97]

Before the primary, African American, Latino, Jewish, and other Brooklyn clergy and civic leaders had attended the first of two Clergy for Dinkins fund-raising breakfasts, where "a lot of praying and politicking" went on, according to news accounts.[98] A number of prominent Jewish religious leaders endorsed Dinkins in August, including Rabbi Gilbert Klaperman, former president of the New York Board of Rabbis. Gardner Taylor, pastor of Concord Baptist Church in Brooklyn, introduced Dinkins. Reminiscent of Harold Washington's 1983 campaign for mayor of Chicago, Dinkins the candidate spoke of "bringing the divided city of New York together" and "the possibilities and necessities for constructive change."[99] Harry Belafonte also stumped at the breakfast in support of Dinkins. He represented "a bridge of historical continuity" between those who had participated in the freedom movement of the 1950s and 1960s and those involved in the political empowerment movement of the 1980s and 1990s.

On September 29, Clergy for Dinkins held its second fund-raising breakfast at the Sheraton Center in Manhattan. The Reverend Herbert Daughtry served as the group's political strategist and called for several initiatives to get Dinkins elected. He challenged each member of Clergy for Dinkins to pledge $1,000 from his or her religious institution that would raise in total $1 million for the Dinkins campaign to purchase television time. Daughtry encouraged pastors to leverage their mailing lists and inquire if the people on them were eligible and registered to vote. Each member of a clergy's congregation would contact one other person about that person's voter-registration status. Daughtry suggested that ministers establish a coordinator to communicate with the Dinkins campaign headquarters. Each church could enlist volunteers to work at phone banks and provide transportation to polling sites as well as knock on doors on election day. The group agreed to organize a clergy fund-raising day on October 15 and an ecumenical Clergy for Dinkins rally on October 22 at the Sheraton with ministers inviting other colleagues to the event. Daughtry called for members of the group to go beyond their religious institutions and organize election rallies in each of the boroughs.[100]

GENERAL ELECTION

Bill Lynch understood that while the Progressives in Latinos for Dinkins had played a critical role in winning the primary, Dinkins would have to move toward the center in order to gain the support of Independents and moderates in the general election. The Republican primary had been won by a well-known prosecutor, Rudolph Giuliani. Born in East Flatbush, Brooklyn, Giuliani was a second-generation Italian American, a Roman Catholic, a high-profile former U.S. attorney for the Southern District of New York, and a former assistant attorney general under Ronald Reagan. Giuliani ran on a reputation as being an honest crime-fighting former federal prosecutor in Manhattan. In 1985, Giuliani, in his role as U.S. attorney, had announced indictments of the top mob bosses and the entire Mafia Commission, all of whom he helped convict and send to prison with lifetime sentences. He tried to convince voters that he would be more honest and tougher on crime then Dinkins, whom he called a typical clubhouse politician.[101]

In order to beat Giuliani, both Lynch and Dennis Rivera realized that Dinkins would need to attract Independents and white ethnic "Koch Democrats." They understood that racism would drive many of these voters away, but to make Dinkins viable they needed only a small percentage to come aboard.

Following the primary, Lynch issued orders that all the campaign offices were to start working with former supporters of Ed Koch. "I started letting the Koch people in because like every other race we had to move to the right to win the general election," Lynch recalled.[102] At the same time, Rivera selected Ada Castro to head the citywide Latinos for Dinkins operation. Castro had worked for Rivera and helped to advance his agenda, even though she did not share the same principles of the original leftist activists that became part of Latinos for Dinkins. Because of this, Castro became a contentious figure. Her detractors say she was an outsider with no leftist credentials or interest in a long-term program for Latino political empowerment. The rank-and-file members of Latinos for Dinkins viewed Castro as a reminder of how Lynch and Rivera had moved to the center and marginalized the left-of-center activists who had helped them win the primary. Most important, Rivera alienated and pushed out Zoilo Torres, the architect who had built the political infrastructure in the Latino communities, replacing him with someone who knew nothing about mobilizing voters for Dinkins or advancing the larger original vision of Latino political empowerment.[103] The original members of Latinos for Dinkins confronted Rivera about what they considered to be his strong-arm tactics in naming Castro. "He listened and said fine, and did not change anything," Sandy Trujillo added. Lynch did not get involved, which Trujillo concedes was the right thing to do. "This was our movement and, at the end of the day, Dennis had a lot more to deliver than we could in terms of resources and muscle."[104]

Not only were the original members of the Latinos for Dinkins campaign pushed out of leadership roles, but their offices were almost immediately filled with former Koch loyalists and professional campaign staff for whom they had nothing but contempt. Trujillo remembers the day after the primary, "We had all these real sleazy Dems . . . go into the campaign office the next day with their briefcases . . . saying, 'Okay, we are all Democratic Party members now. What can we do to help?'" It was difficult to accept this intrusion given the Koch campaign's unethical behavior during the primary. A particularly heated debate broke out in the Bronx office when the Latinos for Dinkins team was told to work with Luis Miranda and others who were viewed as unprincipled mercenaries who had betrayed the city's Latino community during the primaries for a paycheck. "We did not trust them, but we were given the directive that it was big tent and we had to welcome everyone," says Trujillo.[105]

The structure of the campaign shifted abruptly from being democratic and egalitarian, a culture that many grassroots activists recognized from their work with the PSP and El Comité, to professional and hierarchical in the model of other high-profile elections. While Lynch and Rivera's actions angered some in the leftist coalition, many understood that this was a small price to pay for their own long-term political empowerment. Torres, however, remembers having "a really bad falling out with Dennis" over these decisions, and he decided to leave the campaign to focus on building the political action committees.[106] He was not the only former member of Latinos for Dinkins who walked away disillusioned. Lynch admits that black leftists left the campaign, too, but says that didn't matter to him. "I'm thinking about winning," says Lynch, and the political calculus dictated that he needed to trade a handful of leftists for a truckload of moderates.[107]

During the primary, Democratic Party regulars in Brooklyn never really embraced the Latinos for Dinkins movement, José Candelario says. Several times during the primary campaign in 1989, local party bosses who supported Dinkins asked Candelario and other members of the Latinos for Dinkins office in Williamsburg to "submit" to their leadership and "we refused," says Candelario: "They pressured us to relinquish control of our work to them but the Dinkins campaign supported us. The [local] Democratic party apparatus [in Brooklyn] had become keenly aware of the potential we had for mounting a permanent Latino political empowerment structure [in Williamsburg and Sunset Park] during the primary which confirmed to us the value of our operations." Right after winning the primary, the local party bosses "descended on us like hawks. But again, the Dinkins campaign stood firmly on the principle that they would continue to work with those of us who helped win the primary."[108]

The former Koch supporters like Miranda, brought on board by Lynch and Rivera, did bring resources to the Dinkins campaign. They were able to mobilize conservative Democrats and get access to the city's key radio stations. Miranda even set up an effective public-relations operation out of the Latinos for Dinkins office in the Bronx. Democratic regulars like Stanley Simon and others from the Bronx borough president's office also lent their support. On one occasion, Simon came to the Latinos for Dinkins office to deliver bags of street money, cash given to political operatives to ensure a large voter turnout in a community. Democratic regulars came with flyers, posters, and other campaign necessities that were in short supply in the Latinos for Dinkins office in the Bronx.

At this time, American political campaigns were undergoing a major shift, becoming more technologically sophisticated and dependent on television advertising. Recognizing this trend, Lynch advocated for putting a huge amount of money into media advertising. The campaign's Bronx coordinator, Vicente Alba, argued instead for more spending on the campaign's ground game—street-level outreach and events. But Lynch refused to back down. By 1989, new technologies and tactics had begun to undermine the historical importance of county party bosses, district leaders, political clubs, and activists.[109] Under the old party structure, a candidate would work through party bureaucracy to get the necessary support to win. [110] But not anymore. Now candidates would have to raise enough money themselves to appeal directly to the masses.

The infamous "Willie Horton" report, which devastated Michael Dukakis's presidential aspirations the year before, had convinced Lynch that television advertising (the so-called air game) was absolutely necessary for winning elections in the modern political environment. During his tenure as governor of Massachusetts, Dukakis instituted a weekend pass program for prisoners with good behavior. One of those passes went to Willie Horton, an African American who was serving a life sentence for a brutal homicide during a robbery. Horton escaped while on his weekend pass and kidnapped a white couple, killing the man and repeatedly raping the woman. During the presidential election, George H. W. Bush's campaign ran an ad that featured a large image of Horton's mug shot and suggested that Dukakis would not keep Americans safe from black criminals. The advertisement contributed to Dukakis's collapse and drew Independents and moderate Democrats into the Bush camp.[111]

The Willie Horton spot is widely believed to have been conceived by Roger Ailes, Bush's media strategist in the 1988 election and a top adviser to Giuliani in his 1989 mayoral campaign. (Ailes is now the president of the Fox News Channel and chairman of the Fox Television Stations Group.) Ailes first entered New York City politics in 1989 as a media consultant for the cosmetic magnate Ronald Lauder's failed bid for the Republican nomination for mayor. Once Lauder dropped out of the race, Ailes joined Giuliani's team, reviving what had been a weak campaign. Early in the Republican mayoral primary, Giuliani had faltered numerous times, sounding both equivocal and inexperienced. In addition, his campaign was running short of funds. To get Giuliani through the primaries, Ailes gave him "intensive sound-bite training and limited him to one media event a day" to practice staying on message.[112] Moreover, Ailes devised a campaign strategy that included a series of talking points and negative television advertisements aimed directly at his opponents in Republican primary.[113]

After Giuliani secured the nomination, Ailes focused on how to dismantle Dinkins. Ailes studied the tense ethnic standoff that had followed the murder of Yusef Hawkins in Bensonhurst and the protests organized by Al Sharpton and Sonny Carson. He developed a narrative that played repeatedly on television and radio spots, in print articles, and in stump speeches. The narrative labeled Carson an anti-Semite and connected Dinkins to Carson (a move meant to scare off Jewish voters from supporting Dinkins). Most important, however, it also turned Carson into the Willie Horton of New York City by reminding voters that he instigated the "Day of Outrage" protests and the confrontation that followed between black militants and the NYPD. Ailes mentioned that the Dinkins campaign had given Carson $9,500 afterward, which Ailes referred to as "hush money."[114]

After the "Day of Outrage" protest in Brooklyn, Lynch met with the controversial Carson. Carson had served as county chairperson for CORE in Brooklyn, participated in the school-board struggles in the 1960s, helped found and support Medgar Evers College, and organized the Black Men's Movement Against Crack when that scourge hit the ghettos. Carson had served a fifteen-month sentence in Sing Sing Correctional Facility in 1974 for allegedly kidnapping a man suspected of stealing money from one of Carson's organizations. (The case was extremely political, having been built on evidence from a COINTELPRO operation.) Carson also even admitted to being anti-Semitic and anti-white.[115] Torres says that Dinkins could not afford to have Carson as an opponent because he could mobilize thousands of voters in Bushwick and Bed-Stuy alone. Torres recalls that Lynch gave Carson that $9,500 in "walking around money" to be used in a targeted get-out-the-vote operation.[116]

Lynch denied that this was what Ailes referred to as "hush money" and insisted that the Dinkins campaign paid Carson's organization as part of street money—funds historically allocated to grassroots voter-turnout operations on election day. Carson used the funds to mobilize voters in housing projects and in low-income areas where the typical campaign volunteer would likely be unwilling to go. Voting returns in those precincts showed that Carson's organization had done a superb job. The Giuliani campaign demanded to see receipts for the money, but some of the cash given to volunteers for meals as well as other expenses for transportation and childcare could not be easily tracked down. "Street money is a time-honored political tradition," wrote the *Amsterdam News*, "in which every candidate who seeks to win an election provides food, transportation, and sometimes" small salaries for the volunteers who dedicate substantial time to working on a campaign. For the Giuliani camp to suggest that Carson, who headed the Brooklyn CORE, "who has written a book about his life, done time in jail, who worked for Nelson Rockefeller on two campaigns . . . who worked closely with Jews during that time of his life as an anti-Semite, who sold out his people for so little money is an outrage." Moreover, a Jewish woman helped Carson write his autobiography, "and fully half of the people who followed him on freedom rides [down South during the civil rights movement] were Jews."[117] When asked about the comparison between Carson and Horton, Ailes said, "They're both felons and they're both black, but that's not my fault."[118] The strategy played on the fears of middle- and working-class whites and conservative Latinos who had long formed the backbone of Koch's coalition, and whom the Giuliani camp hoped to win over.[119]

In addition to Carson, Ailes decided to use Dinkins's relationship with Jesse Jackson to paint Dinkins as anti-Semitic and hopefully push Jewish Democrats into voting for Giuliani. There was useful footage from Dinkins's primary victory celebration at which Jackson and other black political leaders monopolized the podium for hours. Dinkins himself didn't take the stage to give his acceptance speech until after midnight when most of the television audience had already gone to bed. From the beginning of the general election, Giuliani referred to Dinkins as a "Jesse Jackson Democrat" and used footage from Jackson's speech on Dinkins's behalf in his advertisements. A month before the general election, Ailes put a campaign ad in a Yiddish newspaper, the *Algemeiner*, with photos that compared Giuliani with President Bush and Dinkins to Jackson; the caption stated, "Let the people choose their own destiny."[120] Ailes directed a steady stream of images at New York's Jewish population that linked Dinkins to Jackson's anti-Semitic comments about "Hymietown" in 1984 as well as Carson's open declaration of being both anti-white and anti-Jewish.

Despite the efforts of the Giuliani campaign, the City Council's only Orthodox Jewish members, Susan Alter and Noach Dear of Brooklyn, endorsed Dinkins. In doing so, they opposed some powerful Orthodox Jewish leaders in Kings County. Alter had been a civil rights activist and since 1978 had represented a district that was 80 percent African American. Dear had represented Brooklyn's Borough Park and Bensonhurst neighborhoods since 1978. Alter and Dear resisted right-wing Orthodox fears and warnings against electing a black mayor, particularly one with ties to Jesse Jackson, and enthusiastically supported Dinkins. Dear argued that Dinkins held Jewish New Yorkers and Israel in high regard, adding, "maybe he'll get some of the pro-Palestinian militant blacks to reconsider their position."[121] The longtime New York Jewish Democratic political strategist Philip Friedman added that the worst you can call Dinkins is a clubhouse politician, but "he is not a radical," not threatening, and "no Jesse Jackson."[122]

The relentless negative ads from Ailes and the Giuliani campaign proved effective. Dinkins started the general election with plenty of money and a nearly 20-point lead in the polls. Both dwindled as election day approached. The conventional wisdom had been that an African American candidate could not get more than 40 percent of the vote in the primary, but Dinkins had won more than 50 percent. As the Democratic nominee, Dinkins also had a huge advantage in the overwhelmingly Democratic city. In fact, New Yorkers had not elected a Republican mayor since John Lindsay in 1965. But Ailes unleashed an incredibly potent ethnocentric campaign that the New York media used to sell newspapers and magazines and boost ratings. In their coverage of the campaign, *Newsweek* acknowledged that the New York press had been harder on Dinkins since Ailes's attack campaign began.[123]

Just weeks before election day, the press began investigating Dinkins's finances and his ties to Sonny Carson. Giuliani complained that Dinkins had gotten off easy in the media during the campaign; members of the media took the bait and went trolling deeper for scandals in Dinkins's past. For his part, Ailes said that he hesitated to use his "toughest stuff against Dinkins" for fear that it could cause Giuliani negative repercussions on election day.[124] Nevertheless, Ailes's tough attacks whittled Dinkins's lead over Giuliani down to single digits by election day.

In addition to the fear tactics of the Ailes operation, the nomination of a black candidate for mayor caused an ethnic fragmentation within the Democratic Party that possibly persists to this day, but Bill de Blasio's election in 2014 might hopefully alleviate this bias: his wife is African American, his two children are mixed-race, and his winning campaign spoke of a "blueprint for progress." Nonetheless, in 1989, faced with the possibility of an African American mayor from Harlem, working-class Italians in Brooklyn decided to cross party lines to vote for one of their own. One voter rhetorically asked, "Who do you trust more to crack down on drugs and crime, a white Italian guy from Brooklyn or a liberal black politician from Manhattan?"[125] The most ethnocentric members of Latinos for Koch also abandoned the Democratic Party in 1989 to help the white candidate. Some remained registered Democrats but voted Republican, while others left the party and became Independents or Republicans. Sandy Trujillo noticed that a number of key Latinos for Koch supporters joined the Giuliani campaign. Although no statistical evidence exists regarding just how many went over to the Giuliani camp,[126] an exit poll taken after the 1989 Democratic primary reported that "six in ten Democrats who voted for Mayor Koch would support a Republican in a general election rather than vote for a black politician."[127]

In the end, Dinkins won by the narrowest of margins: 51 percent for Dinkins to 48 percent for Giuliani. The growing strength of the Latino electorate, and the capacity of Progressive Latino leaders to visualize a new direction for the city and break from the Latino leaders within the Koch-run Democratic machine, catapulted Dinkins into office. Progressives formed coalitions and garnered institutional support from within the labor movement, which turned out large numbers of Latino voters for Dinkins. The ability to deliver the vote for Dinkins drew a response from

Democratic regulars, political bosses, and clubs. By the late 1980s, Latino Progressives had undergone both a quantitative and a qualitative political transformation with Latinos voters going from a relatively small portion of the electorate to a substantial percentage of the winning margin, making this one the closest mayoral election in twenty years.[128] Dinkins received 91 percent of the black vote, 65 percent of the Latino vote, and 27 percent of the white vote.[129] As Dinkins puts it, he started with an incredible lead, "And yet, in the general election against Rudy, I win by the skin of my teeth. Reporters used to say to me, 'Why do you think it was so close?' I used to say, 'Why do you ask?' In more recent years, when they ask me, I say, 'Racism, pure and simple.'"[130]

LEGACY OF THE DINKINS ADMINISTRATION

In 1989, when it started to seem likely that David Dinkins would win the general election, career civil servants, bureaucrats, policy wonks, and lobbyists descended on the campaign. Neither Dinkins nor Bill Lynch had anticipated this onslaught, focused as they had been for the previous six months on building the black and Latino coalition necessary to defeat Ed Koch in the primary. The team was overwhelmed and incapable of making considered responses. This was the first of many instances when the Dinkins administration would find itself back on its heels due to a lack of governing experience.

Once the general election was over, the problems intensified. Dinkins, Lynch, and Dennis Rivera had been so completely focused on winning that the transition team was largely unprepared and unable to hit the ground running.[131] The leadership had not, for example, given any thought to how it should deal with requests from decision makers on the City Council or elites in the real-estate and financial industries. These forces came straight at the mayor-elect with demands, suggestions, offers, and veiled threats. The transition team lacked people experienced in parsing the words and actions of all these heavy-hitting players.

Victor Manuel Quintana, who joined the new administration as the director constituency affairs, confirms that Dinkins, Lynch and others at the center of the campaign had developed and implemented a movement-building strategy for winning but not for sustaining the movement while governing. Most critically, perhaps, they did not recognize the importance of continuing to service and build the black and Latino coalition responsible for Dinkins's electoral victory. After winning, Dinkins immediately began fighting for his political survival. The administration had a severe economic crisis to deal with, which required a budget that negatively affected Dinkins's political base and working-class black and Latino communities across the city.

Lynch, now deputy mayor, had the responsibility of delivering news of the cuts in social services to the media. The media attacked the administration daily because it "had no confidence in Dinkins's ability or the abilities of the blacks and Latinos in the mayor's office to run the city efficiently," says Trujillo. "As soon as he got in, [the press] came after him with full guns blazing," says Quintana. Articles focusing on the high levels of crime in the city and the government's increasing financial crisis forecast doomsday scenarios.[132] Most New York City news outlets had endorsed Dinkins for mayor but once he took office, his opponents continually raised questions about Dinkins's creditability and integrity.[133] Thanks to Roger Ailes's attacks during the campaign, after Dinkins took office the press continued to hound him about his personal financial mismanagement, including questions about stock transfers to his son and old unfiled tax returns. The press went after him for how much money he spent on a headboard for the master bedroom in Gracie Mansion.[134] "In this town," says Lynch, "if you don't have the press with you, forget it."[135]

In the meantime, the coalition began to show strains. Some Latino activists said that once Dinkins took office, he started taking his Latino base for granted.[136] According to Julio Pabon, several months after Dinkins became mayor, he and other activists noted that Dinkins had still not made one Latino appointment. "Not one! We called Dennis [Rivera] and said, 'You have to do something. What is happening?'"[137] Latinos who later joined the administration complained that they were marginalized. For example, Willie Nieves ran Mayor Dinkins's newly created Latino Affairs Department (Chicago's mayor-elect Harold Washington had created a similar department in 1983); he resigned in October 1991 to protest his lack of access to the mayor, arguing publicly that the mayor was not being responsive to his Latino constituency.[138] A number of Latino activists broke with Dinkins when his administration agreed to a plan that would construct a medical-waste incinerator on 138th Street and Locust Avenue in the Port Morris industrial-park section of the South Bronx. That initiative convinced Vicente Alba and other supporters that they should expect business as usual under Dinkins.[139]

The record shows that some of these accusations are without merit. More Latinos served in the Dinkins administration than under any mayor before or since. Dinkins subsequently named Sally B. Hernandez-Pinero as the deputy mayor for finance and economic development; Dr. J. Emilio Carrillo as president of the Health and Hospitals Corporation; Carlos M. Rivera as the commissioner of the Fire Department; Gladys Carrion as commissioner of the Community Development Agency; and Dennis DeLeon as commissioner of human rights.[140]

The Dinkins administration also actively supported Latino political empowerment initiatives in the city. The year Dinkins took office, the city went through a charter revision and the number of seats on the City Council increased from thirty-five to fifty-one. The Dinkins administration supported a subsequent redistricting that resulted in the creation of new, predominately black and Latino voting districts. Dinkins also helped to create a political environment that allowed Dominicans to become more active in New York City politics, and, following the election, members of Latinos for Dinkins founded four Dominican political clubs in newly formed districts.

By the late 1980s, Latino Progressives had undergone both a quantitative and a qualitative political transformation, with Latino voters going from a relatively small portion of the electorate to a substantial percentage of the winning margin. Between 1989 and 2010, the number of Latino elected officials at the local and state level in New York City doubled.[141] Guillermo Linares became the first Dominican member of the City Council; Richard Rivera became the first Puerto Rican civil court judge in the city's history.[142] Javier Nieves (no relation to Willie Nieves) won a seat in the New York State Assembly; José Serrano won the seat in Congress representing the Bronx that Robert Garcia had vacated in a 1990 special election. Two years later, Nydia Velázquez became the first Latina elected to serve in the U.S. House of Representatives.[143]

In Brooklyn alone, there are now eleven Latino elected officials where only two served before 1989. Today, young, Progressive, and independent

Latinos like Pablo Rivera, state senator José Peralta, and Councilwoman Annabel Palma are nurturing their own local organizations and encouraging civic involvement through groups like the Latino Leadership Institute. They are savvy about electioneering, technology, and policy making—and are taking aim at the culture of corruption and cronyism in Albany.[144]

Dinkins was not able to hold the black–Latino coalition together for many reasons. For one, as early as the transition period, his administration failed to deliver a satisfying volume of improvements and political appointments to the Latino groups within the original coalition who supported him. Thus four years after his historic victory, Dinkins faced a reelection campaign—a rematch against Rudolph Giuliani—with a reduced Latino voter turnout.[145] As a result, in 1993 Giuliani became the 107th mayor of New York by less than 2 percentage points, or some 44,000 votes, the closest margin of victory in the history of the city's mayoral politics. Giuliani won 50.7 percent of the vote to Dinkins's 48 percent. An analysis of the ethnic breakdown of the voting results shows that Dinkins gained 95 percent of the African American vote and 65 percent of the Latino vote; Giuliani captured 77 percent of the largest voting bloc, that of whites. Giuliani would go on to win reelection in 1997.[146] He was succeeded by Republican-turned-Independent Michael Bloomberg. And in November 2014, voters in New York City elected a Democratic mayor, the first since Dinkins left office in 1993.

* * *

New York City's experiences between 1955 and 1995 teach us much about the nature of black and Latino coalition building in the United States. In 1959, black and Latino hospital workers developed solidarity as workers, suffering the same injustices, indignities, and aspirations. The workers gained the right to collective bargaining and more equitable pay only through the combined support of black and Latino political clubs, labor leaders, activists, entertainers, civil rights leaders, and elected officials. Similarly, blacks and Latinos were able to work together during the 1960s and 1970s on behalf of school reform, tenants' rights, and antipoverty programs, driven by immediate need and shared suffering.

Indeed, coalitions happen when necessity forces people together. Black and Latino neighbors work together to get the lights turned on in their buildings and to get the trash removed from their shared streets. Black and Latino students fight for the right to be seen on college campuses and study non-Eurocentric curricula. When the great migrations from the South and the Caribbean first occurred, immigrants remained isolated within their own ethnic groups. But as they became acculturated to their new surroundings, they started to branch out and learn from one another. They began to see their shared plight and collective power.[147]

It remained an open question whether the black and Latino constituencies, organizations, and communities that had come together and fallen apart so many times would be able to join forces once again to have a voice in the 2013 mayoral election. Bill de Blasio as the Progressive candidate was not black or Latino, but he had the capacity to learn from the experiences of politicians who had risen to power on the shoulders of these ethnic groups. De Blasio was able to build a coalition with representatives from all sectors of New York City's "gorgeous mosaic." He received endorsements from Local 1199 and DC 37 and benefited from their impressive get-out-the vote operations. De Blasio had the support of fast-food workers, who represent perhaps one of the most mobilized group of young and politically conscious laborers across the city today. On the campaign stump, de Blasio championed a living wage for the working poor as essential to improving the city's economy, and he called for an investigation into the labor practices and wages of fast-food restaurant chains operating in the city. In addition, he called for an end to the city's use of random arbitrary fines against mom-and-pop restaurants and vowed to create family-owned, business-friendly policies, all of which attracted operators of bodegas, pizza shops, and other types of small food-related businesses to vote for him.

The Progressive movements and coalitions covered in this book changed the city's history. Culminating in the election of David Dinkins in 1989, they provided new templates for advancing Progressive movements and building winning electoral majorities. The electoral infrastructure laid out in 1989 provided a road map for further independent campaigns, but the question still remains: Can a similar coalition form today and revitalize and improve, with the use of new technologies, the infrastructure built from 1959 to 1989?

CONCLUSION

I
N 1989 WITH the election of David Dinkins, the ethnic fragmentation of
the Democratic Party in New York City began. Before 1989, there had
been only white Democratic candidates for mayor. Democrats who con-
sciously or unconsciously viewed white candidates more positively than
non-whites and believed that they were better able to govern the city had no
difficult choices to make when they voted for mayor.[1] However, to date, the
1989 election was an anomaly. In that election and each following one, Democratic voters have consistently supported white candidates over non-white
candidates regardless of the candidate's party affiliation. Elections in 2005 and
2009 pitted a white against a non-white candidate. As the longtime Democratic political strategist Bill Lynch says, "When you put color in it, it changes
the nature of the election. When you put a person of color against somebody
who is white, most often the white candidates will win."[2] The meaning of 1989
for Democratic Party politics in New York City has been profound: Republicans have since been elected mayor of New York City when black and Latino
Democrats stay home and don't vote. Democratic Party turnout on election
days in the city fell almost 50 percent between 1993 and 2009, and Republicans have controlled City Hall during the same time period.[3]

FERNANDO FERRER'S CAMPAIGN FOR MAYOR

Democratic voter apathy in the changing face of New York City politics
revealed itself in 1997 in the Democratic primary for mayor of New York.

The Bronx borough president, Fernando Ferrer, ran in the hopes of unseating the Republican incumbent, Rudolph Giuliani. Some suspected that African American and Latino power brokers had cut a deal back when David Dinkins ran in 1989 and 1993; Latino political operatives in New York's Democratic Party would support an African American mayoral candidate, and, thereafter, African Americans would do likewise for Latino candidates—primarily, the Puerto Rican candidate Ferrer. But support for Ferrer from fellow elected Latino politicians remained lukewarm. In the Bronx, Ferrer had been a supporter of a corrupt machine, which had stained his reputation. He came up as a successor to Stanley Friedman, the Bronx Democratic Party leader, and Stanley Simon, then the Bronx borough president. Ferrer had backed the machine candidate (or remained silent) when Jesse Jackson ran for the Democratic nomination for president in 1984 and 1988 and when José Serrano ran against Simon as an insurgent in the Democratic primary for Bronx borough president in 1985. When Simon went to jail on a political corruption conviction, Ferrer became borough president by appointment; he kept Simon's staffers and appointees in power instead of cleaning house. In 1989, Ferrer also reluctantly came out in support of Dinkins in the Democratic mayoral primary. Activists remembered Ferrer's record, and many refused to support his campaigns for mayor in 1997, 2001, and 2005. The same remained true among African American politicians and activists who reluctantly, if at all, supported and worked for Ferrer's campaigns.[4]

At the start of the 1997 Democratic primary season, Zoilo Torres went to Ferrer's campaign office with a group of other activists. "We were all happy to get the old Dinkins activists together and get the first Puerto Rican elected mayor," Torres recalls. "I had some public differences with Ferrer in the past. But I went as an act of conciliation to volunteer for his campaign. But I didn't even get a call from the guy!"[5] So he and the other activist worked for Ferrer's opponent in the primary, the Jewish Progressive Manhattan borough president Ruth Messinger. For activists like Torres, Messinger was a better candidate because she was clearly left-of-center politically and did not have Ferrer's tainted reputation as a machine politician. "I broke with the old [Puerto Rican] nationalistic alliances" at that point "out of principle," says Torres.[6]

During the primary campaign, Messinger condemned another mayoral candidate, Al Sharpton, for not condemning the Nation of Islam's leader,

Louis Farrakhan, as an anti-Semite. Farrakhan had called Jews "bloodsuck-ers" and Judaism a "gutter religion."[7] Sharpton regarded Messinger's con-demnation as an example of how she was introducing racial politics into the Democratic primary and playing the race card to attract white Democratic voters "at the expense of racial sensitivities in this city."[8] In 1997, Sharpton received substantial support from Latino leaders as well as African Ameri-cans who had supported Ferrer until he dropped out of the race in May. Fer-rer's departure gave Sharpton's campaign "a big boost" as he gained enough black and Latino votes to be called a coalition candidate.[9] In fact, Ferrer dropped out because his campaign could not sustain the necessary fund-raising to be competitive in the primary, but publicly Ferrer insisted that his departure from the primary race would help unify the Democratic Party and thereby ensure Giuliani's defeat in the general election.[10] When Sharp-ton ran for the U.S. Senate in 1994, he received the endorsement of *El Diario*, the city's largest Spanish-language newspaper, and gained 60 percent of the Latino vote in that campaign. After Ferrer left the race, he, like many lead-ing African American Democrats, endorsed Messinger. Nonetheless, Fer-rer's support of her campaign can best be described as apathetic.[11]

Like Ferrer, Dinkins and Representatives Charles Rangel and Major Owens endorsed Messinger. While campaigning, Sharpton criticized Mess-inger for having refused to support Jackson in 1988 and for playing the race card against him, and this action negated the impact of Dinkins's, Rangel's, and Owens's endorsement of Messinger. In addition, DC 37, the city's larg-est public-employee union, endorsed the incumbent mayor, Giuliani, thus denying Messinger access to thousands of campaign volunteers and phone banks that the union operated.[12] In a low turnout, even though Messinger had a larger war chest than Sharpton, she struggled to capture the necessary 40 percent of the primary vote to avoid a runoff. Messinger defeated Sharp-ton in the primary, winning 39 percent.[13]

Sharpton's lawyers first filed suit, demanding that the Democratic run-off be held and citing fraud and irregularities in the primary; they later dropped the suit. Sharpton would go on to campaign for Messinger in the general election against Giuliani. But the possibility of that lawsuit repressed voter turnout in the general election among the black and Latino voters who had supported Sharpton and who viewed Messinger as attempting to steal the election from him. In the end, Sharpton's followers gave Messinger lukewarm support at best in the general election. Before the primary, Sharpton correctly predicted that the African Americans who did not turn out to support Dinkins's reelection bid in 1993 would also not turn out for Messinger in 1997.[14] In addition, Messinger was too far to the left for many white Democratic voters. Messinger's stump speech called for building more affordable housing in the city, ending economic and racial inequalities, stopping police brutality, and supporting immigrants' rights.[15] The Progressive coalition that did form and support Messinger paled in contrast with the one Dinkins had enjoyed. The Messinger coalition failed miserably to get working-class black and Latino voters to turn out and vote on election day; as a result, Giuliani enjoyed a landslide victory because the base of the Democratic Party stayed home.

In 2001, a coalition formed in support of Ferrer, although one without several important Latino and African American Progressives who again refused to support his candidacy. The primary election that year fell on September 11, and due to the terrorist attack on the World Trade Center that morning, voting was postponed. When the election took place weeks later, Ferrer failed to obtain the necessary 40 percent of the vote to avoid a runoff with the second-place vote-getter. In the runoff, Ferrer faced off against Public Advocate Mark Green, but during the race a polarizing political cartoon surfaced of Ferrer kissing Al Sharpton's rear end. The source of the cartoon is unknown, but African Americans and Latinos believed that Green's campaign had created and released the flyer. The image mobilized white working-class Democrats to vote for Green, who went on to win the primary with the majority of white Democratic votes.[16] As in 1997, black and Latino working-class voters, unimpressed with either Ferrer or Green, stayed at home. After the primary victory, Green met with Ferrer's campaign team. He condescendingly told them, "I don't need your votes; I need you to help me govern," reported the political strategist Bill Lynch, who attended the meeting. In the general election, the billionaire Republican challenger Michael Bloomberg's money and Green's "arrogance got him killed," according to Lynch.[17]

Bloomberg outspent Green by tens of millions of dollars. In an expensive media market like New York City, historically potential candidates can't run for mayor or win an election unless they have money, a lot of money. A former registered Democrat, Bloomberg was neither a liberal nor a conservative but a venture capitalist whose fortune went a long way in defeating Green. Bloomberg also won because Green had no viable Progressive coalition to mobilize his party's base. The weak black and Latino coalition that had supported Ferrer had collapsed after the racially polarizing primary campaign. And again, the majority of working-class black and Latino voters stayed home on election day in 2001. In the 2001 general election, Bloomberg received 719,819 votes, or 50 percent, and Green received 676,560 or 47 percent, in an election marked by overall low voter turnout in a city where Democrats outnumbered Republicans 8 to 1. In 2001, African American voters supported Green 3 to 1, while half of the Latino vote went to Bloomberg.[18] The Messinger and Green losses proved that Democrats could not elect a mayor without support and voter turnout from the black and Latino communities.

MICHAEL BLOOMBERG, THE BILLION-DOLLAR CANDIDATE

In 2005, Fernando Ferrer finally won the Democratic nomination for mayor, but his political past hounded him once again. He was unable to gain unanimous support among Latino activists and African Americans who continued to view his support for David Dinkins as having been lukewarm. Additionally, he had been out of office for four years and had a hard time reigniting black and Latino members of his base. Despite the obstacles, Ferrer won the Democratic primary and ran against the incumbent, Michael Bloomberg. It is hard to defeat an incumbent, especially a popular and wealthy one, and in 2005, Ferrer was further hampered by white working-class Democratic voters crossing party lines and electing a white candidate instead of supporting a Latino member of their own party. All told, Ferrer lacked a strong Progressive coalition to mobilize voters or the money to match Bloomberg's campaign war chest.

The same thing happened in 2009, when the African American Bill Thompson, the city comptroller, ran against Bloomberg. Thompson received tepid support from some Latinos and got no support from the recently elected President Barack Obama. Thompson could not match Bloomberg's campaign funds, and behind the scenes, Bloomberg had been "making promises, cutting deals, and buying influence," with community organizations and grassroots groups across the city, remembers Hector Soto. Bloomberg also carried out a "carpet-bombing campaign" that "obliterated any opposition."[19] Despite these challenges, Thompson ran a surprisingly more competitive campaign against Bloomberg than had Mark Green in 2001 and Ferrer in 2005, winning 46 percent of the vote.

ORGANIZED LABOR AND BLACK AND LATINO COALITIONS

The twelve years of Ed Koch's mayoralty followed by twenty years of Republican mayors in New York City under Rudolph Giuliani and Michael Bloomberg devastated organized labor in New York City. By Bloomberg's final year in office, all the city's 152 public-sector union contracts had expired. Many unions threw their support to Bill de Blasio, who won the mayoral election and was inaugurated on January 1, 2014. But in the process of waiting for the end of the Bloomberg era, many union members became demobilized. Workers in the food industry showed themselves to be among the most militant and savvy in the city's labor movement, but their organizing efforts and demands for higher wages and better working conditions had been hampered by lack of money and political support.[20] In 2012, union membership across the country had declined to its lowest level since 1916 (percentages of membership decline in New York City did not exist at the time of publication). The Bureau of Labor Statistics reported that union membership last year fell drastically, despite increases in the nation's employment rates.[21]

Without campaign finance reform, politicians uninterested in increasing opportunities for working-class black and Latino communities in the city will continue to maintain control of City Hall and elsewhere. However, developing strategies to mobilize black and Latino working-class voters seems the most cogent way of electing a candidate responsive to the Progressive coalition that put him or her in office. From 1959 to 1989, organized labor benefited from what can best be described as pragmatic and shrewd Democratic and Republican candidates (for boroughwide, citywide, and statewide elections) who needed workers' support to get elected and reelected. That was the case for Democratic mayor Robert F. Wagner Jr., Republican governor Nelson Rockefeller, and Republican mayor John Lindsay. However, this state of affairs began to change with the rise of neoliberalism in the late 1970s and early 1980s. Even the Democrat Ed Koch benefitted from the support of real-estate interest groups during his first campaign and relied less on union support. He implemented Reagan-style policies in New York, which worked against the interest of organized labor, which included, by the 1980s, an increasing number of blacks and Latinos. Organized labor in Progressive coalitions with former radicals mobilized to help defeat Koch when he ran in the 1982 Democratic primary for governor of New York against Mario Cuomo. The election of Cuomo helped soften some of the hardships that working-class black and Latino residents suffered in New York City under Reagan and Koch. Organized labor benefitted from the fact that Cuomo remained beholden to them to get reelected. As a result, the governor supported many of the policies and candidates that Progressive coalitions, which included the city's largest labor unions, supported. And so for the twelve years under Bloomberg, the unions had no leverage because he owed them nothing.

The problem was that the majority of candidates that these coalitions backed from 1959 to 1989 were not Progressives but pragmatic, centrist politicians. From Wagner in 1954 to Koch in 1977, they backed just enough Progressive policies and candidates to gain the endorsement and support of Progressive coalitions. The politicians did not resist, reject, or refuse the support of wealthy corporations or individuals who paid for their campaigns, especially those in the banking and real-estate sectors. The few Progressives elected to public office in New York City—like Gilberto Gerena Valentín, Al Vann, David Dinkins, and Ruth Messinger—found little support among other elected officials and/or the New York City press corps for their policies or their reelection campaigns.

BLACK AND LATINO ELECTED OFFICIALS POST-1989

There were a number of black Latino Progressive coalitions that waged battles before the creation of Latinos for Dinkins. David Dinkins's campaign victory and his administration's support for the political reapportionment and increase in the number of seats in the City Council from thirty-five to fifty-one have ensured that blacks and Latinos are today well represented among New York City elected officials. But representation in higher citywide or statewide offices still remains elusive, largely because of racial fragmentation within the Democratic Party.

A number of problems remain among black and Latino elected officials in Albany. They need to clearly articulate issues relevant to the communities they represent, but, most of all, their efforts and reputations have been seriously hampered by the rampant corruption in Albany. Officials have to do a better job investigating allegations of improprieties among elected officials. For example, just as the 2013 New York mayoral election began to rev up, corruption scandals and the arrest of black and Latino legislators from New York City rocked Albany. "You have a better chance" of being led out of the Assembly or the Senate in Albany in "handcuffs than you do being voted out of office," says Ken Lovett, Albany bureau chief for the *Daily News*.[22]

In order to regain the strength that had helped Dinkins into office, black and Latino elected officials need to mobilize around issues important to Progressives in the same way that labor leaders did in hospitals in the 1950s and 1960s, as student activists did on college campuses in the late 1960s, as activists did on the streets and in tenements in the 1960s through the 1980s, and as various groups did in 2012 (under the aegis of Occupy movements that first began in New York City).

The demands of black and Latino Progressive coalitions from 1959 to 1989 were consistent and remain important concerns today: a living wage in which to provide better housing, health care, food, and educational opportunities for them and their families; the end of police brutality; and greater black and Latino representation among elected officials. On the question of ending police brutality, Progressive coalitions have been engaged in a campaign for almost two decades to end the NYPD's stop-and-frisk crime-prevention program. It is viewed as a civil rights violation, which police officers most often carry out against male youth in black and Latino communities across the city. In fact, stop-and-frisk remained a constant part of the debate among candidates vying for the Democratic nomination for mayor of New York.[23]

THE FOUNDATION OF POLITICAL SUCCESS

Coalitions occur when individuals and communities recognize that victory requires partners with similar interests; otherwise, forging ahead alone will mean defeat. As the elections of Harold Washington and David Dinkins and the success of Jesse Jackson's Rainbow Coalition show, powerful coalitions include key players with the ability to bring different community leaders together.

Granted, some coalitions succeed and others fall apart. But the coalitions that last the longest are those with individuals and groups that show the capacity to expand their concern beyond their own opinions, feelings, and views, and embrace and validate those of their coalition partners. After achieving a goal, obtaining a list of demands, and/or winning an election, many successful and enduring coalitions develop a collective approach to allocating resources, making appointments, keeping the lines of communication open, and obtaining advice. They also have fund-raising resources to finance their issues, and they respect the needs of the coalition partners who have contributed to their success.[24] Especially in today's fragmented political landscape, no candidate can win any office of importance without the support of like-minded, if diverse, coalitions. Labor unions and other organizations with large numbers of working-class black and Latino members cannot advance their interests without political support from elected officials.

In the 2013 campaign for New York City mayor, the Manhattan-born and Massachusetts-raised Bill de Blasio was able to put together a viable coalition. De Blasio earned degrees from New York University and Columbia University; he served as a councilman and as New York City public advocate, and surprised many by gaining support from a coalition that includes black, Latino, and white Progressives. He is married to an African American and has the necessary street and professional credibility to pick up the mantle that Dinkins left behind in 1993. De Blasio has lived most of his adult life in the Park Slope section of Brooklyn. In 1989, he entered politics for the first time, serving as a volunteer coordinator for the Dinkins campaign in Brooklyn. After Dinkins's election, de Blasio served as an aide on Dinkins's City Hall staff and worked on Dinkins's 1993 reelection campaign, before going on to hold positions on the staff of Charles Rangel in Harlem and Peter Vallone, a Democrat from Queens. Since his days as a volunteer on the Dinkins campaign, de Blasio had gained a reputation as the savvy New York political strategist from Brooklyn. As result, in 1996 President Bill Clinton hired him to run the Clinton–Gore reelection campaign in New York. In 1997, Clinton appointed him as his regional director for New York and New

Jersey in the U.S. Department of Housing and Urban Development (HUD) under Andrew Cuomo, then HUD secretary. While at HUD, de Blasio ran for public office for the first time, winning a seat on Community School Board 15 in Brooklyn in 1999. In 2000, Hillary Clinton named him to run her Senate campaign, supervising all aspects of her candidacy, including political strategy, daily events, and the get-out-the-vote operation on election day. In 2001, de Blasio won a seat on the New York City Council, where he represented the Thirty-ninth Council District in Brooklyn. De Blasio served on the City Council from 2002 to 2010, and then won a citywide office as the New York City public advocate, the position he held when he announced that he was running for mayor in 2013. He won that election with more than 73 percent of the vote.[25]

De Blasio won the Democratic primary for mayor of New York in no small part due to a campaign commercial featuring his fifteen-year-old charismatic son, Dante. In the ad, the tall, confident youth sports a large Afro hairdo and champions de Blasio's political platform, which calls for affordable housing, increased taxes on the wealthy to pay for universal preschool, and ending the NYPD's stop-and-frisk crime-prevention policy, which disproportionally focuses on stopping black and Latino youth who look like Dante. As the ad ends, it shows Bill de Blasio at home with his wife, Chirlane McCray, and his children, Ciara and Dante, with Dante saying into the camera: "Bill de Blasio will be a mayor for every New Yorker, no matter where they live, or what they look like," followed by a closing scene of father and son walking down the street with de Blasio placing his arm around him. Dante delivers the clincher: "And I'd say that even if he weren't my dad."[26]

NOTES

INTRODUCTION

1. Frank D. Bean and Marta Tienda, *The Hispanic Population of the United States* (New York: Russell Sage Foundation, 1987); Laird W. Bergad and Herbert S. Klein, *Hispanics in the United States: A Demographic, Social, and Economic History, 1980–2005* (Cambridge: Cambridge University Press, 2010); Jorge Duany, *Blurred Borders: Transnational Migration Between the Hispanic Caribbean and the United States* (Chapel Hill: University of North Carolina Press, 2011).

2. Leon Fink and Brian Greenberg, *Upheaval in the Quiet Zone: A History of Hospital Workers' Union, Local 1199* (Urbana: University of Illinois Press, 1989). Very little exists on the coalitions, even among the most recent labor histories published. David Goldberg and Trevor Griffey, eds. *Black Power at Work* (Ithaca, N.Y.: Cornell University Press, 2010).

3. Ralph Ellison, *Invisible Man* (New York: Vintage International, 1995); V. P. Franklin, ed., "The History of Black Student Activism," special issue, *Journal of African American History* 88, no. 2 (2003). Some works discuss the activist but not in depth: Shelly L. Anderson, "An Uneasy Alliance: Blacks and Latinos in New York City Politics" (Ph.D. diss, Ohio State University, 2002). Most are devoid of Latino activist participation, such as Latinos for Jackson discussed in the last two chapters of this book. See, for example, John Jairo Betancur, *The Collaborative City: Opportunities and Struggles for Blacks and Latinos* (New York: Routledge, 1999); and Chris McNickle, *To Be Mayor of New York: Ethnic Politics in the City* (New York: Columbia University Press, 1993).

4. Bill Platt, *Black and Brown in America: The Case for Cooperation* (New York: New York University Press, 1997); Juan F. Perea, "The Black/White Binary Paradigm of Race," in *The Latino/a Condition: A Critical Reader*, ed. Richard Delgado and Jean Stefancic (New York: New York University Press, 1998), 359–68; Paula D. McClain and Joseph Stewart Jr., *"Can We All Get Along": Racial and Ethnic*

Minorities in American Politics, 1998, 2nd ed. (Boulder, Colo.: Westview Press, 1998); Nicolás C. Vaca, *The Presumed Alliance: The Unspoken Conflict Between Latinos and Blacks and What It Means for America* (New York: HarperCollins, 2004); J. Phillip Thompson III, *Double Trouble: Black Mayors, Black Communities, and the Call for Deep Democracy* (New York: Oxford University Press, 2006); Neil Foley, *Quest for Equality: The Failed Promise of Black-Brown Solidarity* (Cambridge, Mass.: Harvard University Press, 2010). Scholarship on coalition building gleaned from Jill M. Bystydzienski and Steven P. Schacht, eds., *Forging Radical Alliances Across Difference: Coalition Politics for the New Millennium* (New York: Rowman & Littlefield, 2001); and Gerald Horn, *Black and Brown: African Americans and the Mexican Revolution, 1910–1920* (New York: New York University Press, 2005).

5. Address by Dr. Martin Luther King Jr. to Prayer Pilgrimage, July 22, 1962, 1, Folder Committee for Justice to Hospital Workers & Prayer Pilgrimage July 22, 1962, Box 48 Strike—Ten Hospitals—May 1960, collection 5510, Kheel Center for Labor-Management Documentation and Archives, Cornell University, Ithaca, N.Y.

1. JOURNEYS

1. Harvey Brett, "Report on Cuban Population in N.Y.C.," 1, 3–4, November 25, 1935, "Feeding the City Project Collection" WPA NYC Unit (hereafter FCWPA), Roll 269; Strong, "Puerto Rican Colony in N.Y.," 1935(?), 2, FCWPA, Roll 269; "Spanish American Restaurants," 2, FCWPA, Roll 144, Eating Out Foreign Restaurants Research Folder; Irma Watkins-Owens, *Blood Relations: Caribbean Immigrants and the Harlem Community, 1900–1930* (Bloomington: Indiana University Press, 1996), 4; Geoffrey Jacques, "CuBop! Afro-Cuban Music and Mid-Twentieth-Century American Culture," in *Between Race and Empire: African Americans and Cubans Before the Cuban Revolution*, ed. Lisa Brock and Digna Castañeda Fuertes (Philadelphia: Temple University Press, 1998), 253.

2. Strong, "Puerto Rican Colony in N.Y."

3. Ramón Grosfoguel and Chloé S. Georas, "Latino Caribbean Diasporas in New York," in Mambo Montage: The Latinization of New York, ed. Agustín Laó-Montes and Arlene Dávila (New York: Columbia University Press, 2001), 105.

4. Ibid.

5. Winston James, *Holding Aloft the Banner of Ethiopia: Caribbean Radicalism in Early Twentieth-Century America* (London: Verso, 1998), 197.

6. R. H. Leavell, T. R. Snavely, T. J. Woofter, Jr., W. T. B. Williams, and Francis D. Tyson, *Negro Migration in 1916–17* (Washington, D.C.: Government Printing Office, 1919), 87, 104–105; Michael Perman, *Struggle for Mastery: Disfranchisement in the South, 1888–1908* (Chapel Hill: University of North Carolina Press, 2001), 269.

7. Leavell et al., *Negro Migration*, 101, 105, 107, 28–31. On the Great Migration in general, see Carole Marks, *Farewell—We're Good and Gone: The Great Black Migration* (Bloomington: Indiana University Press, 1989). On the migration to Chicago, see James Grossman, *Land of Hope: Chicago, Black Southerners, and the Great Migration* (Chicago: University of Chicago Press, 1989). On Westchester County, see Andrew Wiese, *Places of Their Own: African American Suburbanization in the Twentieth Century* (Chicago: University of Chicago Press, 2004), chap. 2. On Harlem, see Gilbert Osofsky, *Harlem: The Making of a Ghetto, Negro New York, 1890–1930* (New York: Harper Torchbooks, 1964). On Cleveland, see Kenneth L. Kusmer, *A Ghetto Takes Shape: Black Cleveland, 1870–1930* (Urbana: University of Illinois Press, 1976).

8. 1930 Federal Census of the Village of North Tarrytown, N.Y.

9. Ibid.

10. Cheryl Lynn Greenberg, *Or Does It Explode? Black Harlem in the Great Depression* (New York: Oxford University Press, 1991).

11. Osofsky, *Harlem*.

12. Grosfoguel and Georas, "Latino Caribbean Diasporas in New York," 107.

13. Ibid.

14. Edwin Cruise, interview with author, 2006.

15. Louis A. Perez, Jr., *Cuba Between Reform and Revolution* (New York: Oxford University Press, 1995), 288–312.

16. Francisco Corona, interview with author, 2006.

17. George Priestly, interview with author, 2006.

18. Ibid.

2. UPSETTING THE APPLE CART

1. Leon Fink and Brian Greenberg, *Upheaval in the Quiet Zone: A History of Hospital Workers' Union, Local 1199* (Urbana: University of Illinois Press, 1989), 1, 6; Frederick Douglass Opie, "Eating, Dancing, and Courting in New York: Black and Latino Relations 1930–1970," *Journal of Social History* 42, no. 1 (2008): 80.

2. Ken Downs, Montefiore Hospital interview transcript, 1975, Box 5680OH, 1, 14, Sub-Series X-D, 33, 47, 22, 47, 49, 50, 54, Kheel Center for Labor-Management Documentation and Archives, Cornell University, Ithaca, N.Y.

3. Fink and Greenberg, *Upheaval in the Quiet Zone*, 47, 48.

4. Ted Mitchell, Montefiore Hospital interview transcript 1, 1975, Box 5680OH, 1, 43, Sub-Sub-Sub-Series X-A-1-i, 1, 37.

5. *New York Amsterdam News*, December 6, 1958, March 21, 1959, January 24, 1959.

6. Hilda Joquin, Mount Sinai Hospital interview transcript, 1977, Box 5680OH, Sub-Series X-B, 7, Kheel Center Archives.

7. Julio Pagan, interview with author.

8. Nellie Morris, interview with author.

9. Ibid.; Emerito Cruz, interview with author.

10. Henry Nicholas, Mount Sinai interview transcript, 8, 9.

11. Joquin, Mount Sinai interview transcript, 5.

12. Moe Foner with Dan North, foreword by Ossie Davis, *Not for Bread Alone: A Memoir* (Ithaca, N.Y.: Cornell University Press, 2002), 55.

13. Joquin, Mount Sinai interview transcript, 16, 18.

14. Salvadore Cordero, Montefiore interview transcript, 3, 5.

15. Joseph Brown, Montefiore interview transcript, 35.

16. Foner, *Not for Bread Alone*, 37–38.

17. Mitchell, Montefiore interview transcript 1, 14.

18. Foner, *Not for Bread Alone*, 38.

19. Ibid. See also Fink and Greenberg, *Upheaval in the Quiet Zone*, 17–18.

20. Foner, *Not for Bread Alone*, 38, 39.

21. Mitchell, Montefiore interview transcript 1, 31.

22. Thelma Bowles, Montefiore interview transcript, 21, 25–26, 11, 31, 33, 3.

23. Brown, Montefiore interview transcript, 2, 5–6, 22–23, 31, 24–25, 29, 3, 25–26, 31–32, 36.

24. Fink and Greenberg, *Upheaval in the Quiet Zone*.

25. Downs, Montefiore interview transcript, 18, 29, 44.

26. Bowles, Montefiore interview transcript, 27.

27. Downs, Montefiore interview transcript, 40.

28. Cordero, Montefiore interview transcript, 12, 19; Cruz, Montefiore interview transcript, 14.

29. Cordero, Montefiore interview transcript, 19, 13; Mitchell, Montefiore interview transcript 1, 33, 34.

30. Mitchell, Montefiore interview transcript 1, 18.

31. Ted Mitchell, Montefiore Hospital interview transcript 2, 1976, Box 5680OH, 1, 44, Sub-Sub-Sub-Series X-A-1-i, 2, 17–18, Kheel Center Archives.

32. Fink and Greenberg, *Upheaval in the Quiet Zone*, 36.

33. Mitchell, Montefiore interview transcript 1, 9–10, and Montefiore interview transcript 2, 32.

34. Fink and Greenberg, *Upheaval in the Quiet Zone*, 38.

35. Ibid., 41.

36. Foner, *Not for Bread Alone*, 42.

37. Mitchell, Montefiore interview transcript 2, 35.

38. Foner, *Not for Bread Alone*, 40–41, 45; Fink and Greenberg, *Upheaval in the Quiet Zone*, 41.

39. Foner, *Not for Bread Alone*, 55, 43.

40. Fink and Greenberg, *Upheaval in the Quiet Zone*, 44–45.

41. Foner, *Not for Bread Alone,* 43; Fink and Greenberg, *Upheaval in the Quiet Zone,* 44–46.

42. Pagan, Mount Sinai interview transcript, 14–17.

43. Nicholas, Mount Sinai interview transcript, 2, 18.

44. Joquin, Mount Sinai interview transcript, 6–8, 13, 15, 17.

45. Quoted in "You Don't Get Anything on a Silver Platter," *1199 News,* December 1999, 15.

46. Foner, *Not for Bread Alone,* 45.

47. Ibid.

48. Fink and Greenberg, *Upheaval in the Quiet Zone,* 55–56, 61; Brown, Montefiore interview transcript, 38.

49. Brown, Montefiore interview transcript, 40; Endorsement of Bronx State Assemblyman Felipe N. Torres to Chairman 1199 Bronx Strike Committee Joseph Brown, June 11, 1959, Collection 5510, Box 46, Folder Messages from Unions, Org, Ind. Re Strike, Kheel Center Archives; Fink and Greenberg, *Upheaval in the Quiet Zone,* 47.

50. Foner, *Not for Bread Alone,* 47.

51. Fink and Greenberg, *Upheaval in the Quiet Zone,* 63.

52. Nicholas, Mount Sinai interview transcript, 16–17.

53. Bowles, Montefiore interview transcript, 52.

54. Foner, *Not for Bread Alone,* 55; Pagan, Mount Sinai interview transcript, 22.

55. Officials and Executive Board of Local 585 to Members, May 13, 1959, Collection 5510, Box 46, Folder Contributions Food, Kheel Center Archives.

56. Fink and Greenberg, *Upheaval in the Quiet Zone,* 66, 67, 79.

57. Ibid., 72–73.

58. Shirley Gray, interview with author, August 2008; *New York Times,* January 7, 1987.

59. Leroy Archibald, interview with author, January 2011.

60. Santos Crespo, interview with author, August 2008.

61. Thomas Russell Jones, vice president Bedford-Stuyvesant Political League to Local 1199, June 10, 1959, Collection 5510, Box 46, Folder Contributions Food, Kheel Center Archives.

62. Gowanus Spanish American Club, Food Contribution to Local 1199, June 11, 1959, Collection 5510, Box 46, Folder Contributions Food, Kheel Center Archives.

63. Food Contribution List, ca. May 1959, Collection 5510, Box 46, Folder Contributions Food, 2, Kheel Center Archives.

64. Mitchell, Montefiore interview transcript 2, 36.

65. Quoted in "You Don't Get Anything on a Silver Platter," 15.

66. Foner, *Not for Bread Alone,* 45.

67. Ibid., 49.

68. Ibid., 49, 45.

69. Mitchell, Montefiore interview transcript 1, 16.

70. Foner, *Not for Bread Alone,* 45.

71. Fink and Greenberg, *Upheaval in the Quiet Zone*, 79.

72. L. Joseph Overton, president New York NAACP, Press Release, May 17, 1959, Collection 5510, Box 46, Folder Messages from Unions, Org, Ind. Re Strike, Kheel Center Archives.

73. L. Joseph Overton, president New York NAACP, to Juan Sanchez, president Federation of Hispanic Societies, Inc., May 19, 1959, Collection 5510, Box 46, Folder Messages from Unions, Org, Ind. Re Strike, Kheel Center Archives.

74. *New York Amsterdam News*, July 14, 1962; List of Hispanic Contacts for Operation Humanity, ca. May 1959, Collection 5510, Box 46, Folder Messages from Unions, Org, Ind. Re Strike, 2, Kheel Center Archives.

75. Foner, *Not for Bread Alone*, 49; Fink and Greenberg, *Upheaval in the Quiet Zone*, 79.

76. Fay Bennett, executive secretary National Sharecroppers Fund, press release, June 1, 1959, Collection 5510, Box 46, Folder Contributions Food, Kheel Center Archives.

77. Local 32-E and Bronx NAACP Flyer, "Giant Outdoor Rally," ca. June 10, 1959, Collection 5510, Box 46, Folder Messages from Unions, Org, Ind. Re Strike, 1–2, Kheel Center Archives.

78. *New York Amsterdam News*, May 16, 1959.

79. Fink and Greenberg, *Upheaval in the Quiet Zone*, 93–95.

80. Foner, *Not for Bread Alone*, 56–57.

81. A. Philip Randolph to Friends of the Committee, June 22, 1962, Collection 5510, Box 46, Folder Messages from Unions, Org, Ind. Re Strike, Kheel Center Archives.

82. Bayard Rustin, interview transcript, 1977, Box 56900H, 2, 56, Sub-Sub-Series X-F-4, 15, 5, Kheel Center Archives.

83. *New York Times*, November 19, 2005; Sherrie Baver, "Puerto Rican Politics in New York City: The Post–World War II Period," in Jennings and Rivera, *Puerto Rican Politics in Urban America*, ed. James Jennings and Monte Rivera (Westport, Conn.: Greenwood Press, 1984), 44–46.

84. William K. De Fossett, report on the Emergency Action Convention on June 29, 1962 in the office of A. Phillip Randolph, Bureau of Special Services, July 2, 1962, Box 6140, 3, 38, Malcolm X File, 1–3, Kheel Center Archives; Joseph Monserrat and A. Philip Randolph to Friends of the Committee, July 30, 1962, Collection 5510, Box 48 Strike—Ten Hospitals—May, 1960, Folder Committee for Justice to Hospital Workers & Prayer Pilgrimage July 22, 1962, Kheel Center Archives; "Cleveland Robinson Obituary," *New York Times*, September 1, 1995; Cora T. Walker Obituary, *New York Times*, July 20, 2006.

85. "Malcolm X Labor's Ally?" *1199 News*, Winter 1993, 27.

86. De Fossett, report on the Emergency Action Convention, 1.

87. Ibid., 2–3.

88. Foner, *Not for Bread Alone*, 60.

89. Quoted in "Malcolm X Labor's Ally?" 27.

90. Dr. Martin Luther King, Jr., Address to Prayer Pilgrimage, July 22, 1962, Collection 5510, Box 48 Strike—Ten Hospitals—May, 1960, Folder Committee for Justice to Hospital Workers & Prayer Pilgrimage July 22, 1962, 1–2, Kheel Center Archives.

91. Fink and Greenberg, *Upheaval in the Quiet Zone*, 113.

92. Resolutions Adopted by the Committee for Justice to Hospital Workers, July 21, 1962, Collection 5510, Box 48 Strike—Ten Hospitals—May, 1960, Folder Committee for Justice to Hospital Workers & Prayer Pilgrimage, July 22, 1962, 1, 2, Kheel Center Archives.

3. DEVELOPING THEIR MINDS WITHOUT LOSING THEIR SOULS

1. The theoretical aspects of this essay are based on Frederick Douglass Opie, "Eating, Dancing, and Courting in New York: Black and Latino Relations, 1930–1970," *Journal of Social History* 42, no. 1 (2008): 79–109.

2. Bayard Rustin, "Black Folks, White Folks," in *Report from Black America*, ed. Peter Goldman (New York: Simon and Schuster, 1969), 144.

3. Ibid. See also Stokely Carmichael and Charles V. Hamilton, *Black Power: The Politics of Liberation in America* (New York: Vintage Books, 1967), 37–38, 44, 46; and Komozi Woodard, *A Nation Within a Nation: Amiri Baraka (LeRoi Jones) and Black Power Politics* (Chapel Hill: University of North Carolina Press, 1999), 32, 86.

4. Donald Alexander Downs, *Cornell '69: Liberalism and the Crisis of the American University* (Ithaca, N.Y.: Cornell University Press, 1999), 4; Stefan Bradley, "'Gym Crow Must Go!' Black Student Activism at Columbia University, 1967–1968," in "The History of Black Student Activism," ed. V. P. Franklin, special issue, *Journal of African American History* 88, no. 2 (2003): 165–167; Peniel E. Joseph, "Dashikis and Democracy: Black Studies, Student Activism, and the Black Power Movement," in "The History of Black Student Activism," ed. V. P. Franklin, special issue, *Journal of African American History* 88, no. 2 (2003): 191. A recent book that does a much better job of clarifying exclusiveness is Martha Biondi, *The Black Revolution on Campus* (Berkeley: University of California Press, 2012).

5. Ralph Ellison, *Invisible Man* (New York: Vintage International, 1995).

6. Bradley, "'Gym Crow Must Go!'" 168.

7. C. Wright Mills, *The Puerto Rican Journey: New York's Newest Migrants* (New York: Russell & Russell, 1967), 220–221; Opie, "Eating, Dancing, and Courting in New York," 80–81; Joseph, "Dashikis and Democracy," 197.

8. Edward J. Escobar, "The Dialectics of Repression: The Los Angeles Police Department and the Chicano Movement, 1968–1971," *Journal of American History* 79, no. 4 (1993): 1490.

9. Ibid., 1491, 1492. See also Basilio Serrano, "Rifle, Cañón, y Escopeta!": A Chronicle of the Puerto Rican Student Union," in *The Puerto Rican Movement: Voices from*

the Diaspora, ed. Andrés Torres and José E. Velázquez (Philadelphia: Temple University Press, 1998), 125; and Vicki Ruíz and Virginia Sánchez Korrol, *Latinas in the United States: A Historical Encyclopedia* (Bloomington: Indiana University Press, 2006), 728.

10. Allen B. Ballard, *The Education of Black Folk: The Afro-American Struggle for Knowledge in White America* (Lincoln, Neb.: iUniverse, 2004), 65–67, 68.

11. *Campus*, December 20, 1967.

12. Lillian Jiménez, "Puerto Ricans and Educational Civil Rights: A History of the 1969 City College Takeover," *Centro Journal* 21, no. 2 (2009): 163–164.

13. Annual Reports 1967–1968, and 1968–1969 SEEK Program, SEEK File, Special Collections, Leonard Lief Library, Lehman College, Bronx, N.Y.

14. Victor Manuel Quintana, interview with author, November 2011.

15. *Meridian*, October 13, 1967, 2.

16. Miguel "Mickey" Melendez, *We Took the Streets: Fighting Latino Rights with the Young Lords* (New York: St. Martin's Press, 2003), 74–76; Mark Naison, interview with author, 2008.

17. Ballard, *Education of Black Folk*, 68.

18. Ibid.

19. Ibid., 68–69.

20. Quintana, interview with author.

21. *Meridian*, November 13, 1967, 5.

22. Jiménez, "Puerto Ricans and Educational Civil Rights," 160–161, 166–167; Xavier Totti, interview with author, February 2012.

23. Totti, interview with author.

24. Piri Thomas, *Down These Mean Streets* (1967; repr., New York: Vintage Books, 1997), 121, 123.

25. Zora Neale Hurston, *Folklore, Memoirs, and Other Writings* [online] (New York: Library of America, 1995), 674.

26. Frederick Douglass Opie, *Hog and Hominy: Soul Food from Africa to America* (New York: Columbia University Press, 2008), 125–128; Mark Naison, *White Boy: A Memoir* (Philadelphia: Temple University Press), 80–81.

27. José Candelario, interview with author, August 2011.

28. Edwin Cruz, interview with author, December 2006.

29. *Meridian*, November 13, 1967, 5.

30. *Meridian*, February 4, 1970.

31. Ballard, *Education of Black Folk*, 67.

32. Ibid.

33. *New York Amsterdam News*, August 20, 1966.

34. Quoted in *Campus*, November 16, 1967, 1.

35. Quoted in ibid., 1, 4, 5.

36. Quoted in *Tech News*, October 3, 1967, 2, 6.

37. Quoted in ibid., 6.
38. Quoted in *Tech News*, October 24, 1967, 1.
39. Ibid., 7.
40. Downs, *Cornell '69*, 4.
41. Bradley, "Gym Crow Must Go!" 167.
42. "Forty Years After Historic Columbia Strike, Four Leaders of 1968 Student Uprising Reflect," *Democracy Now!* [radio show], April 25, 2008, http://www.democracynow.org/2008/4/25/forty_years_after_historic_columbia_strike.
43. Juan González, interview, *Democracy Now!* April 25, 2008; Naison, *White Boy*, 38.
44. González, interview.
45. Naison, *White Boy*, 90–91.
46. *Meridian*, Tuesday, April 18, 1969.
47. Naison, *White Boy*, 91; Bradley, "'Gym Crow Must Go!'" 172, 176; Vertamae Smart-Grosvenor, *Vibration Cooking, or, The Travel Notes of a Geechee Girl* (Athens: University of Georgia Press, 2011), 110.
48. Naison, *White Boy*, 91.
49. Bradley, "Gym Crow Must Go!" 169.
50. Louis Lusky and Mary H. Lusky, "Columbia 1968: The Wound Unhealed," *Political Science Quarterly* 84, no. 2 (1969): 201–202.
51. Bradley, "Gym Crow Must Go!" 165–166.
52. *Tech News*, April 30, 1968, 176.
53. Ibid., 169.
54. Wendell E. Pritchett, *Brownsville, Brooklyn: Blacks, Jews, and the Changing Face of the Ghetto* (Chicago: University of Chicago Press, 2002), 223.
55. Jason Epstein, "The Issue at Ocean Hill," *New York Review of Books*, November 21, 1968; Pritchett, *Brownsville, Brooklyn*, 223, 228.
56. *New York Times*, September 6, 1968, October 10, 1968; Jerald E. Podair, *The Strike That Changed New York: Blacks, Whites, and the Ocean Hill-Brownsville Crisis* (New Haven, Conn.: Yale University Press, 2002), chap. 4; *New York*, October 10, 1983, 41.
57. *City Limits*, November 1997; Jitu Weusi, "Warrior Educator Interview, Part 1," November 20, 2006, H-Net, http://h-net.msu.edu/cgi-bin/logbrowse.pl?trx=vx&list=h-afro-am&month=0611&week=c&msg=IJNEcgfoRpFRfDHjPcKKSQ&user&pw.
58. Weusi, "Warrior Educator Interview."
59. Charles B. Rangel and Leon E. Wynter, *And I Haven't Had a Bad Day Since: From the Streets of Harlem to the Halls of Congress* (New York: St. Martin's Press, 2007), 129–131; Pritchett, *Brownsville, Brooklyn*, 229.
60. Pritchett, *Brownsville, Brooklyn*, 229.
61. Ibid. See also "'Blast from the Past' with Rhody McCoy," excerpt from Sarah-Ann Shaw, interview with McCoy, *Say Brother*, March 20, 1975, Open Vault: WGBH Media Library and Archives, http://openvault.wgbh.org/saybrother/MLA001112/

index.html; and Paul Ritterband, "Ethnic Power and the Public Schools: The New York City School Strike of 1968," *Sociology of Education* 47, no. 2 (1974): 252.

62. Pritchett, *Brownsville, Brooklyn*, 230.

63. "Profile of New York City School Reform Handbook," Open Planner, http://www.openplanner.org/node/206.

64. *Tech News*, October 16, 1968, 1–2.

65. *New York Amsterdam News*, November 2, 1968; Pritchett, *Brownsville, Brooklyn*, 235.

66. *New York*, October 10, 1983, 39.

67. *Meridian*, September 20, 1968, 6.

68. Ibid.

69. Ibid.

70. *Meridian*, October 25, 1968, 3.

71. Interviews with former members of the UNICA organization revealed no indication that any part of what seems like an acronym in reality represented a Spanish, Puerto Rican, Latino, or Hispanic equivalent for "student organizations" (*organización de estudiantes*) or related words.

72. Jiménez, "Puerto Ricans and Educational Civil Rights," 160–161, 166–167; Totti, interview with author.

73. Like Columbia and CCNY students, UNICA engaged in the community control movement, volunteering with Puerto Rican youth in the Bronx to prepare them for campus life and discussing different teacher-student conflicts that existed in impoverished city's schools. UNICA members also supported University of Puerto Rico (UPR) students engaged in their own struggle to add content about Puerto Rican revolutionaries (such as Pedro Albizu Campos) to the curriculum. Students in Puerto Rico also mobilized against the draft, the Vietnam War, and colonialism and gave their support to independence and antipoverty programs on the island. College students on the island resented that they could be drafted into the American armed forces and yet had no representation in the U.S. Congress nor could they vote in presidential elections. Thus, they considered the draft an example of a tax paid in blood without representation.

74. *Meridian*, November 15, 1968, 1.

75. Ibid.

76. Rita O'Hare, interview with author, 2008; *Meridian*, October 25, 1968, 3.

77. Charlotte Morgan-Cato, "Black Studies in the Whirlwind: A Retrospective View," in *A Companion to African American Studies*, ed. Lewis Gordon and Jane Anna Gordon (Malden, Mass.: Blackwell, 2006), 54.

78. *Tech News*, November 13, 1968, 1.

79. Quoted in ibid., 1, 2.

80. Quoted in *Campus*, November 20, 1968, 3.

81. Jiménez, "Puerto Ricans and Educational Civil Rights," 167–168; Julio Pabon, interview with author, January 2011; Frank Espada, interview with author, May 2012.

82. Quoted in Jiménez, "Puerto Ricans and Educational Civil Rights," 163, 167–168.
83. Quoted in ibid., 168.
84. Serrano, "Rifle, Cañón, y Escopeta!" 126.
85. *Campus*, October 30, 1968, 1, 4.
86. Quoted in ibid, 1.
87. Quoted in ibid, 1, 9, 6.
88. Quoted in *Tech News*, December 16, 1968, 3.
89. *Tech News*, February 19, 1969, 1.
90. Ibid.
91. Ibid.
92. *Tech News*, April 18, 1969, 1; Jiménez, "Puerto Ricans and Educational Civil Rights," 168.
93. Susan Polirstok, interview with author, January 2008.
94. *Tech News*, April 23, 1969.
95. Ibid.; Serrano, "Rifle, Cañón, y Escopeta!" 126; Jiménez, "Puerto Ricans and Educational Civil Rights," 170.
96. Jiménez, "Puerto Ricans and Educational Civil Rights," 170.
97. Karen Hess, *The Carolina Rice Kitchen: The African Connection* (Columbia: University of South Carolina Press, 1992), 96.
98. Ibid.
99. *Meridian*, February 21, 1969, 3.
100. *New York Amsterdam News*, July 19, 1969, February 21, 1970.
101. Bradley, "Gym Crow Must Go!" 172–173.
102. *Meridian*, February 5, 1969, 3.
103. *Meridian*, November 15, 1968, 2.
104. *Meridian*, March 7, 1969, 3.
105. *Meridian*, February 21, 1969, 3.
106. *Meridian*, March 7, 1969, 3.
107. *Meridian*, March 14, 1969, 1.
108. Morgan-Cato, "Black Studies in the Whirlwind," 54.
109. *Meridian*, March 21, 1969, 1.
110. *Meridian*, April 1, 1969, 1.
111. Morgan-Cato, "Black Studies in the Whirlwind," 54.

4. YOUNG TURKS

1. Frank Espada, interview with author, May 2012.
2. Bill Lynch, interview with author, August 2011.
3. Phillip Thompson III, *Double Trouble: Black Mayors, Black Communities, and the Call for Deep Democracy* (New York: Oxford University Press, 2006), 179–180; Lee

A. Daniels, "The Political Career of Adam Clayton Powell," *Journal of Black Studies* 4, no 2 (1973): 119–120; *City Limits*, November 1997.

4. Charles V. Hamilton, "Needed, More Foxes: The Black Experience," in *Urban Politics New York Style*, ed. Jewel Bellush and Dick Netzer (Armonk, N.Y.: Sharpe, 1990), 375–376.

5. Ibid.

6. Sandra (Sandy) Trujillo, interview with author, October 2010.

7. Hector W. Soto, interview with author, September 2010.

8. Philip S. Foner, *History of the Labor Movement in the United States: From Colonial Times to the Founding of the American Federation of Labor* (New York: International, 1991), 71–75; Gregory A. Butler, *Disunited Brotherhoods: . . . Race, Racketeering and the Fall of the New York Construction Unions* (Lincoln, Neb.: iUniverse, 2006), 33, 36–37.

9. Brian Purnell, "'Revolution Has Come to Brooklyn': The Campaign Against Discrimination in the Construction Trades and Growing Militancy in the Northern Black Freedom Movement," in *Black Power at Work: Community Control, Affirmative Action, and the Construction Industry*, ed. David Goldberg and Trevor Griffey (Ithaca, N.Y.: Cornell University Press, 2010), 23–47.

10. Butler, *Disunited Brotherhoods*, 9, 32, 34, 35.

11. Ibid., 32; Samuel C. Florman, *Good Guys, Wiseguys, and Putting Up Buildings: A Life in Construction* (New York: Macmillan, 2012), 240.

12. Mark Naison, interview with author, January 2011.

13. Leroy Archibald, interview with author, January 2011.

14. Ramon Jimenez, interview with author, January 2011.

15. Naison, interview with author.

16. *New York Amsterdam News*, January 27, 1979.

17. Quoted in *New York Amsterdam News*, September 6, 1979.

18. *Bronx Free Press*, December 14, 2011.

19. *New York Amsterdam News,* June 14, 1980, July 12, 1980, August 16, 1980.

20. Quoted in *Bronx Free Press*, December 14, 2011.

21. Ibid.; Karl Linn, *Building Commons and Community* (New York: New Village Press, 2007), 162–163.

22. Miguel "Mickey" Melendez, interview with author, September 2010. For more, see Max Elbaum, "What Legacy from the Radical Internationalism of 1968?"*Radical History Review* 82 (2002): 38, 41, 46, 51.

23. Melendez, interview with author.

24. Miguel "Mickey" Melendez, *We Took the Streets: Fighting Latino Rights with the Young Lords* (New York: St. Martin Press, 2003), 84–87; Melendez, interview with author; Luis Garden Acosta, interview with author, June 2012.

25. Young Lords Party, Resolutions & Speeches: Puerto Rican Revolutionary Workers Organization (November 1972), Box 11, Folder 11, Lourdes Torres Papers, Archives

of the Puerto Rican Diaspora, Centro de Estudios Puertorriqueños, Hunter College, CUNY, New York, N.Y.

26. Ibid.

27. Ibid.

28. Julio Pabon, interview with author, January 2011.

29. Ibid.

30. Jerald E. Podair, *The Strike That Changed New York: Blacks, Whites, and the Ocean Hill-Brownsville Crisis* (New Haven, Conn.: Yale University Press, 2002), 67, 175.

31. César J. Ayala and Rafael Bernabe, *Puerto Rico in the American Century: A History Since 1898* (Chapel Hill: University of North Carolina Press, 2007), 243; Rose Muzio, "Puerto Rican Radicalism in the 1970s: El Comité-MINP" (Ph.D. diss., City University of New York, 2008).

32. Pabon, interview with author.

33. Ibid.

34. Andrés Torres and José Velazquez, *The Puerto Rican Movement: Voices from the Diaspora* (Philadelphia: Temple University Press, 1998), 48–50; José Candelerio, interview with author, February 2012.

35. Ramón Bosque-Pérez and José Javier Colón-Morera, *Las carpetas: Persecuión política y derechos civiles en Puerto Rico* (Río Piedras: Centro para la investigación y promoción de los derechos civiles, 1997), 255–265; Cesar Ayala, "Political Persecution in Puerto Rico: Uncovering Secret Files," *Against the Current*, April 30, 2000, 41.

36. Ayala and Bernabe, *Puerto Rico in the American Century*, 244; Zoilo Torres, interview with author, August 2011.

37. Zoilo Torres, interviews with author, September 2010 and January 2013; Bosque-Pérez and Colón-Morera, *Las carpetas*, 255–265, 290–292.

38. *New York Times*, October 8, 1969, October 14, 1969, November 24, 1969, March 16, 1971, May 21, 1972; *Boston Globe*, December 22, 1974.

39. Quoted in *New York Times*, May 21, 1972.

40. *Boston Globe*, December 22, 1974.

41. Zoilo Torres, interview with author, February 2012.

42. José Candelerio, interview with author, August 2011.

43. Torres, interviews with author, 2010 and 2011; Candelario, interview with author, August 2011.

44. Candelario, interview with author, August 2011.

45. Torres, interviews with author, 2010 and 2011; Candelario, interview with author, August 2011; Saul Nieves, interview with author, October 2010.

46. Nicole P. Marwell, *Bargaining for Brooklyn: Community Organizations in the Entrepreneurial City* (Chicago: University of Chicago Press, 2007), 51–53; *New York Times*, October 3, 1993.

47. José Candelario, interview with author, October 2011.

48. Nieves, interview with author, 2011.

49. Candelario, interview with author, October 2011.

50. Jaime Estades, interview with author, September 2010; Candelario, interview with author, October 2011.

51. Estades, interview with author.

52. Torres, interview with author, 2011.

53. Candelerio, interview with author, August 2011; Torres, interview with author, 2010; Estades, interview with author.

54. "Negro, Puerto Rican Rally Builds Unity," February 16, 1964, El Centro, Box 9, Folder 14, Jesus Colon Papers, Archives of the Puerto Rican Diaspora Centro de Estudios Puertorriqueños, Hunter College, CUNY, New York, NY.

55. Saul Nieves, interview with author, January 2013.

56. Charles Earl Jones, *The Black Panther Party [Reconsidered]* (Baltimore: Black Classic Press, 1988) 43, 316; Jeffrey O. G. Ogbar, *Black Power: Radical Politics and African American Identity* (Baltimore: Johns Hopkins University Press, 2005), 199; Leonard Nathaniel Moore, *Carl B. Stokes and the Rise of Black Political Power* (Urbana: University of Illinois Press, 2002), 5.

57. Ibid.; *New York Times*, August 7, 1985, December 27, 2009; Charles B. Rangel and Leon E. Wynter, *And I Haven't Had a Bad Day Since: From the Streets of Harlem to the Halls of Congress* (New York: St. Martin's Press, 2007), 126, 134.

58. Rangel and Wynter, *And I Haven't Had a Bad Day Since*, 126, 134.

59. Lynch, interview with author.

60. Herman Denny Farrell Jr., interview with author, October 2011.

61. Henry Garrido and Oliver Gray, interview with author, August 2008; *Christian Science Monitor*, November 7, 1983, May 1, 1984, December 21, 1987.

62. Lewis Zuchman, interview with author, June 2011.

63. Ibid.; *New York Times*, January 6, 1985, February 17, 1985, May 26, 1985, August 7, 1985; Bill Platt, *Black and Brown in America: The Case for Cooperation* (New York: New York University Press, 1997), 124, 144; Thompson, *Double Trouble*, 138.

64. Thompson, *Double Trouble*, 139.

65. Ayala and Bernabe, *Puerto Rico in the American Century*, 240; Archibald, interview with author, Pabon, interview with author; Zuchman, interview with author; Espada, interview with author; *New York Times*, December 3, 2008.

66. *New York Times*, December 3, 2008.

67. *New York Times*, April 11, 1985, December 3, 2008.

68. Pabon, interview with author.

69. Ibid.

70. Archibald, interview with author.

71. Pabon, interview with author.

72. Ibid.

73. José Ramón Sánchez, *Boricua Power: A Political History of Puerto Ricans in the United States* (New York: New York University Press, 2007), 109, 114, 124, 131, 159; Ayala and Bernabe, *Puerto Rico in the American Century*, 240; Torres and Velazquez, *Puerto Rican Movement*, 177; Platt, *Black and Brown in America*, 141–142; Thompson, *Double Trouble*, 180; *New York Times*, April 8, 1984.

74. *New York Times*, April 8, 1984.

75. Ibid.

76. David Dinkins, interview with author, October 2011.

77. Jimenez, interview with author; Vincente "Panama" Alba, interview with author, November 2011.

78. Gerald Meyer, "Save Hostos: Politics and Community Mobilization to Save a College in the Bronx, 1973–1978," *Centro Journal* 15, no. 1 (2003): 82, 89, 92.

79. Jimenez, interview with author.

80. *New York*, August 17, 1981.

81. *New York Times*, June 14, 1984, January 17, 1985, December 27, 2009.

82. Jonathan Soffer, *Ed Koch and the Rebuilding of New York City* (New York: Columbia University Press, 1978), 201; Zenaida Mendez, interview with author, October 2010.

83. Lynch, interview with author.

84. Ibid.

85. Mark Naison, *Communists in Harlem During the Depression* (Urbana: University of Illinois Press, 2004), 66–67; Lynch, interview with author.

86. Lynch, interview with author.

87. *New York Times*, August 27, 1982; *Washington Post*, August 28, 1982; *New York Times*, September 24, 1982.

88. *New York Times*, August 27, 1982, September 17, 1982.

89. Luis Garden Acosta, interview with author, May 2012; Espada, interview with author; Records of the Puerto Rican Legal Defense and Education Fund, Part 1: Executive and Administrative Records, online edition.

90. Acosta, interview with author; Espada, interview with author.

91. Acosta, interview with author; *New York Times*, August 27, 1982; September 17, 1982, September 22, 1982.

92. *New York Times*, August 27, 1982.

93 Lynch, interview with author.

94. Acosta, interview with author; Espada, interview with author.

95. Torres, interviews with author, 2010 and 2011.

96. Dennis Rivera, interview with author, October 2011.

97 Candelerio, interview with author, August 2011.

98. Ibid.

99. Ibid., August and October 2011.

100. Giovanni Puello, interview with author, November 2010.

101. Mendez, interview with author.
102. Ibid.
103. On Vieques, see Torres and Velazquez, *Puerto Rican Movement*, 330–339.
104. Espada, interview with author.
105. Ibid.; Torres and Velazquez, *Puerto Rican Movement*, 331; Trujillo, interview with author.
106. Torres and Velazquez, *Puerto Rican Movement*, 331; Espada, interview with author; Trujillo, interview with author.
107. Trujillo, interview with author.
108. Ibid.; Torres, interview with author, 2011; Angel Garcia, interview with author, October 2011; Jimenez, interview with author. For more on the NCPRR, see Torres and Velazquez, *Puerto Rican Movement*, 62, 189, 306, 309, 339.
109. Trujillo, interview with author.
110. Mendez, interview with author.
111. Candelerio, interview with author, August 2011.
112. Ibid; Torres, interview with author, 2010; Estades, interview with author; Ernesto Maldanaldo, interview with author, March 2010.
113. Trujillo, interview with author.
114. *1199 News*, November 1999, 21.
115. *New York Times*, December 9, 1998.
116. Stanley Hill, interview with author, August 2008
117. Hamilton, "Needed, More Foxes," 375–376; Hill, interview with author; Santos Crespos, interview with author, August 2008.
118. Hill, interview with author.
119. Ibid.
120. *New York Times*, December 9, 1998.
121. Crespo, interview with author.
122. *Public Employee Press*, March 6, 1981.
123. *Public Employee Press*, March 8, 1985.
124. *Public Employee Press*, March 14, 1980.
125. Ibid.
126. *Public Employee Press*, March 6, 1981
127. Hill, interview with author.
128. *Public Employee Press,* November 11, 1984.
129. Ibid.
130. *Public Employee Press*, February 22, 1985.
131. *Public Employee Press*, March 8, 1985.
132. Hill, interview with author.
133. Ibid.
134. *Public Employee Press*, March 13, 1987.
135. *Public Employee Press*, February 22, 1985.

5. THE CHICAGO PLAN

1. Richard W. Simpson, remarks at "Harold Washington: Exploring a Legacy" (panel discussion), WBEZ (Chicago Public Radio), October 25, 2003; rebroadcast, April 12, 2008.

2. Gilberto Cárdenas, *La Causa: Civil Rights, Social Justice, and the Struggle for Equality in the Midwest* (Houston: Arte Público Press, 2004), 89–92; Jim Carl, "Harold Washington and Chicago's Schools Between Civil Rights and the Decline of the New Deal Consensus, 1955–1987," *History of Education Quarterly* 41 (2001): 315; *People's World*, June 13, 2003, peoplesworld.org.

3. Cárdenas, *La Causa*, 91.

4. Jesse Jackson, interview with Madison Davis Lacy Jr., April 1989, Henry Hampton Collection, Washington University Libraries, St. Louis, Mo.

5. Marion Stamps, interview with Madison Davis Lacy Jr., June 1989, Henry Hampton Collection.

6. Renault Robinson, interview with Madison Davis Lacy Jr., April 1989, Henry Hampton Collection.

7. Ibid.

8. Joseph Gardner, interview with James A. DeVinney, April 1989, Henry Hampton Collection.

9. "Black Power in American Cities: The Proceedings of a Dynamic Conference Addressing the Issues of Mayoral Politics and Afro Americans" (report, December 1983), Harold Washington: Black Research Site on the First Black Mayor of Chicago, http://eblackchicago.org/HAROLD/pdf/proceedings.pdf#zoom=60.

10. Ibid.

11. Stamps, interview.

12. *Chicago Tribune*, August 31, 1982, August 30, 1982, September 12, 1982.

13. *Chicago Tribune*, August 31, 1982.

14. "Black Power in American Cities."

15. *Chicago Tribune*, August 30, 1982; Gardner, interview.

16. Lou Palmer, interview with Madison Davis Lacy Jr., April 1989, Henry Hampton Collection.

17. *Chicago Reader*, September 3, 1998; Dempsey J. Travis, *Harold: The People's Mayor: An Authorized Biography of Mayor Harold Washington* (Chicago: Urban Research Press, 1989), 60, 65; Carl, "Harold Washington and Chicago's Schools," 311.

18. *Chicago Tribune*, October 15, 1982.

19. Travis, *Harold*, 60, 65, 120; Carl, "Harold Washington and Chicago's Schools," 311.

20. Travis, *Harold*, 87; David Stovall, "From Hunger Strike to High School: Youth Development, Social Justice, and School Formation," in *Beyond Resistance! Youth Activism and Community Change: New Democratic Possibilities for Practice and Policy for America's Youth*, ed. Shawn Ginwright, Pedro Noguera, and Julio Cammarota (New York: Routledge, 2006), 105.

21. Pierre Clavel, *Activists in City Hall: The Progressive Response to the Reagan Era in Boston and Chicago* (Ithaca, N.Y.: Cornell University Press, 2010), 114.

22. Travis, *Harold*, 87–90.

23. Dick W. Simpson, interview with author, August 2012; Travis, *Harold*, 87–90.

24. *Chicago Tribune*, March 4, 1979; *New York Times*, January 17, 2002.

25. Jackson, interview.

26. Salim Muwakkil, remarks at "Forging a Rainbow Coalition: The Legacy of Harold Washington" (panel discussion, presented by Public Square [Illinois Humanities Council]), WBEZ (Chicago Public Radio), February 9, 2008, http://www.wbez.org/episode-segments/forging-rainbow-coalition-legacy-harold-washington; Stamps, interview.

27. Timothy W. Wright and Alice J. Palmer, remarks at "Harold Washington: Exploring a Legacy."

28. Muwakkil, remarks at "Forging a Rainbow Coalition"; Stamps, interview.

29. Jesús "Chuy" Garcia, remarks at "Harold Washington: Exploring a Legacy."

30. Jackson, interview.

31. *Chicago Tribune*, October 1, 1982.

32. Simpson, interview with author; Jaime Dominguez, "Latinos in Chicago: A Strategy Towards Political Empowerment (1975–2003)" (Ph.D. diss., University of Illinois at Chicago, 2007), 95–96; Cárdenas, *La Causa*, 91.

33. *New York Times*, April 3, 1983.

34. Simpson, interview with author; Dominguez, "Latinos in Chicago"; Cárdenas, *La Causa*.

35. *Time*, July 8, 1985.

36. Simpson, interview with author; Dominguez, "Latinos in Chicago"; Cárdenas, *La Causa*.

37. Simpson, interview with author; *Chicago Tribune*, April 29, 1981, February 15, 1982, March 15, 1982; Cárdenas, *La Causa*.

38. Muwakkil, remarks at "Forging a Rainbow Coalition."

39. Cárdenas, *La Causa*, 91–92; Simpson, interview with author.

40. María de los Angeles Torres, remarks at "Eight Forty-Eight Explores Harold Washington's Legacy" (panel discussion), WBEZ (Chicago Public Radio), November 23, 2007, http://www.wbez.org/story/news/politics/eight-forty-eight-explores-harold-washingtons-legacy.

41. Garcia, remarks at "Harold Washington: Exploring a Legacy."

42. Simpson, remarks at "Harold Washington: Exploring a Legacy."

43. Cárdenas, *La Causa*; *Christian Science Monitor*, November 7, 1983.

44. Sheila D. Collins, *The Rainbow Challenge: The Jackson Campaign and the Future of U.S. Politics* (New York: Monthly Review Press, 1986), 113; "Black Power in American Cities."

45. Zoilo Torres, interview with author, September 2010.

46. *New York Amsterdam News*, April 30, 1983.

47. Ibid.

48. *New York Amsterdam News*, May 21, 1983; Torres, interview with author.

49. *New York,* October 10, 1983.

50. Jesse Jackson, interview by Blackside, April 11, 1989, for *Eyes on the Prize II: America at the Racial Crossroads, 1965–1985*, Film and Media Archive, Henry Hampton Collection.

51. Howard Jordan, interview with author, October 2010.

52. Collins, *Rainbow Challenge*, 141.

53. Ibid.

54. *New York Times*, March 18, 1982.

55. Armando Gutierrez, "The Jackson Campaign in the Hispanic Community: Problems and Prospects for a Black-Brown Coalition," in *Jesse Jackson's 1984 Presidential Campaign: Challenge and Change in American Politics*, ed. L. Jefferson Barker and Ronald W. Walters (Urbana: University of Illinois Press, 1989), 115.

56. Collins, *Rainbow Challenge*, 189.

57. Gutierrez, "Jackson Campaign in the Hispanic Community," 115, 116.

58. Michael C. LeMay, *Guarding the Gates: Immigration and National Security* (Westport, Conn.: Praeger Security International, 2006), 173.

59. Gutierrez, "Jackson Campaign in the Hispanic Community," 115.

60. *New York Amsterdam News*, February 18, 1984.

61. Recorded versions of the song are available on YouTube. See, for example, www.youtube.com/watch?v=w_owXd-j280.

62. *New York Amsterdam News*, February 18, 1984.

63. *New York Amsterdam News*, March 10, 1984, June 23, 1984.

64. *New York Amsterdam News,* April 14, 1984.

65. Evelina Antonetty and Alfred L. Woodards, "History of United Bronx Parents," Box 2, Folder 15, United Bronx Parents, Inc., Records, Archives of the Puerto Rican Diaspora, Centro de Estudios Puertorriqueños, Hunter College, CUNY, New York, N.Y.

66. Ramon Jimenez, interview with author, January 2011.

67. *New York Amsterdam News*, March 31, 1984.

68. *New York Amsterdam News*, April 14, 1984.

69. Jimenez, interview with author; *New York Amsterdam News*, April 7, 1984.

70. José Candelario, interview with author, August 2011.

71. *New York Amsterdam News*, March 10, 1984; *Washington Post*, April 1, 1984.

72. *New York Amsterdam News*, April 7, 1984.

73. Ibid.

74. Ibid.; *New York Amsterdam News*, May 12, 1984.

75. *New York Amsterdam News*, April 14, 1984.

76. Ibid.

77. Dennis Rivera, interview with author, October 2011.
78. William Lynch, interview with author, August 2011.
79. Collins, *Rainbow Challenge*, 186.
80. Jimenez, interview with author.
81. Collins, *Rainbow Challenge*.
82. Ibid., 187.
83. Gutierrez, "Jackson Campaign in the Hispanic Community," 113.
84. Ibid.; Collins, *Rainbow Challenge*, 186, 188–189.
85. Gutierrez, "Jackson Campaign in the Hispanic Community," 123.
86. Collins, *Rainbow Challenge*.
87. Gutierrez, "Jackson Campaign in the Hispanic Community," 123, 304.
88. Saul Nieves, interview with author, October 2011.
89. Collins, *Rainbow Challenge*, 304–305.
90. Gutierrez, "Jackson Campaign in the Hispanic Community," 123–124.
91. Collins, *Rainbow Challenge*, 305.
92. *New York Amsterdam News*, August 18, 1984.
93. *New York Amsterdam News*, September 22, 1984.

6. WHERE THE STREET GOES, THE SUITS FOLLOW

1. *City Limits*, November 1997.
2. *New York*, October 10, 1983.
3. *New York Times*, July 8, 1983; *New York*, October 10, 1983; *New York Amsterdam News*, May 19, 1984, November 17, 1984; *New York Times*, January 6, 1985; *New York Amsterdam News,* January 19, 1985, January 26, 1985.
4. Ramon Jimenez, interview with author, January 2011.
5. Lewis Zuchman, interview with author, June 2011.
6. Hector W. Soto, interview with author, September 2010; Howard Jordan, interview with author, October 2010; Zuchman, interview with author; Julio Pabon, interview with author, March 2009.
7. *New York*, October 10, 1983; Basil Paterson, interview with author, October 2008; *New York Times*, June 15, 1984, July 12, 1984.
8. *New York Times*, April 14, 1984, June 15, 1984, June 14, 1984.
9. Basil Paterson, interview with author, July 2011.
10. *New York Times*, July 8, 1983.
11. *New York Times*, December 8, 1984; *New York*, October 10, 1983; *City Limits*, November 1997.
12. *New York Times*, December 8, 1984.
13. *New York Amsterdam News*, June 29, 1985.
14. Jimenez, interview with author; *New York Amsterdam News*, December 14, 1985.

15. *New York*, October 10, 1983; Pabon, interview with author.
16. Paterson, interview with author, 2008; David Dinkins, interview with author, October 2011.
17. *New York Times*, December 8, 1984.
18. Jimenez, interview with author.
19. Sandra (Sandy) Trujillo, interview with author, October 2010.
20. *New York Times*, April 8, 1984.
21. Dinkins, interview with author.
22. Jimenez, interview with author.
23. Ibid.
24. *City Limits*, November 1997.
25. Herman Denny Farrell Jr., interview with author, October 2011.
26. Dinkins, interview with author.
27. Paterson, interview with author, 2011.
28. William Lynch, interview with author, August 2011; *New York*, October 10, 1983; *New York Times*, February 17, 1985.
29. Lynch, interview with author.
30. *New York Amsterdam News*, April 27, 1985; *New York Times*, May 26, 1985.
31. *New York Amsterdam News*, August 3, 1985.
32. Paterson, interview with author, 2011.
33. *New York Amsterdam News*, August 3, 1985.
34. Ibid.; Lynch, interview with author.
35. *New York Times*, February 17, 1985.
36. *Newsweek*, February 25, 1985.
37. *New York Times*, February 17, 1985.
38. Farrell, interview with author.
39. *New York Amsterdam News*, June 29, 1985.
40. Ibid.
41. *New York Amsterdam News*, September 7, 1985.
42. Ibid.
43. *New York Times*, May 26, 1985; *New York Amsterdam News*, August 31, 1985; *New York Times*, September 15, 1985; *City Limits*, November 1997; Juan Cartagena, "Voting Rights in New York City, 1982–2006," *Southern California Review of Law and Social Justice* 17, no. 2 (2007): 559–560.
44. *New York Times*, September 24, 1984, May 26, 1985, June 4, 1985; *New York Amsterdam News*, August 31, 1985; *New York Times*, September 12, 1985; *New York Amsterdam News*, September 14, 1985; *New York Times*, September 15, 1985; Suleiman Osman, *The Invention of Brownstone Brooklyn: Gentrification and the Search for Authenticity in Postwar New York* (New York: Oxford University Press, 2011).
45. *City Limits*, November 1997.
46. *New York Times*, September 12, 1985, September 15, 1985.

47. *New York Times*, September 12, 1985.

48. *New York Times*, February 10, 1985.

49. Farrell, interview with author.

50. Erica Gonzalez, in Box 34, Folder Series 6: Writing and Publications, Richie Perez Papers, Archives of the Puerto Rican Diaspora, Centro de Estudios Puertorrique-ños, Hunter College, CUNY, New York, N.Y.

51. Shirley Gray, interview with author, August 2008.

52. Jimenez, interview with author.

53. *New York Amsterdam News*, September 6, 1986; *La Prensa* (New York), June 11, 1993; *New York Times*, June 20, 1993; *Bond Buyer*, August 12, 1993; *New York Times*, September 13, 1993, October 19, 1993; Lynch, interview with author.

54. Dinkins, interview with author; *Daily News* (New York), November 16, 2011, online blog, http://www.nydailynews.com/blogs/dailypolitics/2011/11/herman-badillo-back-with-the-democrats.

55. *New York Amsterdam News*, March 31, 1984.

56. Ibid.

57. *New York Times*, January 6, 1985, February 17, 1985, May 26, 1985; Jimenez, interview with author; Zuchman, interview with author.

58. Pabon, interview with author.

59. Ibid.

60. Ibid.

61. *New York Times*, September 27, 1985, November 5, 1985.

62. Paterson, interview with author, 2011.

63. Leroy Archibald, interview with author, January 2011.

64. Angel Garcia, interview with author, October 2011.

65. I made several attempts to interview Representative Serrano for this book, but his office failed to follow up on the request.

66. *New York Times*, March 29, 1985.

67. Ibid.; *New York Amsterdam News*, April 20, 1985; *New York Times*, August 15, 1985.

68. *New York Amsterdam News*, August 31, 1985; Lynch, interview with author.

69. *New York Amsterdam News*, August 31, 1985.

70. Zoilo Torres, interview with author, September 2010.

71. *New York Times*, March 29, 1985.

72. Arnaldo "Arnie" Segarra, interview with author, October 2010.

73. *New York Amsterdam News*, April 20, 1985, August 31, 1985.

74. *New York Amsterdam News*, September 7, 1985.

75. *New York Times*, August 15, 1985, April 20, 1985, September 7, 1985.

76. *New York Amsterdam News*, September 14, 1985; *New York Times*, September 15, 1985.

77. Miguel "Mickey" Melendez, interview with author, September 2010; *New York Amsterdam News*, September 14, 1985; *New York Times*, September 15, 1985.

78. *New York Amsterdam News*, April 26, 1986.

79. Zenaida Mendez, interview with author, October 2010.

80. Trujillo, interview with author.

81. Mendez, interview with author.

82. Trujillo, interview with author.

83. Dennis Rivera, interview with author, October 2011.

84. *New York Times*, May 26, 1982; *New York Amsterdam News*, September 1, 1984, January 12, 1985, February 9, 1985; *New York Amsterdam News*, April 12, 1986; *New York Times*, October 26, 1987.

85. Lynch, interview with author.

86. *New Yorker*, December 10, 1990. See also *New York Times*, May 10, 1992.

87. *New York Amsterdam News*, February 9, 1985; *New Yorker*, December 10, 1990; Rivera, interview with author.

88. *New York Times*, November 30, 1987.

89. *New York Amsterdam News*, January 12, 1985.

90. Ibid.

91. *New York Amsterdam News*, February 9, 1985.

92. *New Yorker*, December 10, 1990; Lynch, interview with author.

93. Lynch, interview with author.

94. *New York Amsterdam News*, April 26, 1986.

95. *New Yorker*, December 10, 1990; *New York Times*, May 10, 1992.

96. *New York Times*, December 3, 1984; *New York Amsterdam News*, April 27, 1985; *Chicago Tribune*, August 20, 1985; *Los Angeles Times*, November 20, 1985; *Washington Post*, August 28, 1986; *New York Times*, September 30, 1986.

97. Quoted in *New York Amsterdam News*, April 9, 1988.

98. *New York Times*, April 17, 1988; *Michigan Citizen* (Detroit), April 30, 1988; Garcia, interview with author.

99. *New York Amsterdam News*, April 9, 1988; *New York Times*, April 17, 1988, April 18, 1988.

100. Quoted in *New York Amsterdam News*, January 30, 1988.

101. *New York Times*, March 22, 1988; *New York Amsterdam News*, March 26, 1988.

102. *Michigan Citizen*, April 30, 1988.

103. Quoted in *New York Amsterdam News*, April 16, 1988.

104. Ibid.

105. Jordan, interview with author.

106. Shelly L. Anderson, "An Uneasy Alliance: Blacks and Latinos in New York City Politics" (Ph.D. diss., Ohio State University, 2002), 137.

107. Torres, interview with author.

108. *New York Times,* April 18, 1988.

109. Asther Arian, Arthur S. Goldberg, John H. Mollenkopf, and Edward T. Rogowksy, *Changing New York City Politics* (New York: Routledge, 1991), 67.

110. Lynch, interview with author; Rivera, interview with author.

111. Zuchman, interview with author; Jordan, interview with author.

112. Bill Piatt, *Black and Brown in America: The Case for Cooperation* (New York: New York University Press, 1997), 145; Arian et al., *Changing New York City Politics*, 44; Anderson, "Uneasy Alliance," 137.

113. Anderson, "Uneasy Alliance," 136.

114. *New York Times*, April 17, 1988; David Dinkins, interview with Brian Lehrer, *The Brian Lehrer Show*, WNYC (New York Public Radio), July 29, 2009; Paterson, interview with author, 2011.

7. LATINOS FOR DINKINS

1. *New York Times*, October 23, 1979; *Los Angeles Times*, June 3, 1981; *Washington Post*, November 14, 1985.

2. *New York Times*, July 13, 1989.

3. *Guardian* (London), September 14, 1989; *New York Amsterdam News*, February 18, 1989; *New York Times*, July 29, 1989; January 1, 1990; David Dinkins, interview with author, October 2011; Wilbur C. Rich, *David Dinkins and New York City Politics: Race, Images, and the Media* (Albany: State University of New York Press, 2007), 26–27.

4. *New York Amsterdam News*, February 18, 1989; *New York Times*, July 29, 1989; Dinkins, interview with author.

5. After Dinkins won the election, *Newsweek* and later the *New York Times* ran stories that Dinkins (and Koch before him) had mismanaged city funds in the process of decorating and running Gracie Mansion, the mayor's home. See, for example, *New York Times*, February 22, 1991.

6. *New York Amsterdam News*, October 7, 1989; *Jerusalem Post*, November 10, 1989; *Australian Financial Review*, November 10, 1989.

7. Philip Kasinitz, *Caribbean New York: Black Immigrations and the Politics of Race* (Ithaca, N.Y.: Cornell University Press, 1992), 249; Chris McNickle, *To Be Mayor of New York: Ethnic Politics in the City* (New York: Columbia University Press, 1993), 312, 323; Shelly L. Anderson, "An Uneasy Alliance: Blacks and Latinos in New York City Politics" (Ph.D. diss., Ohio State University, 2002), 135, 139.

8. Anderson, "Uneasy Alliance," 135, 139.

9. Kasinitz, *Caribbean New York*, 249.

10. McNickle, *To Be Mayor of New York*, 312.

11. Basil Paterson, interview with author, July 2011.

12. Zoilo Torres, interview with author, September 2010.

13. Jamie Estades, interview with author, September 2010.

14. William Lynch, interview with author, August 2011; Dennis Rivera, interview with author, October 2011.

15. Paterson, interview with author.

16. Lynch, interview with author; Rivera, interview with author.

17. Lynch, interview with author; Rivera, interview with author; Dinkins, interview with author.

18. Dinkins, interview with author.

19. Lynch, interview with author.

20. Ibid.

21. Zenaida Mendez, interview with author, October 2010.

22. Giovanni A. Puello, interview with author, November 2011.

23. Mendez, interview with author.

24. Puello, interview with author, 2011.

25. Sandra (Sandy) Trujillo, interviews with author, October 2010 and August 2011.

26. Ibid.

27. Lynch, interview with author.

28. Jaime Estades, interview with author, August 2011.

29. Torres, interview with author.

30. Arnaldo "Arnie" Segarra, interview with author, October 2010.

31. Torres, interview with author; Segarra, interview with author.

32. José Candelario, interview with author, August 2011.

33. Anderson, "Uneasy Alliance," 136.

34. Estades, interview with author, 2010.

35. Torres, interview with author.

36. Ibid.

37. *New York Amsterdam News*, September 9, 1989.

38. *New York Times*, August 20, 1989.

39. Candelario, interview with author, August 2011.

40. Torres, interview with author.

41 Miriam Jimenez inspired this theory: Miriam Jimenez, interview with Howard Jordan, *The Jordan Journal*, WBAI, March 12, 2010. See also my earlier work on ethnocentrism in the Iberian world, migration, creolization, and cultural retentions: *Hog and Hominy: Soul Food from Africa to America* (New York: Columbia University Press, 2008), i, 19, 30, 137, 141–152, and *Black Labor Migration in Caribbean Guatemala, 1882–1923*, Florida Work in the Americas Series (Gainesville: University Press of Florida, 2009), 9–11.

42. Frederick Douglass Opie, "Eating, Dancing, and Courting in New York: Black and Latino Relations, 1930–1970," *Journal of Social History* 42, no. 1 (2008): 99–100.

43. Saul Nieves, interview with author, October 2011.

44. Andy Gonzalez, interview with author, September 2010.

45. Ibid.

46. *Washington Post*, September 9, 1989.

47. Mendez, interview with author.

48. *New York Times*, August 20, 1989.

49. Estades, interview with author, 2010.

50. *New York Times*, August 20, 1989; Estades, interview with author, 2010.

51. Estades, interview with author, 2010.

52. Victor Manuel Quintana, interview with author, November 2011.

53. *New York Amsterdam News*, September 9, 1989.

54. Giovanni A. Puello, interview with author, November 2010.

55. Ibid.

56. Mendez, interview with author.

57. Ibid.

58. Trujillo, interview with author, 2011.

59. Torres, interview with author.

60. Puello, interview with author, 2010.

61. Trujillo, interview with author, 2011; Mendez, interview with author.

62. Quoted in *New York Amsterdam News*, September 9, 1989.

63. Quoted in *New York Times*, August 14, 1989, August 20, 1989.

64. *New York Amsterdam News*, September 9, 1989.

65. Quoted in ibid.

66. Quoted in *New York Times*, August 20, 1989.

67. Trujillo, interview with author, 2010.

68. Angel Garcia, interview with author, October 2011; Trujillo, interview with author, 2011.

69. Garcia, interview with author.

70. Vicente "Panama" Alba, interview with author, November 2011.

71. Trujillo, interview with author, 2011.

72. Garcia, interview with author.

73. Ibid.

74. Julio Pabon, interview with author, March 2009.

75. *Los Angeles Times*, August 24, 1989, August 25, 1989; *New York Times*, August 25, 1989.

76. *New York Times*, August 25, 1986.

77. *New York Times*, August 25, 1989; *Chicago Tribune*, August 31, 1989; *New York Amsterdam News*, September 2, 1989.

78. *Independent*, September 1, 1989; *New York Amsterdam News*, September 16, 1989, September 23, 1989.

79. *City Journal*, Summer 1991; *Village Voice*, December 31, 2002.

80. *Independent* (London), September 1, 1989.

81. Quintana, interview with author.

82. *Washington Post*, September 14, 1989.

83. *New York Amsterdam News*, September 2, 1989.

84. *New York Amsterdam News*, September 9, 1989; *Philadelphia Tribune*, September 15, 1989.

85. Dinkins, interview with author.

86. Lynch, interview with author.

87. *Los Angeles Times*, September 13, 1989.

88. Ibid.; *Washington Post*, September 14, 1989.

89. Quoted in *New York Times*, September 13, 1989.

90. *Los Angeles Times*, September 13, 1989.

91. Quoted in *New York Times*, September 13, 1989.

92. *Washington Post*, September 15, 1989.

93. *Chicago Tribune*, September 14, 1989.

94. *New York Times*, September 13, 1989.

95. *Guardian*, September 14, 1989.

96. *New York Amsterdam News*, September 23, 1989, October 21, 1989.

97. *New York Amsterdam News*, September 30, 1989.

98. *Michigan Citizen* (Detroit), August 19, 1989.

99. *New York Amsterdam News*, September 9, 1989; *Michigan Citizen*, August 19, 1989.

100. *New York Amsterdam News*, October 7, 1989.

101. *Wall Street Journal*, July 17, 1989; *New York Times*, November 8, 1989. The most detailed account of his tenure as a U.S. attorney is in *New York Amsterdam News*, November 11, 1989.

102. Lynch, interview with author.

103. Trujillo, interview with author, 2011; Candelerio, interviews with author, August and October 2011; Estades, interview with author, 2011.

104. Trujillo, interview with author, 2011.

105. Ibid.

106. Torres, interview with author.

107. Lynch, interview with author.

108. José Candelario, interview with author, January 2013.

109. *Adweek*, February 6, 1989; *Independent*, September 1, 1989; Garcia, interview with author.

110. Quintana, interview with author.

111. *Washington Post*, September 15, 1989; *Newsweek*, November 6, 1989.

112. *Washington Post*, September 11, 1989.

113. *Independent*, September 1, 1989. For more on Ailes, see Gabriel Sherman, *The Loudest Voice in the Room: How the Brilliant, Bombastic Roger Ailes Built Fox News—and Divided the Nation* (New York: Random House, 2014).

114. *Washington Post*, October 20, 1989.

115. *Washington Post*, October 20, 1989; *Village Voice*, December 31, 2002; *New York Times*, December 23, 2002.

116. Torres, interview with author; *City Journal*, Summer 1991.

117. *New York Amsterdam News*, October 21, 1989.

118. *Washington Post*, October 20, 1989.

119. *Independent*, September 1, 1989.

120. *New York Times*, September 26, 1989; *Newsweek*, October 9, 1989; *Washington Post*, October 20, 1989.

121. Quoted in *Jerusalem Post*, November 10, 1989.

122. Quoted in *New York Times*, October 10, 1989.

123. *Newsweek*, November 6, 1989.

124. Ibid.

125. Quoted in *Washington Post*, September 14, 1989.

126. Trujillo, interview with author, 2011.

127. *Independent*, September 15, 1989.

128. Candelario, interview with author, 2013; Torres, interview with author.

129. *New York Times*, November 9, 1989.

130. Dinkins, interview with author.

131. Quintana, interview with author.

132. Ibid.

133. Lynch, interview with author.

134. Lynch, interview with author; Quintana, interview with author.

135. Lynch, interview with author.

136. Alba, interview with author; Candelario, interview with author, August 2011; Pabon, interview with author.

137. Pabon, interview with author.

138. *New York Times*, February 10, 1991.

139. *New York Times*, September 8, 1992; Alba, interview with author.

140. *New York Amsterdam News*, November 18, 1989; *New York Times*, December 9, 1989; *New York Amsterdam News*, April 7, 1990.

141. Candelario, interview with author, 2013.

142. Ibid.; Torres, interview with author.

143. *New York Amsterdam News*, March 24, 1990, November 14, 1992.

144. Ibid.

145. Candelario, interview with author, 2013; *Washington Post*, September 14, 1989; *India-West* (San Leandro, Calif.), November 12, 1993.

146. *New York Amsterdam News*, November 6, 1993; *La Prensa* (New York), November 11, 1993.

147. Hector W. Soto, interview with author, September 2010.

CONCLUSION

1. Basil Paterson, interview with author, July 2011; William Lynch, interview with author, August 2011; Arnaldo "Arnie" Segarra, interview with author, October 2010.

2. Lynch, interview with author.

3. *Nation*, May 6, 2013.

4. Hector W. Soto, interview with author, September 2010; Zoilo Torres, interview with author, September 2010.

5. Torres, interview with author.

6. Ibid.

7. *New York Times*, April, 5, 1997.

8. *Daily News* (New York), April 6, 1997.

9. *New York Amsterdam News*, May 17, 1997.

10. Ibid.

11. Ibid.

12. Ibid.; *New York Times*, September 12, 1997.

13. *Daily News*, September 18, 1997.

14. *Daily News*, September 19, 1997.

15. Torres, interview with author.

16. Lynch, interview with author.

17. Ibid.

18. *Newsweek*, November 7, 2001; *Independent* (London), November 8, 2001.

19. Soto, interview with author.

20. *Nation*, May 6, 2013.

21. *New York Times*, June 19, 2013.

22. Ken Lovett, interview with Brian Lehrer, *The Brian Lehrer Show*, WNYC (New York Public Radio), May 6, 2013.

23. Soto, interview with author.

24. Segarra, interview with author; "Harold Washington: Exploring a Legacy" (panel discussion), WBEZ (Chicago Public Radio), October 25, 2003; rebroadcast, April 12, 2008).

25. Jose Candelario, interview with author, August 2011; *Daily News*, December 4, 1999.

26. *Salon*, August 16, 2013, http://www.salon.com/2013/08/16/the_fro_that_shook_a _city_dante_de_blasios_pride/.

INDEX

Italicized page numbers refer to recipes.